IMAGINING CENTRAL AMERICA

IMAGINING CENTRAL AMERICA

Short Histories

SERENA COSGROVE
and
ISABEAU J. BELISLE DEMPSEY

University of
CINCINNATI | PRESS

About the University of Cincinnati Press
The University of Cincinnati Press is committed to publishing rigorous, peer-reviewed, leading scholarship accessibly to stimulate dialogue among the academy, public intellectuals and lay practitioners. The Press endeavors to erase disciplinary boundaries in order to cast fresh light on common problems in our global community. Building on the university's long-standing tradition of social responsibility to the citizens of Cincinnati, the state of Ohio, and the world, the Press publishes books on topics that expose and resolve disparities at every level of society and have local, national and global impact.

ISBN 978-1-947602-93-9 (paperback)
ISBN 978-1-947602-94-6 (OA)
ISBN 978-1-947602-95-3 (ePUB)

Names: Cosgrove, Serena, 1963- author. | Belisle Dempsey, Isabeau J., author.
Title: Imagining Central America : short histories / Serena Cosgrove and
    Isabeau J. Belisle Dempsey.
Description: Cincinnati, Ohio : University of Cincinnati, [2022] | Includes bibliographical
    references and index.
Identifiers: LCCN 2022005488 (print) | LCCN 2022005489 (ebook) |
    ISBN 9781947602939 (paperback) | ISBN 9781947602946 (OA) |
    ISBN 9781947602953 (epub) | ISBN 9781947602960 (PDF)
Subjects: LCSH: Central America—History.
Classification: LCC F1436 .C67 2022 (print) | LCC F1436 (ebook) |
    DDC 972.8—dc23/eng/20220310
LC record available at https://lccn.loc.gov/2022005488
LC ebook record available at https://lccn.loc.gov/2022005489

Designed and produced for UC Press by Julie Rushing
Typeset in Adobe Text Pro and Espinosa Nova
Printed in the United States of America
First Printing

TABLE OF CONTENTS

IMAGINING CENTRAL AMERICA
Short Histories

CHAPTER ONE

Imagining Central America

[The] isthmian nations [of Central America] have much of their history,
global contexts, and political and economic development in common.
... These common attributes demonstrate that Central America exists
within a larger world dynamic that similarly constrains its component
states.[1]

INTRODUCTION

The Central American isthmus—the land bridge that connects North America
to South America—is comprised of seven countries: Belize, Guatemala, El
Salvador, Honduras, Nicaragua, Costa Rica, and Panama. Mountain ranges
run north-south along the spine of the isthmus, dividing the region into nar-
row Pacific plains along the western coast, the highland interior, and wider
Caribbean coastal plains to the east, all of which have informed the locations
and movements of cultures, population centers, infrastructure, and sites for
economic development and political strongholds throughout centuries. The
geography of the region has played a significant role in how the region as a whole
and each country have evolved through time, particularly how the physical and
economic isolation of parts of the region contributed to difficulty unifying the
region as a federation in the early nineteenth century.[2] The barriers to traveling
from the Pacific coast to the Caribbean coast, for example, meant that often
there was little communication between the coasts, which, in turn, influenced
the settlements and political expansion of Indigenous peoples in pre-Columbian
times, the Spanish colonization of the Pacific coastal areas and highlands, British extractivism on the Caribbean coast, the strategic position of the region for
European and United States interests regarding agro-exports and transconti-
nental canal plans in the late nineteenth century, and the eventual construction
of a canal across Panama in the early twentieth century.

Early in the colonial period, Central America was integrated into the world
economy and enjoyed "a certain amount of free commerce and intercolonial

trade."[3] For example, woven textiles and thread made in the western highlands of Guatemala were sold around the world.[4] Early Spanish colonization focused on extraction of silver and gold as well as establishing the *encomienda* system in which Indigenous farmers provided goods and money—often referred to as tribute—and forced labor for export crops such as indigo, cacao, cotton, cattle raising, and sheep farming for wool. During the colonial period, Indigenous labor was supplemented by bringing in African labor in the form of enslaved and free people. Early British colonialists on the Caribbean coast also brought in enslaved Africans where the focus was on extraction, such as logging. This history of extraction has present-day manifestations along with active environmental movements in all countries. Today "the principal themes of the political ecology of the region are . . . extraction of minerals; hydroelectric energy; forestry plantations and extraction of biomass; infrastructure; transnational companies; cross-border disputes; anti-Indigenous racism . . . [and] the many assassinations of activists."[5] Though rich in natural resources, many parts of Central America, including the Caribbean coast, have suffered the environmental impacts of extractivism and mega-development projects. Again, Central America, in general, and the Caribbean coast, in particular, have always been vulnerable to destructive hurricanes from the east, and more and more, the effects of climate change are creating harmful effects and magnifying the impact of natural disasters. Climate change has exacerbated pressures on Indigenous groups as well: for example, the Kuna in Panama have had to leave their ancestral lands due to climate change.[6]

The entire region is volcanic with many active volcanoes today. Frequent seismic events have also affected the region's infrastructure and politics. For example, the 1773 earthquake in present-day Antigua, Guatemala, the original capital of the Spanish Kingdom of Guatemala's *audiencia* or high court, forced authorities to abandon the city and build New Guatemala City in the present-day location of the capital twenty-five miles to the east. The 1972 earthquake in Managua, Nicaragua, and the 1986 earthquake in San Salvador, El Salvador, revealed so much government corruption and so exacerbated existing inequalities that social movements and revolutionary groups were emboldened. These natural disasters from the 1970s and 1980s "occurred within a brief period and precipitated social disasters by aggravating the suffering of the poorer sectors."[7] (See Appendix 1: History of Natural Disasters in Central America.)

For many—including eminent historians and other commentators—Central America is often depicted without Belize and Panama. Proponents of this narrative say that because Panama was originally part of the Republic of Gran Colombia in South America when the United Provinces of Central American declared independence from Spain (and then Mexico) in the early 1800s, it should not be considered part of Central America. Yet, Panama has played a vitalizing role in the Central American economy for over a hundred years and shares many geographical, cultural, and political traits with the rest of the region. On the other hand, Belize is a country that has been simultaneously identified with the Caribbean and claimed by Guatemala. Belize was colonized primarily by the British, and today, the official language is still English. Yet, like all the other Central American countries, the population of Belize includes *mestizos* and Indigenous people, though Belize is 32 percent Afro-descendant.

Readers may also have heard about the troubled "northern triangle," a subregion of Central America that includes Guatemala, El Salvador, and Honduras. Excluding Belize, Nicaragua, Costa Rica, and Panama, the northern triangle narrative of Central America focuses on the rise of violence, drug trafficking, and weak governance in these three countries. Limiting the imaginary of Central America to three countries is problematic because it reifies a version of the region as full of problems for which there are deep historical explanations, including international meddling going back centuries. Again, these challenges are not unique to these three countries, and there are many local civil society, private sector, and public sector efforts to address these challenges. There's another version of Central America that includes Chiapas, the southernmost state of present-day Mexico, and does not include Panama; this is often the Central America that historians of the early colonial period use because this was the area that comprised the Spanish Kingdom of Guatemala.[8] Though variations regarding forms of governance, language, cultural diversity, and natural resources exist between and across the seven countries, this region shares geographies, borders, histories, peoples, and trade relations. It is also important to keep in mind how the long history of foreign policies of colonial and neocolonial powers—from Spain and Great Britain to the United States—have had profound impacts on each of the seven countries. Indeed, the politics and economies of all the Central American countries are very much affected by global forces both in historical and present-day perspective.

In this short history, we propose a narrative or "imaginary" of the isthmus as a region that differentiates the seven countries from each other as well as pointing to the unifying features of Central America as a whole. Instead of a blurry region often appended to Mexico in the minds of uninformed politicians and media pundits, our goal is to help readers more clearly envision a region comprised of different countries: from Guatemala and Belize—who share a border with Mexico to the north—to El Salvador, Honduras, Nicaragua, and Costa Rica to the south, and Panama, which shares a border with Colombia. Given the global interconnections between the region and other countries as well as the interstate connections between the region's countries, we feel that a short, synthetic book will help students, educators, policymakers, journalists, and global citizens alike to develop a more nuanced mental map of the region, including an understanding of its major historical periods, peoples, and institutions. Through reading about the opportunities and challenges that confront the region and the reasons why Central America appears in the global news so often, readers will learn about a vital region of the world, and thus, be more informed and better able to advocate for diplomatic and development policies that support participation, inclusion, democracy building, good governance, and economic development across the region. In recounting the history of the United States and Central America, the historian Aviva Chomsky warns that "If we erase important parts of our own and Central American countries' histories, we can believe that they are simply, inherently, 'shit-hole countries' as President Trump suggested in early 2018."[9] Given the charged political histories of the region as well as colonial and neocolonial interventions with present-day impacts, this book provides a succinct analysis for readers with limited time or country-specific interests. This book is purposely short. Abundant academic scholarship exists about the region that provides extensive analysis for the historical epochs of the region and the countries that comprise it. For this reason, each chapter includes compelling quotes from many of these scholars and a list of recommended readings so that the interested reader can easily identify additional materials that they might like to peruse.

In this introductory chapter, we endeavor to build a regional context so that readers can familiarize themselves with the key themes, trends, and concepts used to analyze the region. We also summarize important regional events and movements in historical perspective, such as peoples and population movements; political elites and the contestation of social movements; and the impacts of foreign powers on the region so that readers can better understand how these factors manifest in the individual countries. In this first chapter, we'll discuss the original peoples of the region, and key events such as the conquest and European colonization of the region, the nineteenth century decolonization movement, the emergence of tensions between early political leaders, early modern statehood, the political and social movements of the twentieth and twenty-first centuries, and the effects of colonial and neocolonial powers on the region past and present. Central America's history is both deeply grounded in models of strong local leadership and yet greatly influenced by North American and European countries.

RACE AND ETHNICITY AND A HISTORY OF COLONIZATION

Prior to the arrival of Columbus, Central America had a large Indigenous population comprised of multiple Indigenous cultures, including Mesoamerican groups and circum-Caribbean groups. These original peoples included the Mayas, Aztecs, Pipils, and Lencas, among others—and thriving economies, including regional trade. Christopher Columbus arrived on the Caribbean coast of Honduras and then travelled southward to Nicaragua and Costa Rica in the early sixteenth century.[10] At that moment, it is estimated that there was a population of 5.6 million people spread from what is present-day Chiapas in southern Mexico to Panama.[11] "The Mayas had been living in the region for millennia and had been producing a substantial surplus to maintain an elite. After the conquest, Spaniards became the new elite, but the colonists were not so unintelligent as to wreck the tribute-producing society that had been and continued to be the basis of civilization in America."[12] The Spanish conquest of Central America "proceeded most briskly in highland areas and along the Pacific littoral. . . . Conversely, conquest was protracted in lowland areas and Atlantic watershed zones, where people lived less sedentary . . . lives."[13] The logic of Spanish colonization was initially informed by goals of extracting precious metals and claiming land for the Spanish crown with the expectation that local inhabitants would pay tribute and provide labor. This meant that Spain did recognize some of the lands held by Indigenous communities; these lands, "communal in character, were ceded to the indigenous peoples by Spanish conquerors in recognition of the ancient laws in place before the Conquest."[14] This is an aspect of Spanish colonization that is different than other forms of European colonization and is something that stayed in place until liberal reforms in the early nineteenth century. This was not benevolence on the part of Spaniards, rather the way they could extract tribute—or taxes—and compulsory labor from local people. Conversion to Catholicism also played a significant role in the subjugation of Indigenous peoples to colonial power.[15] As Santos Zetino, a Salvadoran Indigenous activist, recounts, "Supposedly, we were saved when we were baptized and our sins were pardoned, but now we know that this was a lie. Christianity was the sword that the Spaniards used to subdue us."[16] The original peoples of Central America were subject to forced conversion to Christianity, dispossession, and enslavement, but the most lethal effect of the Spanish conquest was illness. "The decline of Native American populations was rapid and severe, probably the greatest demographic disaster ever. Old World diseases were the primary killer."[17] It is calculated that in most of the Americas, including Central America, Indigenous populations had declined by 89 percent by 1650, a mere 150 years later.[18] In Central America, "the indigenous population shrank from almost 6 million in 1500 to less than 300,000 in 1680."[19] Indeed, Indigenous populations across Latin America did not recover from the conquest: ". . . by the beginning of the nineteenth century

Indians [*sic*] accounted for only 37 percent of Latin America's total population of 21 million."[20]

In present times, however, there remain many Indigenous communities across the region, demonstrating persistence and resistance after centuries of ill treatment. These communities have often been successful in gaining legal recognition of their ancestral lands. Their activism has manifested in broader environmental and human rights demands as well. Indigenous Maya communities in Guatemala, for example, played an important role in the civil war (1960–1996) and movements for greater Indigenous rights in Guatemala coincided with global movements for inclusion as well. "By 1980, the guerrilla groups in Guatemala amounted to more than 8,000 men and women and were supported by a noncombatant civilian base of some 250,000 in the indigenous, overpopulated areas of the central and northwest Highlands. The indigenous mobilization constituted the most significant event of the crisis because it represented both ethnic and national demands and it embodied the greatest indigenous revolt since the Conquest."[21] Indeed, 40 percent of Guatemala is Indigenous Maya, comprised of 22 different groups with their respective languages. In most countries of Central America, there are numerous Indigenous groups, many of whom have achieved some level of autonomy and control over (some) of their ancestral lands. Along the Caribbean coast of Belize, Guatemala, Honduras, and Nicaragua, the Afro-Indigenous Garifuna number over two hundred thousand, most of them in Honduras.

TABLE 1.1

CENTRAL AMERICA BY RACE AND ETHNICITY (PERCENTAGES)

COUNTRY	MESTIZO	AMERINDIAN	AFRO-DESCENDANT	ASIAN	EUROPEAN OR WHITE
Belize (2010)	52.9	11.3	32	4.9	4.8
Guatemala (2018)	56	43.5	0.3	-	-
El Salvador (2007)	83.6	0.2	0.1	-	12.7
Honduras (2013)	90	7	2	-	1
Nicaragua (2021)	69	5	9	-	17
Costa Rica (2011)*	83.6	2.4	1.1	-	83.6
Panama (2010)	65	12.3	9.2	-	6.7

*Mestizo and European or White categories are the same for Costa Rica.

Source: World Fact Book, https://www.cia.gov/the-world-factbook/.
(See endnotes for country-by-country links and additional information.)[22]

Though there is debate among historians about the precise numbers of the Indigenous population of Central America in 1502, the Spanish trafficked large numbers of Africans to increase the local workforce as part of the Atlantic slave trade. Subsequently, the African diaspora in Central America has left a significant imprint on the region. Throughout the seventeenth century in the capital of Guatemala and every major city of Nicaragua, for example, free and enslaved people from Africa and of African descent outnumbered other groups, including Spaniards and Indigenous people.[23] "Yet unlike in many other regions of the African diaspora, these histories were not simply whitewashed, but so often were displaced or denied" in Central America.[24] This phenomenon of exclusion and erasure has multiple causes. First, modern assimilationist narratives of *mestizaje*[25] lauded the mixing of European people with other inhabitants of the region into one people, thereby promoting *mestizo* identity and rendering invisible people of African descent and Indigenous peoples across the region. Second, anti-Black racism as manifest in different epochs and accompanying discriminatory laws and frameworks pushed African descendant communities to the margins. "Central America reveals the importance of place in conceptualizing blackness and diaspora" given that by the late nineteenth century, many Afro-descendant communities on the Caribbean coast of Central America lived in semi-autonomous zones or in U.S. or British enclaves and were treated as if they didn't exist by political leaders in the actual countries where they lived.[26]

When nation states began to "incorporate" these communities in the nineteenth and twentieth centuries, nationalist narratives were used to impose and subsume all ethnic groups into one *mestizo* identity. Given the distant locations many of these communities occupied vis-à-vis Central American capitals, they remained outside dominant narratives of belonging and citizenship. In the late nineteenth and early twentieth centuries, British West Indian migrants from Caribbean countries were encouraged to come and work in the region on major construction projects, such as the Panama Canal and railroad construction across the isthmus, and to work for logging and fruit export companies. Even though these laborers had been invited, there were many times when anti-Black discrimination manifested in racist, exclusionary laws across the region. Over the years, many mixed-race people of African descent were incorporated into *mestizo* or Indigenous identities, which, in turn, corroborates why a more nuanced version of "mixedness" and the Blackness of Central America isn't as well-known as it should be given both the historical record and the contributions of Afro-descendant communities today.[27]

European migration also had an impact on the region, though less is known about the actual numbers of Europeans immigrating to the region during the conquest and early colonial period. One way that the Spanish crown compensated conquistadors for their efforts and enticed them to stay "was the encomienda, a grant of Indians who were required to provide tribute to the Spaniard in the form of labor and goods."[28] Newson explains that "during the sixteenth century, between 250,000 and 300,000 Spaniards migrated to Spanish America, maybe half of them illegally" but there are few studies that track immigration numbers from Europe to individual Latin American countries, including Central America.[29] The historical record does indicate that most of this early migration was male; rape and forced unions with Indigenous and Afro-descendant women occurred across the region.[30] The Spaniards were not the only colonizers and immigrants. The British colonized much of what is present-day Belize and the Caribbean coast of Nicaragua. The British model of colonization was less focused on tribute and more focused on settler colonialism: ". . . rather than ruling over the people they colonized—like the Spanish in Mexico or Peru . . . settler colonial projects were based on eliminating the people who were there and replacing them with a white, European population."[31] Also, throughout much of the nineteenth century, there were sustained immigration flows from German-speaking Central Europe to Guatemala[32] as well as German capital which benefited from the 1896 overproduction crisis.[33] In 1888, there were "6,856 foreigners [in Costa Rica], the majority of whom were Europeans tied to coffee's trade and production," whereas "the importance of foreign hacendados was less in El Salvador and Nicaragua."[34] In Central American countries, governments often offered benefits to Europeans as an incentive to come to the region, propagated by the racist idea that "ingenuity and hard work would come from Europe."[35]

The effects of the Spanish conquest and colonial expansion led to the emergence of a Christian mixed race or *mestizo*[36] population, the descendants of unions between Europeans, Indigenous people, and Afro-descendant people. This mixing or *mestizaje* became a nationalistic discourse used throughout the region to encourage the assimilation of all groups into one and make invisible Indigenous and Afro-descendant communities. "And it has been effectively used to promote national amnesia about or to salve the national conscience in what concerns the dismal past and still colonized condition of most indigenous peoples of Latin America."[37] *Mestizaje* also has gender and class overtones. To justify the subjugation of Indigenous people, for example, *mestizo* leaders would describe them as timid and give them feminine traits while simultaneously discussing the type of mothers that Indigenous women should be, which, in turn, supported patriarchal control of Indigenous fathers over daughters.[38] Some members of this hybrid *mestizo* group with close ties to Europeans came to hold power, and upon independence in the early 1800s, an emergent European-descendant/*mestizo* elite was poised to claim power over poor *mestizos*, Indigenous peoples, and Afro-descendant communities. Called different names in different countries—"the fourteen families" in El Salvador or *los Criollos* in Guatemala—elite families, often with direct connections to Europe, occupied the leadership positions and claimed the wealth of the European colonizers in the United Provinces of Central America beginning with the creation of the federation in the early 1800s. "Power in Central America manifested itself as two forces: political monopoly and bureaucratic arbitrariness. First, elite rule was powerfully rooted in the ownership of land, in agricultural production, and in foreign commitments. The second force, linked to the first . . . [was how] the elite radically separated political ideals and concrete practice, bifurcating the legal formality of the liberal legal code and its concrete contents and daily application."[39] These local elites were not gentle leaders, rather they claimed their wealth to the exclusion of other groups, often using local paramilitary violence to sustain their wealth. "The history of Latin America [including Central America] is endowed abundantly with great men—*caudillos*—who have led their nations to greater achievement or ruin, or simply thrived on . . . charisma and bold leadership to build powerful political machines."[40] This pattern of *caudillo* or "strong-arm" leadership created conflict and protest across the centuries. "Conflict between a privileged elite on the one hand and an oppressed peasantry on the other dates from the Spanish Conquest. Calculated terror has been an established method of control of the rural population for five centuries. Resentful peasants have often responded violently individually, and sometimes touched off widespread revolution and civil war."[41]

ELITE POLITICS: CONSERVATIVES AND LIBERALS

Definitively, the first Central American Liberals came up against colonial structures which they tried to change in their attempts to produce good governments and soon they saw that the future they imagined depended not just on good wishes but on creating States based on extreme inequality. Conservative groups saw bad government in the liberal ideas and therefore dreamed and insisted on a return to the colonial order, managing to convince the popular masses to support their efforts.[42]

Historian Víctor Acuña Ortega argues that early independence leaders were more compelled by self-interest, kinship, and personal loyalties rather than political ideals.[43] As a result, there was no abrupt change with the advent of independence; what took place was a confirmation of the former regime and the belief that the people—popular masses—were not mature enough to govern[44] or to participate democratically, and that Indigenous and Afro-descendant people were only fit to serve as exploitable labor.[45]

In 1821, Central America declared independence from Spain, first forming part of an independent Mexico until 1823, at which time Chiapas stayed with Mexico and the Central American countries of Guatemala, El Salvador, Honduras, Nicaragua, and Costa Rica formed the United Provinces of Central America. Belize remained a contested territory, simultaneously claimed by the British and Guatemala. Costa Rica, under Spanish colonialism, was the furthest way from the colonial capital in Guatemala, making it "the poorest province," which contributed to its homogenous social structure and space to make different decisions about the role and type of government.[46] At this time, Panama formed part of Colombia to the south.

The loose federation of the United Provinces of Central America split apart in 1840. From the beginning, efforts to organize political life were frustrated, leading to civil war and anarchy.[47] Challenges emerged immediately when it came to building a national identity for the region that would bring together these different cities and sub-regions: how "to reconcile or choose between municipal and national sovereignty?"[48] First, "strong provincial loyalties" and *mestizo, caudillo* leadership across the region did not easily lend themselves to compromise and collaboration, both of which would have been needed to sustain the federation.[49] Secondly, "independence ... began with political parties which had long-standing economic differences struggling for control"[50] as exemplified by "cleavages and tensions"[51] between elites. "Conservative" political tendencies celebrated local elite Spanish interests, the connection with Spain, and the role of the Catholic Church; *mestizo* "liberal" goals focused on modernizing the economy and limiting Church power. "The strongholds of partisan Liberalism of the time—El Salvador and Nicaragua (more accurately San Salvador and Leon)—were able to resist Guatemalan centralism from the days of the federation forward."[52] Though both sides extolled political ideals about conservative traditions or liberal enlightenment ideas, respectively, neither side particularly sought the participation of the poor *mestizo* or Indigenous masses; rather this was about tensions between the European-descendant aristocracy and an emergent business class.

Though the short-lived federation split into separate countries in 1840, national elites—organized into the two main political parties mentioned above called the Conservatives and the Liberals—continued to perpetuate economic policies and political formations whose primary objective was to protect elite *mestizo* interests at the expense of the majorities. Though these parties were mainly comprised of elites, they had different approaches to governance and planning. The ideologies of each party informed national politics across the region from early statehood well into the twentieth century. We will unpack their differences here to facilitate understanding regional and country-by-country politics. "These parties—Conservative and Liberal—were factions of a landholding and bureaucratic elite, but they reflected fundamentally different perceptions on how best to develop their country" with a Conservative commitment to maintaining the colonial status quo of the Catholic landed aristocracy and Liberals acting as advocates for modernization and new forms of economic development.[53] "The Conservatives pleaded for moderation, order, and the stability of traditional, familiar institutions," such as respect for the Catholic Church hierarchy, a celebration of Spanish culture, and a status quo that respected small Indigenous land holdings, interestingly, because of the need for their continued tribute and labor to help farm the big estates.[54] The Liberals, on the other hand, "sought to make Central America a modern, progressive state, casting off the burden of Iberian heritage, and to absorb republican innovations from France, England, and the United States."[55] Whereas the Conservatives tended to promote the interests of the landed aristocracy and their agricultural production, the Liberals wanted to restrict the power of the Catholic Church, abolish slavery, promote economic development by lowering taxes on the private sector, modernize the public sector, expand the legal system, offer free education, and commit the government to building infrastructure. Though Conservatives were aligned with protecting the interests of landed elites, the Liberals were not as radical as they tried to appear when considered in historical perspective. "Not only did the Liberals seek political power without radical social or economic change . . . but also they did so from a profoundly illiberal and implicitly racist position."[56]

Even after the dissolution of the United Provinces of Central America, the tensions between Liberals and Conservatives continued until the early twentieth century. Though there had been clear ideological divisions between the two groups in the early 1800s—informed by tensions between Spanish-descendant Conservative leaders who yearned for the colonial status quo and new emergent Liberal leaders familiar with Enlightenment philosophies from Europe—these differences tended to blur as time went by, creating polarized models of strong-arm leadership with ever-changing ideological positions:

> Beyond the thorny questions of ideology Liberals faced other equally serious problems. Leaders switched sides with a facility explainable only on the basis of crass calculations of personal advantage. Worse yet, the Conservatives were not immune to the Liberal arguments in favor of export promotion and private ownership of land. Thus, the same Conservatives who defeated the Liberals in the 1840s, after more than a decade of severe economic difficulties, stood to benefit directly when conditions improved

13

after midcentury. Indeed, they remained in power much longer than they might have had they been, in fact, opposed to the Liberals' most basic economic policies.[57]

Into the twentieth century, "the norm was for elites to fight each other viciously but to close ranks in suppressing any and all lower-class movements that threatened to overturn this predominantly intra class or intraoligarchic political contest of Liberals versus Conservatives."[58] In historical perspective, it is easy to see that the policies of these two parties were informed greatly by the economic interests of their proponents, which often meant the continued subjugation of people on the margins. And the legacy for present-day Central America is the persistence of what Acuña Ortega calls "a political culture based on despotism, militarism, alienation, and deference."[59]

Then and today, most Central American countries have very high levels of income inequality and poverty due to these early political priorities. Costa Rica and Panama present different paths taken: Costa Rica disbanded its army in 1949 and chose to invest heavily in social services such as potable water, education, and healthcare, and today enjoys a much higher standard of living than its neighbors to the north. Panama also has a high standard of living due to multiple factors: income from the Panama Canal as well as the decision to develop a strong banking system and international financial services sector.

NEOCOLONIALISM AND TWENTIETH CENTURY SOCIAL MOVEMENTS

Export crops cultivated under colonialism, such as indigo and cochineal which served the European textile industry, morphed into agro-exports, such as coffee and bananas in the late nineteenth and early twentieth centuries, that sustained elites—tying them to foreign interests as well—and committing the region to a model of economic development that did not spread wealth or social welfare benefits around. In fact, this economic model often meant times of boom and bust when unstable commodity prices plummeted, or other countries moved into production. "Central American coffee production reached its maximum output in the 1880s, producing almost 14 percent of the world coffee yield."[60] But, by the 1920s, the coffee elites "had depleted the possibilities of coffee's development without apparent worry about or knowledge of such limitations."[61] The banana sector didn't fare well either and during times of economic crisis, foreign firms began to buy up huge extensions of land from national growers, leading Central American historian, Edelberto Torres-Rivas, to claim that by the end of the nineteenth century, "foreign interests controlled the Honduran economy."[62]

The region has been subject to the economic pressures and policies of outside powers during pre-Columbian times, throughout colonization, and since independence. A history of incursions of Indigenous peoples from Mexico into Guatemala and further south was leveraged by the Spaniards who used Mexican Indigenous groups to help quell resistance in early colonization efforts. A s d ecolonization moved across Latin America in the early nineteenth century, the role of the United States began to increase given its own emergent territorial interests. Since the 1800s, the role of the United States has had strong reverberations for the region and individual countries. Neocolonialism describes how countries—often in the global north, such as the United States—impose their political agendas, economic interests, and territorial plans of expansion on other countries near and far. Neocolonialism can include the burden of disadvantageous trade agreements; it also encompasses the imposition of foreign economic interests, aid conditionalities and policies, and military aid on countries. In the mid-nineteenth century, for example, William Walker, a U.S. mercenary, declared himself president of Nicaragua and then tried to take power in Honduras and Costa Rica. Ultimately, he was captured, tried, found guilty, and executed in Honduras. But U.S. foreign policy—as well as Great Britain, but to a lesser extent—has informed much of Central American economics and politics in one form or another throughout the nineteenth and twentieth centuries, and into the twenty-first c entury. M any e xamples e xist o f the deleterious effects of these policies for different Central American countries, and these are explored in greater detail in the country chapters. U.S. foreign policy has been justified t hrough official nar ratives of soc ial pro gress, eco nomic development, the cold war fight against communism, and often codified in laws and legal frameworks, such as the Monroe Doctrine, the Roosevelt Corollary, and other strategies such as Dollar Diplomacy under President Taft and the Alliance for Progress under President Kennedy. "At the time Monroe announced the doctrine, the United States occupied only the eastern seaboard of North America. His [1823] statement made it clear that the new country claimed sole rights to colonize the rest of the continent. And the new country immediately set about doing so."[63]

The United States has directly occupied countries with armed troops at many different p oints; N icaragua i s o ne s uch e xample. Th e Un ited St ates pr opped up elite rulers in Guatemala, El Salvador, Honduras, and Nicaragua through the nineteenth and twentieth centuries. During the Cold War, the United States ousted leaders perceived as being soft o n c ommunism, a s i n t he U.S.-led a nd fi nanced coup d'état against President Jacobo Árbenz in Guatemala in 1954—which created the conditions for over 30 years of civil war—or the 1989 invasion of Panama to oust President Noriega because he was not aligned with U.S. interests. The United States also armed and trained repressive government security forces (armies, police, paramilitaries, etc.) across the region throughout the twentieth century. The United States used international aid, military aid, and diplomacy to influence Central American politics towards U.S. anticommunist political goals, and the United States and international financial intermediaries have also imposed economic policies, such as neoliberal structural adjustment and stabilization policies in the late twentieth century onward, which included devaluing local currencies, reducing basic food subsidies, and the deregulation of national economies.[64] To be eligible for bilateral loans and aid, these neoliberal policies require Central American states to meet such conditionalities as the privatization of state-owned businesses, lowering social spending, and cutting social welfare programming. These policies, in turn, have increased poverty and inequality across the region from the 1980s onwards. Explored in greater detail in each country chapter, many scholars agree that U.S. foreign policy has had a powerful impact on Central America, which, in turn, has fomented Central American outbound emigration. Indeed, it is not infrequent to hear that "U.S. foreign policy appears to have been more effective in generating refugees than U.S. immigration and refugee policies have been in preventing their entry."[65]

Remarkably, even with foreign involvement and powerful, local elites, Central America has a long history of activism and social movements, including generally non-violent civil society movements as well as armed, revolutionary groups, which have organized (and fought) for change as exemplified by socialist and communist organizing in the early twentieth century, popular organizing for inclusion and democratic political processes in the mid-twentieth century, and armed revolutions throughout the twentieth century. Often the most extractivist agro-exports created opposition within their own industries, such as banana workers in Honduras and Nicaragua in the early twentieth century seeking to institute a ten-hour workday instead of a fourteen-hour workday and other basic rights. El Salvador's *campesino* rebellion in the 1930s also had reverberations through the region as the Salvadoran government carried out a massacre of thirty thousand farmers, Indigenous people, and workers to put down a popular uprising.[66] Many of the leaders and activists in these movements have come from marginalized groups such as Indigenous peoples, peasant communities, Afro-descendant groups, women, union organizers, and other disenfranchised or excluded groups. Their platforms have included basic worker rights, protests against authoritarianism, and demands for the inclusion of women, Afro-descendant communities, Indigenous groups, and more recently on behalf of gender and sexual minorities. Environmental groups, often in conjunction with *campesino* and Indigenous groups, have protested the land grabs and extractivist practices of foreign companies and local elites such as large-scale monocropping (e.g., sugar, coffee, and African palm) and mining (e.g., gold, silver, and other minerals), past to present.[67]

Tied to protest and the status quo, religion has also played a regional role in culture, politics, and economics. During the colonial period, people were forced to convert to Roman Catholicism as part of the colonial order, but over the centuries this has evolved in interesting ways. During the revolutionary period of the late twentieth century, for example, many Roman Catholic priests, nuns, and lay people, following the tenets of the Second Vatican Council that called for increased solidarity with the poor and disenfranchised, embraced the values and praxis of liberation theology. Liberation theology is a movement within Christianity that posits that the Kingdom of God should be built on earth and not treated as something to be put off until the afterlife. This translated into prioritizing and addressing the social conditions and political exclusions of the poor in Central America. Many Catholic Church leaders, including church leaders, priests, nuns, and lay leaders, began to organize and demand social welfare initiatives, political participation, and inclusive economic policies with and on behalf of the poor majorities. This led repressive governments and paramilitary death squads to respond harshly, including the 1979 assassination of Archbishop Romero in El Salvador, the 1998 assassination of Bishop Gerardi in Guatemala, and present-day government persecution of the Catholic Church for demanding a return to democracy and rule of law in Nicaragua, for example. Other religions have also proliferated in Central America. In fact, today, almost 20 percent of Latin America—with much higher percentages in Central America—self-identify with Protestantism, following Evangelical and Pentecostal faiths.[68]

CENTRAL AMERICAN MIGRATION

In response to poverty, conflict, and the deadly synergy of climate change and natural disasters, there have been Central American population flows within individual countries (rural to urban shifts), within Central America itself (seeking refuge or economic opportunities in neighboring countries), northwards toward Mexico and the United States, and even to Europe during the twentieth and early twenty-first centuries.[69] In the early twentieth century, there was significant migration within Central American countries (and from the West Indies in the Caribbean to Central America) as workers migrated to banana enclaves throughout Central America as well as to Panama for the construction of the canal.[70] Another example is the flow of service sector workers from Nicaragua to Costa Rica over the past couple of decades. Central American migration to the United States began to grow in the 1980s in response to armed conflicts in the region, which the U.S. government fomented with military assistance to governments and armed groups, often supporting those with bad human rights records. "By the end of the 1980s, around 3 million Central Americans had fled from their countries of origin."[71] During the civil wars from the 1970s into the 1990s, a steady flow of Guatemalans and Salvadorans to the United States grew into a mass exodus, but for Honduras, the growth in emigration has been more gradual.[72] According to the Migration Policy Institute, "Immigrants from the Northern Triangle [Guatemala, El Salvador, and Honduras] comprised 86 percent of the Central Americans in the United States. In 2017, Central American immigrants represented 8 percent of the United States' 44.5 million immigrants."[73] According to sociologist José Luis Rocha, whose extensive scholarship about Central American migrations traces the complex drivers of migration, "The latest data available in the U. S. Census Bureau [2019] indicate that the United States is home to 257,343 people born in Nicaragua, 745,838 born in Honduras, 1,111,495 born in Guatemala and 1,412,101 born in El Salvador. To this population must be added their descendents, second and third generation migrants, to total 429,501 Nicaraguans, 1,083,540 Hondurans, 1,683,093 Guatemalans and 2,311,574 Salvadorans by origin. This migration has been fed by new generations of increasing size, the balance of which is reflected in these figures."[74] Today, most Central Americans in the United States—85 percent of whom have come from El Salvador, Guatemala, and Honduras[75]—live in Los Angeles, with substantial numbers in San Francisco; Texas (especially Houston); Washington, D.C.; New York City; Chicago; New Orleans; and Miami.[76]

TABLE 1.2

CENTRAL AMERICANS IN THE UNITED STATES, 1970–2018

YEAR	NUMBER OF IMMIGRANTS
1970	117,700
1980	352,540
1990	1,111,864
2000	1,996,337
2010	2,989,433
2013	3,053,000
2018	3,255,182

Listed population numbers reflect data from each listed year, not the subsequent decade. Data includes documented and undocumented immigrants taken from census data, public-use files of the American Community Survey (ACS), and figures for 2018 come from the Annual Social and Economic Supplement of the Current Population Survey.[77]

TABLE 1.3

COUNTRY OF ORIGIN FOR CENTRAL AMERICAN IMMIGRANTS IN THE UNITED STATES, 2019

COUNTRY	NUMBER OF IMMIGRANTS	SHARE %
Total Central America	3,782,000	100.0%
El Salvador	1,412,000	37.3%
Guatemala	1,111,000	29,4%
Honduras	746,000	19.7%
Nicaragua	257,000	6.8%
Panama	101,000	2.7%
Costa Rica	94,000	2.5%
Belize	44,000	1.2%
Other Central America	16,000	0.4%

Source: Migration Policy Institute (MPI) tabulation of data from the U.S. Census Bureau 2019 American Community Survey (ACS).[78]

Recently, there has been an increase in the number of unaccompanied children and young people traveling from Central America northwards, due to increasing gang violence, especially in the countries of Guatemala, El Salvador, and Honduras. In a nominal attempt to do something about this, President Obama initiated the Central American Minors Refugee Parole Program "allowing a small number of youth to apply for asylum within their own countries."[79] However, under President Trump and his "Border War," the situation only grew more dire as children were separated from their families and sent alone to Office of the Refugee Resettlement camps.[80] The *New York Times* broke the story about this in April 2018.

CENTRAL AMERICA TODAY

The combination of a strategic geographic location in the Western hemisphere, the politically conservative and repressive nature of local elites, and the resistance of oppressed and marginalized groups greatly inform the history of the region. The activism and vibrancy of these social movements has had multiple ramifications, including pressure to end repression, to adopt policies and laws promoting greater inclusion, and to institute environmental safeguards. In his analysis about development and rule of law, Kevin Casas-Zamora writes, "Central America has done many important things, none more so than ending the civil wars. That, however, was the easy part. Ending the civil wars required the will and the courage to sit down and negotiate a settlement. Building more equitable societies, solid

19

democratic institutions, and dynamic economies requires the same attributes over a very long time span. The end of the wars and the democratic transitions in Central America threw a lifeline to the region, but today that lifeline is at risk of being submerged."[81] Presently, Central America faces a complex and interrelated set of opportunities and challenges. The opportunities include increased access to education for most of the region, sustained slow but steady economic growth, and a vibrant civil society, comprised of non-governmental organizations, citizen and community groups, and other special interest groups. Yet sometimes these achievements are not enough to galvanize action given the postconflict challenges that many countries face.[82] The challenges include high levels of poverty, exclusion, and violence due to the civil war era of the late twentieth century; the gang and drug violence of the early twenty-first century; a steady exodus of people from the region seeking better living conditions (see Tables 1.2 and 1.3); and corruption and weak rule of law in some of the countries (see Tables 1.4–1.6).

TABLE 1.4

IMPUNITY RATES IN CENTRAL AMERICA* — 2017
Percentage reflects number of unsolved journalist murders against respective country's population[83]

COUNTRY	RATE (IN %)
Nicaragua	66.34
Honduras	65.04
El Salvador	65.03
Panamá	63.23
Guatemala	62.40
Costa Rica	54.57

*no data available for Belize (it does not generate enough statistical info for study)

TABLE 1.5

TRANSPARENCY RATES IN CENTRAL AMERICA*— 2015–20
Percentages from 0 to 100, where 0 is "highly corrupt" and 100 is "very clean"[84]

	2015	2016	2017	2018	2019	2020
Guatemala	28%	28%	28%	27%	26%	25%
El Salvador	39%	36%	33%	35%	34%	36%
Honduras	31%	30%	29%	29%	26%	24%
Nicaragua	27%	26%	26%	25%	22%	22%
Costa Rica	55%	58%	59%	56%	56%	57%
Panama	39%	38%	37%	37%	36%	35%

*no data available for Belize

TABLE 1.6

RULE OF LAW IN CENTRAL AMERICA —
2014, 2015, 2016, 2017–18, 2019, & 2020
Scores range from 0 to 1, with 1 indicating the strongest adherence to the rule of law[85]

	2014	2015	2016	2017–2018	2019	2020
Belize	*	0.49	0.47	0.47	0.48	0.48
Guatemala	0.52	0.44	0.44	0.44	0.46	0.45
El Salvador	0.49	0.51	0.49	0.48	0.48	0.49
Honduras	*	0.42	0.42	0.40	0.40	0.40
Nicaragua	0.31	0.43	0.42	0.43	0.40	0.39
Costa Rica	*	0.68	0.68	0.68	0.69	0.68
Panama	0.45	0.53	0.52	0.52	0.52	0.52

*no data available

CONCLUSION

This book started as a conversation between the Seattle International Foundation and Seattle University's Central America Initiative. Bill Clapp, one of the founders of the Seattle International Foundation, approached Serena with the idea of a research project that would summarize key events in Central American history to share with policymakers in Washington, D.C. Serena and Isabeau piloted the project with a short history of Nicaragua, which in turn led to this book project. The purpose of this set of histories is to provide our readers with a short and accessible history of a region that often appears in the news; it is our hope that this book and its open access versions will help students, educators, policymakers, and global citizens better understand this important yet frequently misunderstood region. In the chapters that follow, we explore the paths taken by each Central American country in a systematic fashion moving from pre-Columbian times to the twenty-first century. Each country chapter is divided into parts: opening with a map and historical timeline, systematically touching on each historical period, and concluding with a list of recommended readings. All references cited can be found in the bibliography at the end of the book. Chapter Nine, the final chapter, explores present-day manifestations of historical themes and topics that are transversal to the region, connecting people and groups across borders, to help the reader better imagine a region and not just a collection of individual countries. This final chapter engages the following cross-cutting themes: *caudillo* leadership models, impacts of U.S. foreign policy, activism and social movements, and migration.

We authors each have deep roots—personal and professional—in the region; however, to be clear, we are not historians. Rather, we are engaged scholars committed to raising the level of general knowledge about Central America and promoting increased understanding across difference, respectful and responsive diplomacy, international aid that targets Central American priorities, and more inclusive economic development. When we first drafted this manuscript, we were professor and research assistant, now we're friends and collaborators. Throughout the research and book writing process, we have remained committed to a horizontal collaboration as we moved key documents back and forth for analysis and co-authored the chapters. Serena Cosgrove (she/her) is a scholar of Central America from the United States who moved to the region in the mid-1980s and lived there until 1993, monitoring human rights during the conflicts in Nicaragua, El Salvador, and Guatemala. She has returned multiple times a year since then for research, advocacy, applied work, and kinship connections. Isabeau J. Belisle Dempsey (they/them) is half-Belizean and was raised in the United States. As an undergraduate at Seattle University where Serena teaches, Isabeau studied International Studies and Spanish and traveled to Central America. Intergenerational and interdisciplinary, our approach for this book has leveraged our academic interest and experience in Central America, and our personal and kin connections to the region. We have consulted a wide range of academic and primary sources in English and Spanish by a global set of Central Americanist researchers as well as Central American scholars themselves; we read many historical documents and records and analyzed statistics to present as nuanced an interpretation as possible of the region. We dedicate this book to the persistence of Central Americans committed to increased autonomy and inclusion across the region.

Recommended Reading

Alvarado, Karina O., Alicia I. Estrada, and Ester E. Hernández. *U.S. Central Americans: Reconstructing Memories, Struggles, and Communities of Resistance.* Tucson: University of Arizona Press, 2017.

Booth, John A., Christine J. Wade, and Thomas W. Walker. *Understanding Central America: Global Forces, Rebellion, and Change.* Boulder, CO: Westview Press, 2015.

Chomsky, Aviva. *Central America's Forgotten History: Revolution, Violence, and the Roots of Migration.* Boston: Beacon Press, 2021.

Dym, Jordana. *From Sovereign Villages to National States: City, State, and Federation in Central America, 1759–1839.* Albuquerque: University of New Mexico Press, 2006.

Foster, Lynn V. *A Brief History of Central America.* 2nd ed. New York: Checkmark Books, 2007.

Gudmundson, Lowell, and Héctor Lindo-Fuentes. *Central America, 1821–1871: Liberalism before Liberal Reform.* Tuscaloosa: University of Alabama Press, 1995.

Gudmundson, Lowell, and Justin Wolfe. *Blacks and Blackness in Central America: Between Race and Place.* Durham, NC: Duke University Press, 2010.

La Feber, Walter. *Inevitable Revolutions: The United States in Central America*. New York: W.W. Norton, 1993.

MacLeod, Murdo J. *Spanish Central America: A Socioeconomic History, 1520–1720*. Austin: University of Texas Press, 2008.

Martínez, Óscar. *A History of Violence: Living and Dying in Central America*. Brooklyn: Verso, 2016.

Patch, Robert. *Indians and the Political Economy of Colonial Central America, 1670–1810*. Norman: University of Oklahoma Press, 2013.

Pérez-Brignoli, Héctor. *A Brief History of Central America*. Berkeley: University of California Press, 1989.

Sellers-García, Sylvia. *Distance and Documents at the Spanish Empire's Periphery*. Redwood City: Stanford University Press, 2013.

Torres-Rivas, Edelberto. *History and Society in Central America*. Austin: University of Texas Press, 1993.

Woodward, Ralph Lee. *Central America, A Nation Divided*. 3rd ed. New York: Oxford University Press, 1999.

Wortman, Miles L. *Government and Society in Central America, 1680–1840*. New York: Columbia University Press, 1982.

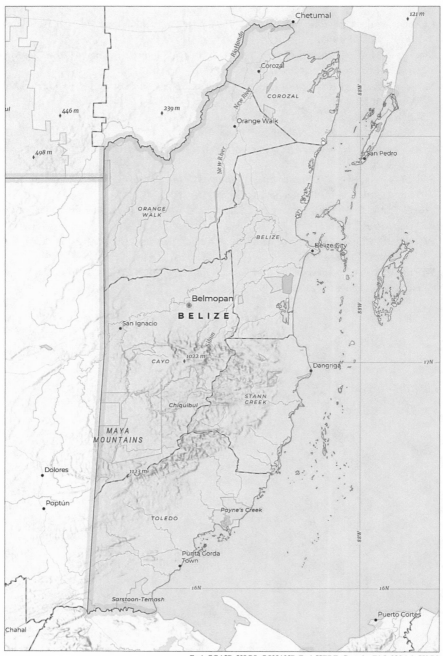

A Brief History of Belize

INTRODUCTION

Known as British Honduras until 1973, Belize is the only Central American country to have been primarily colonized by the British. It is also the only Central American country whose official language is English rather than Spanish; additionally, a form of English Creole, known as Belizean Kriol, is also widely spoken. Belize's population is a mix of *mestizos* (descendants of Spanish settlers and Indigenous Maya), Indigenous Maya, Creoles (descendants of African slaves and English settlers), the Afro-Indigenous group called the Garifuna, Asians (especially Taiwanese and Chinese), and Europeans. The Belizean economy was historically built around mahogany extraction, and a likeness of the tree is featured on the Belizean flag.

Belize has a strained relationship with neighboring country Guatemala, the government of which frequently claims that Belize is Guatemalan territory. This tension has lasted for over a hundred and fifty years and continues today.

TIMELINE OF KEY EVENTS

1508: First known date of Spanish presence; Mayan communities resist Spanish attempts at control of region

1546: Mayan uprising that forcefully expelled the Spanish from Belize

1638: The Baymen (British and Scottish pirates) arrive to Belize coast

1650s: Estimated date of British settlement

1698: Spanish give up attempts to claim Belize, leaving the area

1717–1779: Spanish forces stage various attacks against British settlers

1798: British defeat Spanish in Battle of St. George's Caye

1838: Enslaved people emancipated

1839: Central American Federation disintegrates; Guatemala claims Belize as its territory—Belize was not part of the Federation

1859: Great Britain and Guatemala sign agreement in which Guatemala promises to rescind claims to Belize in exchange for road construction from Guatemala City to Caribbean coast

1862: Belize officially declared a colony of the British Commonwealth, named British Honduras

1893: Mariscal-Spender Treaty delimits border between Mexico and Belize

1945: Belize designated as the 23rd department in Guatemala's new constitution

1949: People's Committee formed to protest devaluation of British Honduran dollar

1950: People's United Party (PUP) formed; minimum age for women voters lowered from 30 to 21

1954: New constitution created that gives Belize full political autonomy, universal adult suffrage, and a two-chamber parliament

1970: Belmopan replaces Belize City as capital

1973: Country officially changes its name from British Honduras to Belize

1981: Belize gains independence from Great Britain with George Price as prime minister; the country remains part of the Commonwealth

1984: First elections since independence; United Democratic Party leader Manuel Esquivel wins

1993: British government announces withdrawal of troops and an end to security guarantee

2005: Unrest caused by tax increases

2008: Dean Barrow elected Belize's first Black prime minister

2012: Dean Barrow re-elected

2018: Referendums held in both Guatemala and Belize to send Belize-Guatemala border dispute to International Court of Justice

2019: International Court of Justice officially presented with Belize-Guatemala border dispute case

2020: Johnny Briceño of the People's United Party becomes prime minister

2021: Froyla Tzalam nominated Governor-General of Belize, becoming first Indigenous Governor-General in Belize

A HISTORY OF BELIZE

Pre-Columbian Era

> Belize, a small nation on the Caribbean coast of Central America, occupies part of the territory in which the Maya civilization flourished during the first millennium [BCE], with an apogee in the Classic Period of 250–900 [BCE].[1]

Prior to the arrival of European colonial powers, Belize was populated by Indigenous groups, particularly the Maya, whose territory extended into present-day Belize's neighbor, Guatemala. At around 850 BCE, it was a thriving region, hosting a population of over three hundred thousand in different city-states throughout much of the present-day country. Maya civilization was mostly agricultural, including crops such as corn and squash, as well as hunting and fishing activities; craft skills such as pottery and jade-carving became popular later. There was some tension and fighting between the different Maya groups: in 1123 BCE, the Yucatec Maya of the north rose up and overthrew the Itzá Maya from the Petén Basin, a region that stretched from northern Guatemala to southeastern México. The other two significant Maya groups were—and still are—the Q'eqchi' and the Mopan.

There are several Maya sites that can be visited throughout the country, such as Altún Ha near present-day Belize City and Xunantunich in Cayo, which is the tallest human-made structure in Belize. Altún Ha was settled around 200 BCE and became a hub of activity, with almost ten thousand people living there. Altún Ha is home to several temples and buildings where priests lived. It is speculated that a peasant uprising took place against the ruling priest class. Xunantunich—which means "Lady of the Rock"—was settled in 300 BCE and boasted fertile lands that were good for farming. Maya civilization declined greatly during the eighth and ninth centuries, their population diminishing significantly. There are many theories as to why this happened, including the spread of disease, droughts devastating the Yucatán and Petén areas, and competition between different city-states.

Colonization and English Rule

> What we today call Belize was in the seventeenth century a remote backwater that attracted British pirates and buccaneers as a base from which to raid ships headed to Spain with their valuable (and typically imaginary) cargoes of gold. The watery lowlands of central and northern Belize were also, however, home to dense stands of logwood, which in the late seventeenth and eighteenth centuries became a highly valuable commodity—a source of dye for the burgeoning

textile industry in England. Some of the early privateers settled in these waterlogged plains, cutting and selling logwood as a means to generating wealth.[2]

Unlike the rest of Central America, Belize's colonizers were from Great Britain rather than Spain. This was mostly due to the Spanish focus on other parts of the region for extraction and development; the Spanish had been the first European presence in Belize, starting excursions in 1508 and later officially declaring conquest in 1542. They were aggressively resisted by the Maya, and were thrown out during a massive uprising in 1546. The Spanish made various attempts to get control of the region, staging several raids against the Maya, destroying their villages and anything to do with Mayan cultural identity.

In 1638, British and Scottish pirates—known as the Baymen—arrived to the coast of Belize in an effort to find a secluded area from which they could attack Spanish ships. The presence of the Baymen on the coast caused the Maya to flee inland. The Baymen settled the coast and soon discovered a sustainable living in cutting, selling, and exporting logwood—a tropical tree found throughout southern Mexico and northern Central America, whose heartwood was used to make a purple-red dye in addition to using the wood for craftsmanship—from Belize to England. The Baymen then introduced slavery to the region in order to support this budding industry, eventually bringing enslaved Africans from the West Indies.

A 1667 treaty in England calling for the suppression of piracy only encouraged the growth of this new logging industry. In 1670, the Godolphin Treaty between England and Spain confirmed English claim to all countries and islands in the Western hemisphere that England had already settled; however, this treaty did not name the coastal area between Yucatán and Nicaragua, where Belize lay. Contention between the European countries continued until 1717 when Spain expelled British loggers from the Bay of Campeche, west of Yucatán. This action had the unanticipated effect of allowing the British settlement near the Belize River to continue growing.

Throughout the eighteenth century, the Spanish attacked the British settlers continuously, forcing them to leave the area on four occasions: in 1717, 1730, 1754, and 1779. In spite of this, the Spanish never officially settled the region, and consequently the British always returned to expand their own trade and settlement. The Battle of St. George's Caye in 1798 was the final Spanish attack against the British settlement in which Spanish governor General Arturo O'Neill led a flotilla of thirty vessels and two thousand troops against the Spanish. The British eventually won the engagement, officially expelling the Spanish from claiming control of the area that comprises Belize today. "[T]he British tried, throughout the 16th and 17th centuries, to secure Belize as a colony away from the Spanish and 'to wipe out all memory of Spanish pretensions, and to encourage exclusively the British way of life'. One of the first outward and visible signs of a British colony in those days was the establishment of the National Church."[3]

British colonialism focused on "extractionism": the practice of systematically identifying and extracting valuable natural resources on a massive scale for capital benefit. The British identified resource-rich land and established colonies in order to extend the reach of the British empire. This method of "indirect colonialism" formed a world-wide network of trade ports and taxable states that benefited the crown, while not demanding a large contingent of settlers.[4]

The British shifted their economic focus from logwood to mahogany extraction near the end of the eighteenth century. While the extraction of logwood was less labor intensive, the mahogany industry demanded more money and land, and consequently more laborers to work that land. Enslaved people in Belize were officially emancipated in 1838, five years after the British Slave Emancipation Act was passed. This put a strain on the growing mahogany industry, and the British found ways to make up for the labor that had been lost upon emancipation: "At the time of emancipation, a boom in the mahogany market created a need for labor, which was dealt with by importing indentured labor and using coercive methods to keep freedmen dependent."[5]

The Garifuna—also known as the Garinagu, an Afro-Indigenous people descended from the Carib people of the Caribbean and Africans who had escaped from slavery and resisted colonialism in the Lesser Antilles—arrived to southern Belize by way of Honduras, reportedly as early as 1802. They settled in the Stann Creek area and became fisherfolk and farmers. Other Garifuna arrived to Belize after a civil war in Honduras in 1832. November 19, 1832, is the date officially recognized as "Garifuna Settlement Day" in Belize, which is celebrated nationally and regionally throughout Central America by Garifuna communities.

In 1854, Britain laid an official claim to the settlement they had established in Belize, shortly following concessions they had made regarding the Bay Islands and the Mosquito Coast in Nicaragua. The Settlement of Belize in the Bay of Honduras was declared a British colony in 1862, officially dubbed British Honduras and put under the governance of the British leaders in Jamaica, another British colony in the Caribbean.

Independence

Belize gained its political independence in September 1981 from the United Kingdom to become the 156th member of the United Nations, a separate member of the British Commonwealth of Nations, as well as an individual member of what [Keith] Buchanan terms the "commonwealth of poverty"—the Third World. Belize is definitely a "Caribbean society" as defined by [David] Lowenthal, although its location on the mainland of Central America has meant that the country's history is very much interwoven with this landmass as well.[6]

The British Honduran economy remained heavily reliant on mahogany extraction, especially due to the interests of investors such as the British-owned Belize Estate and Produce Company, which at one point owned half of all privately-held land. This proved to be detrimental when the Great Depression hit, nearly causing the colony's economy to collapse as British demand for timber plummeted. The damage was exacerbated when a category four hurricane hit Belize in 1931, the deadliest in the country's recorded history. Belize City, the capital, was ravaged.

Conditions worsened further when Britain decided to devalue the British Honduran dollar in 1949. Popular mobilization had been stirring in the wake of the 1931 hurricane because of the lack of government support; the devaluation finally encouraged British Hondurans to organize for the founding of the first local political party, the People's Committee, which would then become the People's United Party (PUP). The PUP protests against devaluation eventually became a campaign demanding independence from Britain, as well as constitutional reforms such as expansion of voting rights to all adults. The colonial government granted universal adult suffrage in 1954, and the first election was decisively won by the PUP. Pro-independence activist George Price became the PUP leader in 1956 and the head of government in 1961. Britain proclaimed "self-government" for Belize in 1964, under a new constitution.[7] In June of 1973, British Honduras was renamed Belize. Although there is no official account of why the name "Belize" was chosen, there are several theories, including that it may derive from a Maya word: possibly "Balix," meaning "muddy waters" in reference to the Belize River, or perhaps "Belikin," meaning "land facing the sea."

Under Prime Minister George Price, Belize began a campaign for full independence, seeking international recognition as a nation. The first United Nations resolution supporting independence for Belize was passed in 1975, with 110 votes in favor, 16 abstentions, and only 9 against; however, none of the Spanish-speaking Latin American countries voted in favor, apart from Cuba. Costa Rica, El Salvador, Honduras, Nicaragua, Panama, the Dominican Republic, and Uruguay all voted no, and the rest abstained. The Central American nations likely voted "no" out of respect for Guatemala and its claims to Belize's territory. Prime Minister Price met with General Omar Torrijos, president of Panama, at the 1976 summit meeting of the Non-Aligned Nations—a group formed in the 1950s in response to the increasingly polarized Cold War-era world of 120 states from the Global South that are not formally aligned with or against any major power bloc, and which still functions as a major international organization today. PM Price's meeting with General Torrijos was an effort to gain the Panamanian government's support for Belizean independence. The Sandinista government of Nicaragua was a major supporter of Belize's bid for independence. By the end of 1980, Belize had gained nearly unanimous international support, and officially gained its independence from Britain on September 21, 1981, almost two hundred years later than the rest of Central America.[8]

Present-Day Belize

In 1984, heads of state of the CARICOM countries (the Caribbean Community and Common Market), including Belize, met in the Bahamas to affirm economic policies contained in the "Nassau Understanding." This statement committed the region to diversifying its exports away from a handful of agricultural commodities (such as sugar) that had experienced deep declines in world prices in the early 1980s. Caribbean governments pledged to adopt nontraditional crops and attract offshore manufacturing from the United States and Europe in order to cushion themselves against volatile monocrop markets.[9]

Under Prime Minister George Price, the People's United Party continued to win elections until 1984, which was the first national election since Belize's independence. In the 1984 elections, the PUP lost to the United Democratic Party (UDP), led by Manuel Esquivel, who succeeded Price as prime minister. In 1985, Prime Minister Esquivel signed an agreement with the U.S. Agency for International Development (USAID), requiring the Belizean government to adopt neoliberal, structural adjustment, economic policies, such as the privatization of state corporations.

The UDP and the PUP continue to dominate Belize's political scene, trading power back and forth across the years. UDP leader Dean Barrow became prime minister in 2008 after a landslide victory in the general elections, with the UDP winning 25 out of 31 seats in the House of Representatives. He was re-elected in 2012. In November of 2020, the PUP defeated the UDP for the first time since 2003, and PUP party leader Johnny Briceño became prime minister. In April 2021, Froyla Tzalam, a Mopan Maya community leader, was nominated to be the Governor-General of Belize. The Governor-General serves as Commander-in-Chief of the Belize Defence Force in addition to being a general representative of the country. Tzalam is the second woman and the first Indigenous person to serve as Governor-General.

In the context of the international community, Belize has continued to have a unique position, difficult to fit in any one regional or cultural community. Indeed, there continues to be a question over whether Belize ought to be considered more a Caribbean country rather than a member of Central America. Its membership in the Caribbean Community and Common Market (CARICOM) only underscores this issue. Belize shares many cultural similarities to Caribbean countries, as well as the historical legacy of being subject to British rather than Spanish colonization. In fact, there is large overlap between those countries who have membership in CARICOM and countries that are, or historically have been, part of the English Commonwealth. CARICOM itself began to emerge after the collapse of British West Indies Federation in 1962; the project for Caribbean integration was initiated in 1965 by the creation of the Caribbean Free Trade Area.[10] Still, Belize also became a full member of the Central American Integration System (SICA) in 1998, so its membership in CARICOM does not necessarily align its identity with the Caribbean community exclusively.

Belize also has the highest Black/Afro-descendant population in the Central American region, with 32 percent of its citizens self-identifying as such.[11] This demographic difference sets Belize apart from most of the other Central American countries, whose populations are primarily *mestizo* and Indigenous. The presence of the Garifuna, an Afro-Indigenous people, certainly play a role in this larger conceptualization of Belize's national identity, both as an Afrodiasporic country and as a Caribbean country, given the Garifuna's intertwined African and Caribbean cultural heritage.[12]

Tourism in Belize

> Cultures have been subsumed, ritualised for the benefit of hordes of camera-wielding, high-spending, experience-seeking people from well-heeled countries anxious to capture every moment on film.[13]

Although the agricultural sector remains Belize's primary source of income, the tourism industry has quickly become a dominating force in the country's economy, particularly "ecotourism." Key and Pillai define ecotourism as "traveling to an undisturbed and pristine natural environment with the object of studying, admiring and enjoying the scenery with its wild plants and animals."[14] Essentially, Belize's natural biodiversity has become its primary commodity. Many present-day tourists travel to countries like Belize in pursuit of "the authentic." While tourism has indeed been an important factor in Belize's modern economic development, there are also concerns over the sustainability of this model, particularly because of tourists' impact on the environment. The increase in tourism has led to the construction of bars, restaurants, and hotels to host foreign visitors. The land is cleared, trees cut, and other natural resources depleted for the sake of accommodating the tourist industry.[15] However, as the question of sustainability comes to the forefront, the government of Belize has begun grappling with how to find a balance between ensuring the sustainability of the environment of Belize and the continued success of the tourism industry.

Though there is certainly a significant benefit to the national economy, on a local level, there is a bit more conflict and nuance to the tourist-host relationship. Some Belizeans maintain a positive view of the industry's effects on local economies, appreciative of the jobs it creates and the opportunities it provides. Still others see the way that an emphasis on tourism has shifted the culture of their communities, enticing "fisherman to take out tourists rather than fish" and barring locals from interacting with the land in ways they have done for generations, such as frequenting beaches that are now closed off as private property.[16]

Social Movements

During popular debates held before independence was achieved in 1981, Garifuna women and men were popular theorists and social spokespersons in favour of the idea that independence politics was going to be the backbone of a new multiethnic and multicultural political entity. Women expressed their views on several occasions, that independence was not only good news for the rights of the Garifuna but also for other ethnic groups established in Belize.[17]

The Garifuna have faced prejudice in Central America; their unique history and cultural expressions set them apart from much of the region, and it is an enduring struggle for this group to retain their identity and dignity. One of the ways that the Garifuna have begun to center their cultural identity is by changing the name of one of their major settlements in the country: sometime in the early 1800s, Garifuna from Honduras traveled north to Belize, where they settled in what became known as Stann Creek Town, the capital of Belize's Stann Creek District. Around 1975, however, Stann Creek Town's name was changed to Dangriga, a Garifuna word that means "standing waters." Dangriga is known as Belize's "cultural capital" for its concentration of Garifuna cultural expressions, particularly punta music.

Maya culture and identity, like the Garifuna, persist today; their most tangible influence is in the momentum of the land rights movement in Belize. Arguably, traction has been gained for this movement in response to an increase in tourism and a renewed sense of responsibility to be stewards of their country in the face of land lost to hotels and ex-pat housing development. One of the turning points regarding both land rights activism and the persistence of Indigenous identity was in April 2015, when the Maya people of Belize's Toledo district won a landmark case in the Caribbean Court of Justice. The Q'eqchi' and Mopan Maya had been fighting for rights to their historical lands for decades. The Caribbean Court of Justice, Belize's highest appellate court, judged that the land be demarcated and registered to the Maya; that damages be awarded to the Maya people to compensate for all material and moral harm inflicted; and that the government of Belize cease and desist all destruction and use of the designated land without first getting the informed consent of the Indigenous population.

Although the government has not always honored this ruling, now the Indigenous communities of Belize have the legal right to confront the wrongdoings of officials. In September 2021, the Garifuna Nation condemned the government for encroaching on Garifuna settlements in the south. The Nation accused the government of constructing a gas station in Seine Bight without consulting the local Garifuna people. Garifuna lands in Belize are not, at the time of writing, demarcated as Maya lands are; however, in light of the government's attempt to construct on Garifuna lands without their consent, the knowledge of legal precedent in the country has encouraged many in the community to stage protests.

Border Dispute with Guatemala

> Guatemala's controversial claim to the territory of Belize, the roots of which lie in a vaguely worded treaty from 1859 between Guatemala and Great Britain, has not only hindered the political development of Belize, but has affected relations between the United States and Britain, and Central America and the Caribbean. Because of the unequal size and might of the two nations, Belize has found it necessary to maintain the military protection of the British government, even though it is now an independent nation.[18]

Unlike many Central American countries who have faced internal strife, often to the point of civil war, Belize's most heated point of contention lies with its neighbor, Guatemala. For over a hundred and fifty years, Guatemala has laid claims to its neighbor's territory; often, maps drawn by the Guatemalan government show Belize as Guatemala's twenty-third department. When the Spanish empire disintegrated in the 1820s, the independent republics that would eventually become Mexico and Guatemala both made claims to the Belizean territory. However, as these claims were made under the 1786 Convention of London—a doctrine applied specifically to Spain and Spanish territories—Britain, the nation that had settled Belize, did not recognize those claims. Mexico eventually dropped its claims, but Guatemala did not.

In 1859, the Wyke-Aycinena Treaty was written, wherein Guatemala agreed to recognize British Honduras (Belize) as a British colony, conceding all supposed "sovereign rights" in exchange for Great Britain's commitment to build a road from Guatemala City to the Belizean town of Punta Gorda, on the Caribbean coast. But an issue arose with the treaty: "While it is clear that Britain and Guatemala agreed to build a road, the phrase used in the treaty, 'mutually agree conjointly,' left unresolved whether Britain was to build the road entirely at its expense."[19] When the treaty was later ratified, Britain claimed that it was released from any obligation to build the road, as well as denying Guatemala's entitlement to Belize. The dispute over this part of the treaty persisted until 1940, when Guatemala "stated that it was no longer a question of whether Article Seven [the disputed section] could be fulfilled. Guatemala now had the right to recovered territory 'ceded' in 1859."[20] Guatemala then created a new constitution in 1945, where it was stated that "any efforts taken towards obtaining Belize's reinstatement to the [Guatemalan] Republic are of national interest."[21]

At the beginning of 1948, Guatemala threatened to invade Belize in order to forcibly annex what they claimed was rightfully theirs. The British, who still protected Belize as their territory and colony, deployed two companies from a British battalion, with one company sent to investigate the border. Although they did not see any evidence of an imminent Guatemalan invasion, the British stationed a company in Belize City just to be safe. Great Britain and Guatemala attempted diplomatic talks between 1961 and 1975, breaking off intermittently as Guatemala continued to issue threats of invasion, as well as occasionally sending troops to the disputed border as a form of intimidation. In 1978, the British proposed an agreement to adjust the territorial boundaries; to this, Prime Minister Price declared, "We will not cede as much as one centimetre of Belize to Guatemala or anyone else!"[22]

When Prime Minister Price met with President Torrijos of Panama during the 1976 Non-Aligned Nations summit about Belize's pending independence, the Guatemalan government broke off relations with Panama.[23] When Belize gained its independence from Britain in 1981, Guatemala did not recognize its nationhood, continuing to claim Belize as Guatemalan territory. Again, about 1,500 British troops were stationed in Belize to prevent any potential invasions; this put stress on the nation's population, as "the continued presence of British military forces, made necessary by Guatemala's irredentist claims, was a painful reminder of the new nation's dependence."[24]

The year of Belize's independence, Prime Minister Price and the PUP government offered several concessions to Guatemala in exchange for dropping its territorial claims, including a sea corridor through Belizean waters, granting access to the Caribbean; passage for pipelines to carry Guatemalan oil to terminals on the Caribbean; and the construction of a road that crosses from the Guatemalan frontier to the coast. However, PUP's opponents, the UDP, attacked the deal, and it was eventually dropped completely.[25]

In 1991, the Government of Guatemala released a statement saying that they recognized Belize's independence, and the two countries were finally able to establish diplomatic relations, with an ultimate goal of settling the territorial dispute. However, in 1999, Guatemala sent a message to Belize stating that, while they did recognize Belize's sovereign nationhood and right to self-determination, Guatemala would still be laying claim to the land that Belize was occupying.

Guatemalan president Jimmy Morales was vocally supportive of Guatemala's claim to Belize. A referendum was held in April 2018 by the Guatemalan government to determine whether to send the territory claim to the International Court of Justice (ICJ)—95.88 percent of voters voted in support of sending the claim, with 25 percent voter turnout. In May 2019, Belize held its own referendum, and just over 55 percent of voters voted in favor of sending the dispute forward. Based on both of these results, in June 2019, the International Court of Justice received the request to resolve the dispute. Due to the COVID-19 pandemic, the timeline for addressing the case has been in flux, but as of writing this chapter, prepared briefs from each country in defense of their positions will be due in summer of 2022. Then the ICJ will move forward with determining how to settle this centuries-old territorial dispute.

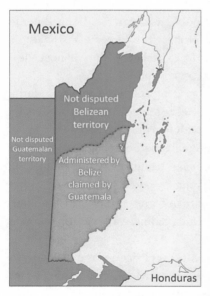

Source: telesurtv.net

TERRITORIAL CLAIMS MAP (TRANSLATION)

This map illustrates the territory that Guatemala claims from Belize and the adjacency line.

- Guatemala claims 12,722 km² of land and 100 km² of the islands from Belize

- For more than 150 years, Guatemala has maintained the territorial dispute

- Belize's governmental system is a constitutional monarchy. It has a prime minister.

- Agriculture is their primary activity; after that is fishing, construction, transportation, and tourism.

- Belize represents 0.74 percent of the total population of Central America. Approximately 311,000 inhabitants.

- Belize's economy occupies the last place among the seven countries of the isthmus.

- Their official language is English, but a large part of the territory speaks Creole or "Kriol." The currency is the Belizean dollar

Recommended Reading

Bolland, O. Nigel. *Colonialism and Resistance in Belize: Essays in Historical Sociology.* Belize City: Cubola, 1988.

Bulmer-Thomas, Barbara, and Victor Bulmer-Thomas. *The Economic History of Belize from the Seventeenth Century to Post-Independence.* Belize: Cubola Books, 2012.

Campbell, Mavis C. *Becoming Belize: A History of an Outpost of Empire Searching for Identity, 1528–1823.* Kingston: University of West Indies Press, 2011.

Dobson, Narda. *The History of Belize.* London: Longman Caribbean Limited, 1973.

Durán, Víctor Manuel. *An Anthology of Belizean Literature: English, Creole, Spanish, Garifuna.* Lanham, MD: University Press of America, 2007.

Edgell, Zee. *Beka Lamb.* Long Grove, IL: Waveland Press, 2015.

Macpherson, Anne. *From Colony to Nation: Women Activists and the Gendering Politics in Belize, 1912–1982.* Lincoln: University of Nebraska Press, 2007.

McClaurin, Irma. *Women of Belize: Gender and Change in Central America.* New Brunswick, NJ: Rutgers University Press, 1996.

Shoman, Assad. *Belize's Independence and Decolonization in Latin America: Guatemala, Britain, and the UN.* 1st ed. Studies of the Americas. New York: Palgrave Macmillan, 2010.

Shoman, Assad. *Thirteen Chapters of a History of Belize.* Belize City: Angelus Press, 1994.

Esri, CGAIR, USGS, CONANP, Esri, HERE, Garmin, FAO, NOAA, USGS

A Brief History of Guatemala

※

INTRODUCTION

Guatemala is the northernmost Spanish-speaking Central American country, sharing borders with Mexico and the Central American countries of Belize, El Salvador, and Honduras. Guatemala is known for its high percentage of Indigenous peoples, who comprise between 40 and 60 percent of the population, depending on year of census and definition of terms. The Indigenous peoples of Guatemala and the *mestizo ladinos* have historically been expected to serve the interests of the European-descendant Creoles or *los Criollos*, Guatemala's land-owning and industrial elite. Much of *los Criollos'* power comes from maintaining economic connections with foreign interests, especially U.S. capital, through agricultural exports, mainly coffee and sugar. Inequality, violence, and poverty—exacerbated by the U.S.-supported, decades-long civil war from 1960–1996—have contributed to high rates of outbound emigration. In fact, it was estimated that 1.6 million Guatemalans live in the United States as of 2010.[1] Importantly, despite discrimination (and genocidal treatment during the civil war) from the economic elites, Indigenous culture remains strong, with over twenty native languages still being spoken today.

TIMELINE OF KEY EVENTS

1523: Conquistador Pedro de Alvarado responsible for the massacre of Indigenous Maya; Guatemala becomes a Spanish colony

~1550: *Popul vuh*, the "Book of the People," written by the Maya K'iche'

1821: Guatemala gains independence

1822: Joins Mexican empire

1823: Becomes part of United Provinces of Central America, along with Costa Rica, El Salvador, Honduras, and Nicaragua

1840: United Provinces of Central America split apart

1844–65: Conservative dictator Rafael Carrera rules

1873–85: Liberal president Justo Rufino Barrios rules

1931–44: Jorge Ubico rules as dictator

1945: Juan José Arévalo becomes first democratically elected president

1951: Colonel Jacobo Árbenz Guzmán elected president, known for landmark agrarian reform program

1954: U.S.-backed coup places Colonel Carlos Castillo in power, following Árbenz's attempt to take some land away from the United Fruit Company as part of a national agrarian reform project

1960: Guatemalan Civil War begins

> **1963:** Castillo assassinated; Colonel Enrique Peralta becomes president
>
> **1966:** César Méndez elected as president
>
> **1970s:** Military-backed Carlos Arana Osorio becomes president; military leaders begin to eliminate people on the left, resulting in over 50,000 deaths
>
> **1981:** Paramilitary death squads kill ~11,000 in retaliation for anti-government guerrilla warfare
>
> **1982:** Military coup puts General Efraín Ríos Montt in power
>
> **1983:** Montt ousted by General Mejía Víctores
>
> **1985:** Marco Vinicio Cerezo elected president
>
> **1991:** Jorge Serrano Elias elected president; Belize restores diplomatic relations with Guatemala
>
> **1992:** Maya K'iche' leader, Rigoberta Menchú, author of *I, Rigoberta Menchú: An Indian Woman in Guatemala,* wins Nobel Peace Prize
>
> **1993:** Serrano forced to resign after attempt to impose authoritarian regime; Ramiro de León Carpio elected president
>
> **1995:** Ceasefire declared by rebels; Guatemalan government criticized for widespread human rights abuses by United Nations
>
> **1996:** Álvaro Arzú elected president and signs peace treaty with rebels, ending 36 years of civil war

1998: Bishop Juan José Gerardi assassinated two days after announcing release of report on victims of the civil war: *Guatemala: ¡Nunca Más!*

2000: Member of right-wing party, the Guatemalan Republican Front, Alfonso Portillo becomes president

2002: Guatemala and Belize hold referendums on drafted settlement in long-standing border dispute

2005: Government ratifies Central American free trade deal with U.S., resulting in street protests

2006: CICIG (Comisión Internacional contra la Impunidad en Guatemala or International Commission against Impunity in Guatemala) created to investigate and prosecute serious crimes in Guatemala, particularly those committed by CIACS organizations (Cuerpos Ilegales y Aparatos Clandestinos de Seguridad or Illegal Clandestine Security Apparatuses)

2011: Guatemala joins Open Government Partnership

2012: Retired General Otto Fernando Pérez Molina elected president. Peréz Molina had deep roots in the repression of the civil war due to his role in the implementation of the scorched earth strategies pursued by the Guatemalan Army during the 1980s.

2013: Ríos Montt convicted of genocide and sentenced to 80 years imprisonment; conviction overturned 10 days later

2015: Retired General and then President, Fernando Pérez Molina accused of corruption and sent to jail along with Vice-President Roxana Baldetti

2016: Jimmy Morales, candidate for conservative party National Convergence Front, elected president

Jan 2019: Morales ends agreement between United Nations and Guatemala regarding CICIG, prematurely expelling CICIG from the country

A HISTORY OF GUATEMALA

Pre-Columbian Era

> The well-known historian of Spanish America, Antonio de Herrera, in describing the first conquest of Guatemala, states that the natives of the province of Utlatlan had 'painted records,' which carried their national chronicles back eight hundred years, that is, to about the year 700 A.D. Utlatlan was the Mexican name of the region in western Guatemala inhabited by the tribe called Quiches, whose capital city, Gumarcaah, was destroyed by Alvarado in 1524.[2]

The region known today as Guatemala was historically settled by Indigenous groups, particularly the Maya, with archeological evidence dating from as early as 12,000 BCE and cultural documents dating back as early as 455 CE. Archeological research continues to unfold today in many sites across the country with recent finds of housing structures and other artifacts dating back to 700–870 CE in Tikal[3] as well as signs of literacy back to the 8th century CE in Xultun.[4] Scholars note the revolt of Buts' Tiliw, known as the greatest leader of the Mayan city-state of Quiriguá, against his predecessor Uaxaclajuun Ub'aah K'awiil, also referred to as Eighteen Rabbit, as a particularly important event in ancient Guatemalan history. The population size at the time of the Spanish conquest is estimated to have been about two million, all of whom were Maya. By 1550, this number had decreased to 427,850 due to conflict with the Spanish and disease.[5]

One of the most important artifacts in Guatemalan culture was a book written in approximately 1550: the *Popul Vuh,* or "The Book of the People," which describes many K'iche' religious and cultural traditions. "The writings brought from the lowlands by the Quiché constituted an *ilbal,* an 'instrument for seeing,' and came to be named Popol Vuh, 'Council Papers or 'Council Book.'"[6] The book contains a calendric system and many mythological stories, such as how the world and humans were created and the triumph of twin heroes Xbalanque and Hunahpu over the Lords of Death. Additionally, it recounts the history of K'iche' migration and settlement, until the invasion of the Spanish in the sixteenth century, when many Mayan books were found and burned. Today, Maya priests or spiritual leaders and students of Maya cosmovision philosophy use the *Popul Vuh,* and the knowledge it contains still resonates with many Indigenous Maya and their allies today. The Maya believed that the sky is held up by trees of different species and colors. The ceiba is the world tree, its branches in the heavens, its trunk on Earth, its roots in the Underworld. If we cut down the ceiba, the firmament will collapse upon us.[7]

Colonization under Spanish Rule

> Of all the agents jointly at work, however, none proved more
> destructive than an array of diseases introduced by Spaniards from the
> Old World to the New [sic] . . . . As many as eight pandemics (smallpox,
> measles, typhus, and plague, alone or in withering combination) lashed
> Guatemala between 1519 and 1632, with some twenty-five episodes
> relating to more localized, epidemic outbreaks recorded between
> 1555 and 1618. . . . Maya depopulation during this period was but one
> downward spiral of a general, though regionally variable, pattern of
> New World [sic] decline.[8]

In the early sixteenth century, the Spanish leader of the conquest of Mexico, Hernán Cortés, granted permits to brothers Gonzalo and Pedro de Alvarado to colonize the region. Pedro ended up at the helm of the effort, at first allying himself with the Kaqchikel nation in order to bring the K'iche' nation to submission before later turning on the Kaqchikel. In 1523, he led a massacre against the Maya people, many of whom had already fallen victim to the new diseases brought by the Spaniards. By 1524, much of what is today called Guatemala was under Spanish rule. And though the impact of Spanish colonization was brutal, it was not new: "A common assumption is that the Spanish encountered in Guatemala culturally pristine societies whose cultures were contaminated and invalidated by their presence. Yet the Highland Maya cultures that flourished during the post-classic period, AD 900 to 1200, had been profoundly affected by repeated invasions from Mexico for at least 1000 years before the Spaniards' arrival."[9]

The early colonial period also marks the origins of the Afro-descendant population in Guatemala, who were brought as enslaved people into the capital of Santiago, greatly influencing the economy and culture through music, food, and art. These people filled any number of labor roles, ranging from domestic workers to supervisors of cacao groves. Not only did the Spanish elites own enslaved people, but also a small population of the native Indigenous people, seeking to emulate the Spanish, participated in this as well, equating ownership of enslaved Africans with a high socio-economic status in society. This is not a well-known history in Guatemala, part of why the contributions of Afro-descendant people invisible. "In both popular and official understandings, Guatemala is not only one of the most Indian countries in Latin America but also one of the least African. The fact that Africans and their descendants were once enslaved in Guatemala is almost entirely absent from national consciousness."[10]

The region during the colonial period was known as *Capitanía General de Guatemala*—the Captaincy General of Guatemala, which was a part of New Spain (present-day Mexico and Central America). "The Spanish capital in Guatemala was Central America's major hub of commerce, transit, in-migration, and hispanization, starting in the sixteenth century."[11] So, present-day Guatemala was the site of the regional capital under Spanish rule; this, in turn, may explain later tensions with leaders from other parts of the region during and after independence as Guatemala was associated with Spain and the colonial legacy. Villa de Santiago de Guatemala, the first capital of the captaincy-general, was founded in 1524, only to be moved three years later to Ciudad Vieja following a Kaqchikel attack on the city. Santiago— which is today called Antigua—found its final location in 1541, next to trade routes in the Valley of Panchoy, which supported the growing cacao trade in the region.

Santiago was home to a diverse community including Spaniards, Indigenous people, *mestizos*, and enslaved Africans and free people. Though gender violence was "both legal and pervasive in colonial Latin America, and infant mortality rates were high, especially among both rural and urban poor,"[12] non-elite women were often able to create independent lives for themselves without having to join convents as corroborated by the work of historians.[13]

During the initial debate over the future of the region after the collapse of Spanish rule in 1821, the traditional Guatemalan landowning and merchant elite used its tremendous influence to push the colony toward annexation by the Mexican empire of Agustín [de] Iturbide. The collapse of this enterprise by 1823, however, discredited this local nobility and allowed a younger, more radical element to play a greater role in the political and economic life of what would become the Central American Federation.[14]

The Captaincy General of Guatemala that had been established by Spain, which consisted of present-day Guatemala, El Salvador, Nicaragua, Honduras, Costa Rica, and the southernmost state of Chiapas in Mexico, achieved independence from Spain in 1821. This union was dissolved a mere two years later, following a failed attempt at annexation into the Mexican Empire. The United Provinces of Central America—also referred to as the Central American Federation and Central American Confederation—was established in 1824. Under the Federation constitution, the federal capital was in Guatemala City, with a president for each of the constituent states: Guatemala, Honduras, El Salvador, Costa Rica, and Nicaragua. In 1825, Liberal Salvadoran army officer Manuel José Arce was elected the first president of the United Provinces.

Though disagreement existed between the Liberals and the Conservatives, they both belonged to an elite Spanish Creole group—*los Criollos*—who Guatemalan historian, Severo Martínez Peláez, claims created and perpetuated economic circumstances that assured prosperity for a few and deprivation for the majority.[15] These circumstances were altered neither by independence in 1821 nor by Liberal reforms following 1871. This inequality perpetuated by elites was based on hierarchies of class and race, and stemmed from the discrimination to which Indigenous people were subjected: "Racism was to become a key element of the new liberal, oligarchic state, in which the Indigenous person—who during the Colonial Period was recognized legally as belonging to a social and racial group and enjoyed a certain amount of autonomy to guarantee the smooth functioning of the corporativist State—loses all their rights and becomes invisible."[16] Tensions developed between Liberal and Conservative elites in Guatemala due to disagreements over how the nation should grow after independence: Conservatives took on a more nationalist approach, wanting to maintain the Guatemala that was made under colonial rule; Liberals were inspired by the Enlightenment, and wanted to convert Guatemala into a "modern, outward-looking ladino state."[17]

Liberals had control of the government from 1823 to 1839, ending their era with Mariano Gálvez when Conservative Rafael Carrera took power by leading an uprising of Indigenous people. Under his leadership, "the legislators closed their first session with more decrees designed to restore Hispanic tradition. They reduced taxes on foodstuffs in another response to popular demand . . . They abolished the head tax altogether" with the goal of returning to the type of treatment of Indigenous peoples as practiced under colonization.[18] Carrera saw the retention of Indigenous customs as the highest priority for his government, rejecting the Europeanization that Liberals sought. He helped this cause through several means: by removing taxes on the Indigenous population, which decreased their need to make money by working on estates and plantations; allowing Indigenous people to hold government positions; and—perhaps most significantly—returning land to Indigenous communities. In 1845, the government declared "all who worked unclaimed lands should receive them," a decree that overwhelmingly favored Indigenous communities.[19]

When Carrera died in 1865, the elite *ladinos* saw it as their chance to reclaim the country—and they achieved this with Liberal President Justo Rufino Barrios, who came to power in 1873. Under Barrios, Western capitalism was introduced into Guatemala. Liberals wanted to nurture budding coffee exports, a crop that was being grown more and more throughout Central America for a global market. "Less inspired by an enlightened belief in liberty than by precepts of progress and order, if not necessarily law, these new coffee liberals, led by Justo Rufino Barrios, enacted land and labor reforms intended to promote coffee cultivation and exportation."[20] Codified in law, this "liberal" era did not serve the interests of women and Indigenous peoples. "Exhibiting a marked 'patriarchal authoritarianism,' second-generation liberals also moved to curtail female independence, enhance male privilege, and promote the patriarchal nuclear family model."[21] And in 1876, President Barrios implemented the *mandamiento* policy, which forcefully conscripted people—specifically men, women, and children from Maya communities—to work coffee plantations. Some hundred thousand Maya migrated for weeks or months at a time to work the plantations: "Land was transformed from a cultural into an economic resource, from community to commodity, by Liberal desires to capitalize on Guatemala's untapped potential as a producer of coffee. . . . Investment by domestic and foreign capital resulted in coffee emerging during the second half of the nineteenth century as Guatemala's principal export crop, a position it has maintained in the national economy from the time of President Barrios until today."[22]

This period of Liberal leadership consolidated a model that prepared the conditions for twentieth century agro-exports based on the exploitation, disenfranchisement, and labor of Indigenous people. "As long as a 'bedrock of subsistence rights' continued to exist, communal divisions could be contained and collective interests defended. In the second half of the nineteenth century, however, a number of factors began to chisel away at this subsistence foundation."[23] Through new laws, reforms, and decrees, the Liberal state took land away from Indigenous communities, creating a mobile work force with no choice but to work on the coffee plantations. "Guatemala's entrance into the nineteenth-century international coffee market remains one of the most brutal in the hemisphere."[24]

Twentieth Century

> Democratization and social reform threatened the power, resources, and status of the small elite that had dominated Guatemala largely unchallenged until the ten-year progressive period that began in 1944. To that elite, the elimination of what they perceived as the communist threat of the Árbenz period (1951–54) also meant a return to their privileged position, a dominance justified by a level of socioeconomic underdevelopment that still required elite 'guidance'. . . . Accordingly, elites and the rest of the right wing used the club of anticommunism, whether cynically or sincerely, to attack left-of-center political parties, labor organizing, and any reforms that might threaten their vested interests.[25]

In 1931, former Minister of War Jorge Ubico Casteñada was elected as president in an election in which he was the only candidate on the ballot. Ubico, intent on pulling Guatemala out of its economic slump, implemented "unprecedented centralization of the state," taking a devout pro-U.S. stance.[26] This newfound alliance facilitated the growth of the United Fruit Company's control over banana production and made this sector Guatemala's most important business. Ubico ruled as a dictator, oppressing his political opponents viciously and massacring Indigenous people who rebelled against him. He was overthrown during the 1944 Revolution, which ended this system of authoritarian government "that had lasted since the republic gained its independence in 1821."[27] The 1944 Revolution later became known as the "Ten Years of Spring," as it was a decade of the only democratically representative government in Guatemala until the end of the civil war in 1996.

Juan José Arévalo was democratically elected in 1945; this made him the first president in Guatemala's post-*caudillo* (military strongman) era. Arévalo called himself a "spiritual socialist," meaning he "conceived of the state as an aggregation of collective interests and values and viewed the function of government as seeing equally the individual and the collectivity."[28] However, he did not identify

46

politically as a socialist or communist, repeatedly clarifying that he was not a Marxist. This did not prevent the United States from becoming nervous about his progressive leanings, especially when he implemented major changes to labor laws, encouraged unionization of major companies such as the United Fruit Company, and set a national minimum wage, among other policies. It's very important to remember the depth and extent of U.S. involvement in the affairs of Guatemala. This influence has unfolded for decades; it includes not just the overthrow of President Árbenz, which you will read about below, but support to the Guatemalan government and armed forces during the ensuing civil war. And this involvement continues up through today, as Gustavo Palma reminds us: "It can be affirmed, without a doubt, that in the last decades of the last century and in the almost two of the current twenty-first century, the political and economic actions of and in Guatemala have been determined by the strategic agenda and interests of the United States."[29]

Colonel Jacobo Árbenz Guzmán, Arévalo's minister of defense, took office in 1951, the first "peaceful and punctual transfer of executive power" in the Guatemalan Republic's 130-year history.[30] Árbenz pledged to continue the reform efforts of Arévalo, wanting to "convert the country from a dependent nation to economic independence; to convert from a 'feudal' to a modern, capitalist economy."[31] Árbenz's focus was energizing the countryside first and foremost: with this in mind, he created the Agrarian Reform Law of 1952, which stated that uncultivated land on estates over 220 acres were subject to expropriation and redistribution. This, of course, agitated the landowning elite, who immediately dubbed the reform "communist"—a charge that quickly caught the attention of the United States, which had already been on alert during the Arévalo administration and quickly moved to overthrow Árbenz. Guatemalan elites grew fearful of growing power among the lower classes due to the reforms, new forms of local leadership, and the potential for rebellion.[32] The United States leveraged this anxiety for the overthrow of Árbenz. "Most [U.S.] 'regime change' operations have achieved their short-term goals. Before the CIA deposed the government of Guatemala in 1954, for example, United Fruit was not free to operate as it wished in that country; afterward it was. From the vantage point of history, however, it is clear that most of these operations actually weakened American security. They cast whole regions of the world in the upheaval, creating whirlpools of instability from which undreamed of threats arose years later."[33]

Árbenz's policy resulted in the expropriation of a sizable portion of United Fruit's land holdings and new highway construction threatened their transportation monopoly. The CIA, or U.S. Central Intelligence Agency, who had close ties with United Fruit, began to plan an intervention. Concerned about the tension, the Árbenz administration went to the Soviet Union for arms in 1954, which the United States took as final proof that the Guatemalan government was under communist control. The U.S. government supplied Guatemalan army exile Colonel Carlos Castillo Armas with military supplies, a small army of mercenaries, and a communications campaign to carry out a coup against Árbenz. Árbenz resigned on June 27, 1954, just ten years after the start of the Revolution, and went into exile in Mexico. "[Castillo Armas'] military background, honest reputation, folk-hero image, and Mayan appearance made him a good choice to lead the invasion. By June 1954, he confidently asserted that he would 'return very shortly' to his homeland. The American government furnished Castillo Armas with all the requisites for the invasion. He received money and an 'army,' among whose ranks were many mercenaries recruited from the area."[34]

The United States installed Castillo Armas into the Guatemalan presidency, his primary supporters being the U.S. State Department, the United Fruit Company, the Guatemalan army, and the Guatemalan elites. Castillo Armas immediately took to reversing most of Árbenz's reforms, returning land to United Fruit and even drawing up a new contract with the company to limit its taxes to just 30 percent of profits.[35] With support from the United States, he also moved to imprison all suspected communists. "Yet the [U.S.] embassy's own research shed doubt on the nature of the 'communist' threat. An anthropologist the embassy itself contracted to investigate the politics of Guatemalans imprisoned by the new regime found that not a single one was a member of Guatemala's communist party, and few had ever even heard of Karl Marx. They were activists, but local activists involved in local issues. Seventy-five percent had participated in political parties, labor unions, peasant leagues, and agrarian committees."[36]

Over one hundred thousand landless rural families, the newly established *campesino* class that had benefited from the 1952 Agrarian Reform, were thrust back into disenfranchisement.[37] Civil unrest grew during the three short but violent years of Castillo Armas' rule—there were several failed coup attempts against him, along with student-led protests, the deadliest of which occurred in 1956, ending with 168 arrests, six deaths, and dozens of wounded, all of which contributed to social, political, and economic instability.[38] On July 27, 1957, Castillo Armas was assassinated by one of his presidential guards. However, albeit briefly, this ten-year period of democracy and programs addressing inequality and access to land, did have national impacts: "A unique alliance of political forces put the power of the state at the service of workers and peasants in order to make a more equitable nation. Peasants, Indians, and workers immediately took advantage of this opening and began a wave of organizing."[39]

In the 1950s, a reformist government attempted to introduce some land reform by appropriating land from wealthy landowners and redistributing it. However, the President, [Jacobo] Árbenz, was ousted from power in 1954 by a CIA backed coup. Following this, a number of left-wing guerrilla movements began to form and a civil war ensued between 1960 and 1996. Over 200,000 people died during the conflict.[40]

In 1958, General Miguel Ydígoras Fuentes, who had previously challenged both Árbenz and Castillo Armas for the presidency, usurped power. His administration was dubbed "a farce of incompetence, corruption and patronage" and 1960 saw the beginnings of insurgent movements comprised of disgruntled members of the military, intellectuals, and students, along with the rural Maya and other left-wing civilian movements protesting the government.[41] The military, in particular, was disillusioned with Ydígoras, and when he agreed to let the United States train an invasion force in preparation for the Bay of Pigs operation in Cuba without consulting members of the military and without sharing the payout received from the United States, the military staged a coup. President Ydígoras was overthrown in 1963, and the military took control.

The military instituted a vicious, oppressive regime, particularly against the Maya, who were seen as "domestic enemies . . . deemed to be the social base for the guerrillas."[42] This perspective stems from the fact that the guerrilla groups sought support from the Indigenous communities, not because they were Indigenous, but rather because they were poor and "stuck in the bottom quintile of an extraordinarily unequal society" which appealed to the revolutionaries as they were fighting, in their view, a class war.[43] The Guatemalan revolutionaries pitted themselves against the national army, who were financially and militarily backed by the United States and Israel; the Guatemalan military received an estimated $30 million in U.S. aid in the 1960s and 1970s[44] and a wide range of military equipment from Israel, including tanks, munitions, and Galil rifles valued at six million dollars.[45] In 1966, the military allowed the democratic election of a civilian government, and Julio César Méndez Montenegro came to power. This resulted in a pause of guerrilla warfare, an "unofficial truce," but the military took this as an opportunity to launch counterinsurgency efforts, and a "state of siege" was declared, suspending civil rights across Guatemala, as well as the placement of all local police and security guards under the Ministry of Defense and implementing strict censorship of the press.

In 1968, Archbishop Mario Casariego y Acevedo was kidnapped, most likely by Guatemalan security forces on orders from the Guatemalan army. The kidnapping seemed to be staged, with the intention of framing the guerrilla forces; the Archbishop, who was an outspoken supporter of the authoritarian regime at the time, may have organized this "self-kidnapping" himself. After the Archbishop's safe return four days later, the war saw a brief lull in political violence, with a small decrease in murders by the death squads, and the "state of siege" reduced to a "state of alarm." This momentary calm ended a few months later when U.S. ambassador John Gordon Mein was assassinated by the guerrilla group, FAR (Fuerzas Armadas Rebeldes or Rebel Armed Forces), although some believe the Guatemalan army was involved in the murder. Regardless, this event led to an increase in U.S. security in the country and harsher counterinsurgency efforts, along with another increase in death squad-killings of the opposition.

A "state of siege" was re-established in 1970 with the election of Carlos Manuel Arana Osorio as president, which led to increased repression. This situation was challenged in 1971 when over twelve thousand students from the University of San Carlos of Guatemala staged a protest against the security forces. The Guatemalan military responded with a raid on the campus, mobilizing eight hundred troops, tanks, and helicopters, searching for weapons caches but ultimately finding nothing. During this time, more death squads were being formed, one of the most infamous being the "Ojo por Ojo" (Eye for an Eye); this death squad killed and tortured civilians suspected of working with the FAR. By the end of 1973, it was estimated that up to forty-two thousand Guatemalan civilians had either been killed or disappeared since the beginning of the war.

The FAR and its supporters were targeted heavily during the U.S.-supported counterinsurgency campaign in the 1960s; in the 1970s, the survivors of this campaign regrouped, and in 1974 formed the EGP (Ejército Guerrillero de los Pobres or Guerrilla Army of the Poor). The EGP received support from some Maya groups, who had felt that the FAR had not taken the racial discrimination against Indigenous peoples sufficiently into account. In 1980, the EGP led an attack against the Guatemalan National Palace as well as on the Guatemalan government headquarters in an attempt to prevent a pro-government demonstration. Six adults and a child died from the explosion of a bomb-filled vehicle, in addition to many more wounded and damage to art pieces in the National Palace. This action was only one of several that guerrilla groups carried out in response to the increased killings by death squads and government forces. General Efraín Ríos Montt took power in 1982 via a coup; in this same year, several guerrilla groups joined efforts to form the URNG (Unidad Revolucionaria Nacional Guatemalteca or National Guatemalan Revolutionary Unity). Montt implemented a scorched earth policy that led to the systemic massacre and forced displacement of many Mayan communities. In this singular year, the military's counterinsurgency regime resulted in seventy-five thousand deaths and the destruction of 440 villages.[46] In 1984, Montt was usurped by his Minister of Defense, General Óscar Humberto Mejía Victores.

End of the War

> Indeed, in its recently published report, the Commission [for Historical Clarification—CEH] concluded that 626 villages had been destroyed, more than 200,000 people were killed or disappeared, 1.5 million were displaced by the violence, and more than 150,000 driven to seek refuge in Mexico. Further, the Commission found the state responsible for 93 percent of the acts of violence and the guerrillas for 3 percent. All told, 83 percent of the victims were Maya and 17 percent were ladino.[47]

Peace talks started in 1986, one year after a new Constitution was drafted and elections were reinstated. Eleven peace agreements were proposed and discarded across a decade and the violence continued. Finally, the twelfth agreement promised to address several key issues that had catalyzed the civil war in the first place, including the human rights of Indigenous communities and agrarian development. This set of peace accords was signed, and in 1996—after the deaths of over 200,000 people, the internal displacement of around 1.5 million Guatemalans, and another 150,000 having fled over the Mexican border—the Guatemalan civil war, one of Latin America's most violent wars, finally came to an end. Of the two hundred thousand-person death toll, 83 percent were Indigenous Maya civilians. Most of these killings were carried out by government officials, death squads affiliated with the government armed forces such as the Secret Anticommunist Army and Mobile Military Police acting on orders to pillage Mayan villages and systematically massacre them. This genocide against the Maya became known as the Silent Holocaust. It is important to note that the genocide had gendered ramifications, and by that, we mean many Maya women were targeted as subversives and Indigenous girls and women were to be raped.[48]

Present-Day Guatemala: Challenges, Opportunities, and Achievements

> In spite of legitimate pessimism, there are noteworthy signs that some things in Guatemala are changing. . . . For example, the last presidential election, in the fall of 2007, was remarkably different from past elections on many levels. Although the subject of tax reform was not broached, the issues of poverty, education, and the rights of women and the Indigenous were front and centre on the platforms for all major parties. . . . Another positive sign of change was the fact that Rigoberta Menchú, 1993 Nobel Peace Prize Winner and Indigenous leader, also campaigned for president in 2007.[49]

Guatemala has made some strides toward political and economic stability since the end of the civil war, but many challenges remain. "By no means the poorest country in Central America in macroeconomic terms, postwar Guatemala has remained among the countries with the highest levels of socioeconomic inequality in the world."[50] This, in turn, is accompanied by weak state institutions, the presence of drug cartels, sustained discrimination against the Indigenous population, deforestation, and one of the highest rates of femicide in the world, all of which also contribute to outbound immigration.

Many argue that there are multiple historical events in Guatemala—Spanish colonization with the support of the Catholic church, early statehood consolidation and the emergence of political and economic elites, and the 36-year civil war (1960–1996)—that contribute to today's high levels of gender-based violence.[51] There are also a number of present-day social factors such as inequality, poverty, discrimination on the basis of gender and ethnicity, as well as high levels of violence due to insecurity, gangs, and drug trafficking, that contribute to the "normalization" of gender violence in the domestic or private sphere as well as in the public sphere. The countries with the highest femicide rates in Latin America are El Salvador, Honduras, and Guatemala.[52] Femicide is the killing of a woman because of her gender; it is an extreme example of gender-based violence, which is on the rise.[53] From 2000 to 2019, 11,519 women were killed violently;[54] the rate of violent deaths of women is growing faster than homicide levels (though homicide rates remain higher than femicide rates). In 2018 alone, 661 women were killed violently in Guatemala.[55] In fact, violence against women is one of the most highly reported crimes in Guatemala, yet impunity rates are abysmally high: only 3.46 percent of cases presented between 2008 and 2017 were resolved according to the International Commission against Impunity in Guatemala.[56] Impunity and structural violence—poverty and discrimination, for example—can keep women from reporting, but this is exacerbated by the absence of witness protection as well.[57]

Gender violence has spurred civil society efforts in which women's organizations across the country and women's groups at the community level are stepping up to hold government offices accountable and simultaneously providing services to women survivors themselves.[58] Women's organizations, including Indigenous women's organizations, have organized across the country, often supporting each other and demanding better laws and their implementation, providing services to survivors, and even providing training to public employees tasked with serving women. Women's organizations have also played a role in the postconflict transition, leveraging their connections across the country.

Indigenous peoples, particularly the Maya, have also been able to sustain community organizing efforts that were encouraged under Árbenz and used to survive the civil war. "Maya from all over Guatemala are uniting around a variety of causes. Language for example is central to the Maya movement."[59] The Maya movement is a vibrant social movement that includes many types of organizations and associations across the country as well as transnational networking and collaboration. "The movement is truly a national, at times transnational, phenomenon. This is in sharp contrast to the community-based allegiances that have long characterized Maya social identity. . . . The movement promotes association based on linguistic groups and then, building on that basis, hopes to foster a pan-Maya, even pan-Native American, identity. By so doing it hopes to peacefully unite Guatemalan Indians into a powerful base that can exert a proportional influence on Guatemalan politics and so claim social and economic justice for all Maya people."[60]

Though 1996 ushered in renewed hope for a peaceful and democratic country, a major event nearing the turn of the century raised concerns about rule of law in Guatemala. This was the assassination of Catholic Bishop Juan José Gerardi, just two years after the end of the civil war. Bishop Gerardi was an outspoken defender of Indigenous rights, working on the REMHI report (Recuperación de la Memoria Historia or Historical Memory Recovery Project), which documented the crimes against humanity committed during the war. The report stated that the vast majority of all human rights violations that occurred were committed by the military. Two days after Bishop Gerardi announced the release of the forthcoming REMHI report, titled *Guatemala: ¡Nunca Más!* or *Guatemala: Never Again*, he was beaten to death in the garage of his house. In 2012, former general and dictator Efraín Ríos Montt was put on trial for genocide and crimes against humanity—including almost 2,000 deaths, 1,500 rapes, and the displacement of 30,000 citizens during his time as president. He was convicted and imprisoned in 2013 on those counts, although the conviction was dropped after only ten days. The trial was reopened in 2015, but he was not re-sentenced due to his deteriorating health. Ríos Montt died in 2018.

After winning the presidential election with 67 percent of votes, Jimmy Morales served as Guatemala's president starting in 2016. Ironically, although he ran his presidential campaign on a platform of fighting corruption, with a campaign slogan of *"Ni corrupto, ni ladrón"* (Neither corrupt nor a thief), Morales was the center of several corruption controversies. In January 2017, his older brother and adviser, Samuel, and his son, José, were arrested for money laundering; the arrests prompted protests demanding Morales' removal, but he refused to resign. In September of the same year, it was revealed that Morales was receiving an additional $7,300 per month on top of his mandated salary from the Ministry of Defense, beginning in December 2016. Although he denied the bonuses were illegal, Morales ultimately returned roughly $60,000 to the government.

At the beginning of 2019, Morales terminated the Guatemalan government's agreement with the United Nations that allowed for the international body, International Commission against Impunity in Guatemala or CICIG, to conduct investigations into crimes committed in the country. "The commission was charged with assisting state institutions in the investigation and dismantling of illegal security groups and clandestine security organizations that had long threatened democracy and peace in Guatemala."[61] CICIG's contract was to last until September of 2019. The Guatemalan elite approved of Morales' decision while the United Nations rejected the termination, as did the Guatemalan Constitutional Court. Morales claimed that CICIG was involved in illegal acts and abuse of authority. These allegations and actions on Morales' part are speculated to be in retaliation against the report CICIG released about his campaign finances in 2016. All of these events demonstrate the ongoing fragility of Guatemala's democracy and governance—particularly rule of law—of the Guatemalan state. This conclusion is further aggravated by the violence of organized crime, high levels of gender violence, and the poverty of the majority Indigenous Maya which fuels outbound emigration. Immigrants, in turn, send remittances back to almost eight hundred thousand families within Guatemala. In 2004, the total amount of these remittances comprised the equivalent of two minimum salaries per month per family. "In this way, the rural population of Guatemala ends up subsidizing the State and its role of 'fighting poverty.'"[62]

Recommended Reading

Asturias, Miguel Ángel. *El Señor Presidente*. Mexico City: Costa-Amic, 1946.

Asturias, Miguel Ángel. *Leyendas de Guatemala*. Madrid: Ediciones Oriente, 1930.

Bazzett, Michael (translator). *The Popol Vuh: a New English Version*. Minneapolis, MN: Milkweed Editions, 2018.

Goldman, Francisco. *The Art of Political Murder: Who Killed the Bishop?* New York: Grove Press, 2007.

Grandin, Greg. *The Blood of Guatemala: A History of Race and Nation*. Latin America Otherwise. Durham, NC: Duke University Press, 2000.

Grandin, Greg, Deborah T. Levenson, and Elizabeth Oglesby, eds. *The Guatemala Reader: History, Culture, Politics*. Durham, NC: Duke University Press, 2011.

Green, Linda. *Fear as a Way of Life: Mayan Widows in Rural Guatemala*. New York: Columbia University Press, 1999.

Jonas, Susanne, and Nestor Rodríguez. *Guatemala-U.S. Migration: Transforming Regions*, Austin: University of Texas Press, 2014.

Kinzer, Stephen. "Chapter 6: Get Rid of This Stinker." In *Overthrow: America's Century of Regime Change from Hawaii to Iraq*, 129-147. New York: Times Books/Henry Holt, 2006.

Menjívar, Cecilia. *Enduring Violence: Ladina Women's Lives in Guatemala.* Berkeley: University of California Press, 2011.

Martínez Peláez, Severo. *La Patria del Criollo: An Interpretation of Colonial Guatemala.* Durham, NC: Duke University Press, 2009.

Menchú, Rigoberta. *I, Rigoberta Menchú: An Indian Woman in Guatemala.* New York City: Verso Books, 1984.

Nelson, Diane M. *Who Counts? The Mathematics of Death and Life after Genocide.* Durham, NC: Duke University Press, 2015.

Saavedra, Alfredo. *Exodus: An Anthology of Guatemalan Poets.* New York: Macondo Book Distributors, 1988.

Sanford, Victoria. *Buried Secrets: Truth and Human Rights in Guatemala.* Basingstoke, UK: Palgrave Macmillan, 2003.

Schlesinger, Stephen, and Stephen Kinzer. *Bitter Fruit: The Story of the American Coup in Guatemala.* Cambridge, MA: Harvard University Press, 2005.

Stavans, Ilan. *Popol Vuh: A Retelling.* Brooklyn, NY: Restless Books, 2020.

Esri, CGAIR, USGS, CONANP, Esri, HERE, Garmin, FAO, NOAA, USGS

CHAPTER FOUR

A Brief History of El Salvador

❈

INTRODUCTION

El Salvador is the smallest of the Central American countries—approximately the size of Connecticut—and the only one that does not border the Caribbean. The majority of the country's population is *mestizo* (descendants of Indigenous peoples and Europeans). El Salvador has been historically dominated by a small group of European-descendant families often referred to as the "fourteen families" who have controlled and still control the prime agricultural land, particularly for coffee production, El Salvador's primary export, as well as major industries and services in the country.

In the late twentieth century, El Salvador was the site of a disastrous civil war which led to the deaths of over seventy thousand Salvadorans and took place between the U.S.-supported Salvadoran Armed Forces and guerrilla insurgents. A vibrant popular movement of community organizations, associations, federations, and non-governmental organizations was active throughout the war in demanding respect for human rights and a return to democracy. This war went on for over a decade (1980–1992). Today, the country is still recovering from the effects of the conflict, both economically and socially. El Salvador also suffers from high rates of violence and gang membership; an estimated 25,000 individuals are members of the MS-13 and Barrio 18 gangs, and the homicide rate averaged 74 per 100,000 from 2015 to 2018. Similar to Guatemala, El Salvador has experienced a lot of outbound emigration during the civil war era and again today, due to violence and poverty;[1] in fact, it is estimated that 2.3 million people of Salvadoran descent currently live in the United States.[2]

TIMELINE OF KEY EVENTS

1524: Conquered by Spanish conquistador, Pedro de Alvarado

1540: Indigenous resistance quelled; El Salvador becomes Spanish colony

1821: El Salvador gains independence from Spain

1823: El Salvador becomes part of United Provinces of Central America

1825: Liberal Salvadoran army officer Manuel José Arce elected as the first president of the United Provinces of Central America

1840: United Provinces of Central America dissolves; El Salvador becomes fully independent

1859–63: President Gerardo Barrios supports the emergent coffee industry

1913–27: The Melendez family dynasty holds executive power

1932: Agustín Farabundo Martí leads peasant and worker uprising, army response led by General Maximiliano Hernández results in over 30,000 deaths

1961: Right-wing group National Conciliation Party (PCN) comes to power after military coup

1969: Increased El Salvador-Honduran tensions following expulsion of thousands of Salvadoran immigrants from Honduras

1977: General Carlos Romero of nationalist National Coalition Party elected president; guerrilla activities by the FMLN (Frente Farabundo Martí para la Liberación Nacional or Farabundo Martí National Liberation Front) commence in wake of growing human rights violations

1979–81: Over 30,000 people killed by state-backed death squads

1979: General Romero ousted in coup by reformist officers; military-civilian junta installed

1980–92: Salvadoran civil war

> **1980:** Archbishop Óscar Romero assassinated; José Napoleon Duarte becomes first civilian president since 1931
>
> **1981:** El Mozote massacre: Salvadoran Army murders 800–1,000 civilians in the eastern department of Morazán
>
> **1982:** Far-right political party ARENA (Alianza Republicana Nacionalista or National Republican Alliance) wins parliamentary elections amidst violence
>
> **1984:** Duarte wins presidential election
>
> **1986:** Duarte begins seeking settlement with FMLN
>
> **1989:** FMLN attacks increase; ARENA candidate Alfredo Cristiani wins elections believed to be rigged; six Jesuits, their housekeeper, and the housekeeper's daughter killed by the Army[3] on the UCA (Universidad Centroamericana "José Simeón Cañas" or Central American University) campus in San Salvador
>
> **1992:** The government and guerrillas sign the United Nations-sponsored peace accord. FMLN recognized as political party.

1993: Government declares amnesty for those implicated in human rights atrocities

1994: ARENA candidate Armando Calderón Sol elected president

2003: El Salvador signs free-trade agreement with U.S., along with Honduras, Nicaragua, and Guatemala

2006: Honduras and El Salvador inaugurate newly defined border, ending 37-year dispute

2009: Mauricio Funes of the FMLN elected president; he is the first FMLN candidate to win the presidency

2011: El Salvador joins Open Government Partnership

2012: Gang truce called by government lasts two years and contributes to a reduction of homicides.

2018: Archbishop Óscar Arnulfo Romero, killed in 1980 by a death squad, is canonized by Pope Francis, becoming Saint Óscar Arnulfo Romero.

2019: Nayib Bukele of the *Nuevas Ideas* (New Ideas) party elected president, signaling first time since the signing of the 1992 Peace Accords that neither of the two traditional political parties controls the presidency

A HISTORY OF EL SALVADOR

Pre-Columbian Era

> When Pedro de Alvarado arrived in 1524 in the Río Ceniza Valley . . .
> of modern-day western El Salvador, he met formidably large, well-
> equipped armies of the Izalcos Pipil. The Izalcos Pipil belonged to the
> Nahua linguistic group . . . Nahuat speakers in Central America were called
> pipil, an ethnic identifier that appears to be related to pipiltin "noblemen."[4]

The region that is now El Salvador was once comprised of three Indigenous nations, several principalities, and various different groupings. El Salvador was originally called Cuzcatlán, which means land of joy or good fortune in Nahuatl. The main inhabitants of Cuzcatlán were the Pipil, who lived in the center of the region, and the Lencas, who lived to the east. Other than the Pipil and Lencas, the region was also inhabited by Incas, Maya, and Aztecs.

It is said that the mythological Toltec Ce Acatl Topiltzin, more familiarly known as Quetzalcoatl, founded the city of Cuzcatlán, capital of the Indigenous kingdom, in 1054 CE. Cuzcatlán was ruled by a head of state called the *Tagatécu* (lord); below the *Tagetécu* were *Tatoni*, princes; then elders and priests; then the commoner caste. Military service was obligatory in Cuzcatlán, starting from fifteen years old until soldiers aged out of service. The economy was mostly agrarian, exporting crops such as cacao throughout the isthmus; there was also gold and silver mining, and trade in handcrafted goods such as textiles.

Colonization and Spanish Rule

> The territory that now comprises El Salvador was conquered by the
> Spanish in 1524–1525 as an offshoot of Hernan Cortes' expedition against
> the Aztec Kingdom of Central Mexico. The Indigenous inhabitants were
> the Pipils and Hauhautls, tribes related to the nomadic Nahua peoples
> of Mexico. The Spanish established, through land grants (encomienda)
> to the colonizers, the system of large landed estates (latifundia) which
> evolved in the 17th and 18th centuries into the hacienda system, and
> which in a specifically capitalist form still dominates the country today.[5]

Spanish conquistador Hernán Cortés, who led the conquest of México, granted permits to brothers Gonzalo and Pedro de Alvarado to explore the region. The Alvarados focused primarily on Guatemala until 1524, when Pedro led an invading army of two hundred fifty Spaniards and three thousand Guatemalan allies into El Salvador to continue the conquest. They were met with resistance from the Pipils, and they engaged in their first battle in Acaxual (present-day Acajutla). Alvarado was seriously injured in the engagement, along with many other Spaniards—but the Indigenous forces suffered far greater casualties. Several more battles followed, including one six days after the Acaxual battle in Tacuxcalco. It took until 1539, with an overwhelming armed force invading Cuzcatlán, for the Spanish to officially conquer the Pipils and subjugate them. The Spanish carried out massacres, destroyed temples to eradicate the Pipils' places of worship, and enslaved those who survived.

Pedro de Alvarado named the region El Salvador ("the Savior") for Jesus Christ. El Salvador was part of the bigger Viceroyalty of Spain, which encompassed much of North and Central America. Pedro's brother, Gonzalo, founded the Villa de San Salvador in 1525, but it was later destroyed during a Pipil uprising in 1526. San Salvador—the present-day capital of the country—was moved to its current location in 1545.

Independence

> In 1821, Spain's Central American provinces declared their independence.
> A Federal Republic of Central America was formed in 1823. Throughout
> Latin America in the early 19th century, the break-up of Spanish

colonialism resulted from the political and economic discontent of a proto-bourgeoisie. . . . The Central American Confederation broke apart by 1838, the year El Salvador emerged as a sovereign nation. By 1880, the Liberals had consolidated their hold on the state apparatus. Between 1880 and 1912, the communal lands of the villages were disentailed, expropriated, and sold to wealthy families at give-away prices. The economic basis of the oligarchy was thus established.[6]

In 1825, Liberal Salvadoran army officer Manuel José Arce was elected as the first president of the United Provinces. Arce wanted to unite the Liberals and the Conservatives, two political factions with opposing ideas about how the United Provinces should be led, but unfortunately he was largely unsuccessful. In 1830, Honduran Liberal Francisco Morazán was elected president of the Federation, serving two terms until 1838. At that point, he was elected the Head of State of El Salvador, and continued trying to keep Central America united. Morazán created the first liberal reforms in Central America, including the right to divorce and religious freedom, among other proclamations, which were evidently intended to benefit the entire republic, although the population did not always accept them: "Some of the . . . legislation and much of that subsequently enacted was of too radical a character for the masses of the nation, who inclined to oppose it because it was new and incomprehensible."[7]

Despite the efforts of Morazán, the situation for the Indigenous peoples in the region continued to be fraught. Many were forcefully displaced from their land yet still had to pay taxes that they were not able to afford. Growing discontent led to several uprisings throughout the area, the most important of which occurred in the department of La Paz, where the Nonualcos—the "tribe of mutes" in Nahuatl—lived. This 1832–1833 uprising was led by Anastasio Aquino, who was called "the rebellious heart of the motherland."[8] Aquino organized the Nonualcos into a fortified army to attack the elites and *mestizos*; Aquino's army took San Vincente and Zacatecoluca, and Mariano Prado, the head of state, fled the country.

In 1840, the Federation was dissolved, and El Salvador, along with its four fellow states, became independent republics. The primary export crop in El Salvador since 1600 had been indigo, which the *mestizo* elite depended on heavily. By the mid-nineteenth century, however, the indigo market declined with the introduction of chemical dyes. In 1846, President Eugenio Aguilar introduced coffee cultivation, an export crop that had been steadily spreading through Central America. "A major step toward economic consolidation occurred between 1870 and 1890 with the privatization of communal and *ejidal* lands . . . inhabited by indigenous subsistence farmers."[9] Land was seized from people—primarily low-income farmers and Indigenous people—based on new vagrancy laws, making a large segment of Salvadorans landless. This land was used for coffee plantations. The expansion of coffee cultivation granted the wealthy land-owning elite a new level of power.

By the late nineteenth century, an oligarchy or ruling class had emerged, referred to as "*las catorce familias*"; these were the fourteen families who controlled the coffee industry and therefore the wealth and power in El Salvador, as well as the "decisions of whomever held political power and they passed the presidency back and forth between their family circles."[10] Heavy handed, "the state used extreme terror in order to ensure the continued hegemony of [a] small agro-export elite, 'one of the smallest, most omnipotent, pugnacious and reactionary in the world.'"[11] The "fourteen families" created the conditions for maximum control over the resources of the nation at the expense of the majority of inhabitants. Historically, then, violence and economic oppression have been intertwined.[12] In addition to the ruling families of the early independence period, European immigration to El Salvador expanded the list to include Hill, De Sola, Sol, Parker, Schonenberg, Dalton, Deinninger, and Duke.[13] To this list of families, Wood adds the D'Aubuisson last name.[14] Today, a short list of the most wealthy and powerful families includes such last names as Cristiani and Llach, Regalado, Wright, Kriete, Poma, Quiñones, Murray Mesa, Simán, and Calleja. Though there may have been exactly fourteen families at some point, today the expression is still used and refers to the eight to ten alliances between very wealthy families from the nineteenth and early twentieth centuries who have amassed most of the wealth and power in the country. Indeed, many of these families retain their dominant position even during border conflicts, civil war, and drastic changes in the international economy.[15] Today, in fact, the concentration of wealth remains constant, and these elites have merely transferred their interests to international capital and real estate, among other investments.

Early Twentieth Century

The period from 1912 to 1932 is generally accounted [as] the Golden Age of the Salvadorean coffee bourgeoisie. . . . A National Guard had been established to police the countryside and put down the periodic uprisings of *colonos* or Indians resisting dispossession. . . . In 1911, a Central American Workers Congress was held in San Salvador. On the heels of the Russian Revolution in 1917, embryonic Communist and Socialist groups appeared. . . . They helped organize El Salvador's first trade union, the Regional Federation of Salvadorean Workers (FRTS), which began in 1920 to organize both urban and rural workers.[16]

The turn of the century saw the United States replacing England as the dominant world power. The United States took interest in Central America for its abundance of raw materials, as well as its strategic location for the construction of a canal that would allow fast and cheap transportation of goods and military forces between the Pacific Ocean and the Caribbean Sea and Atlantic Ocean. In 1908, the United States began construction of a railroad that ran from San Salvador, the capital of El Salvador, to the United States. Plans were also made for a U.S.-military base on the gulf of Fonseca, which borders El Salvador, Honduras, and Nicaragua.

In 1913, Carlos Meléndez took office following the assassination of his predecessor, Manuel Enrique Araujo. The inauguration of Meléndez was the beginning of the Meléndez-Quiñónez dynasty which would last for eighteen years; the presidency was moved back and forth four times between brothers-in-law Carlos Meléndez and Alfonso Quiñónez Molina, then given to Carlos' younger brother in 1919 before Alfonso was re-instated in 1923. The Meléndez-Quiñónez alliance was comprised of coffee growers who strongly encouraged U.S. involvement in El Salvador, which helped to keep them in power. "El Salvador had less blatant dictatorships in the early twentieth century and appeared to encourage some democratic practice along with important expansion of economic opportunity for the middle class, but in reality the coffee elite discreetly monopolized the power, with the Melendez family getting the largest share."[17] The dynasty saw much repression of the common people; there was a mass killing of women, for example, who had gathered to rally support for Miguel Tomás Molina, an oppositional candidate.[18] Toward the end of the dynasty in 1924, the FRTS (Federación Regional de Trabajadores de El Salvador or Regional Federation of Salvadoran Workers) was founded. The dynasty ended in 1927 with the presidency of Pío Romero Bosque, who was a distant relative of the Meléndez-Quiñónez families interested in replacing the tradition of nepotism with democracy.

In 1929, the U.S. stock market crashed, which led to the Great Depression and caused a world-wide economic crisis. El Salvador suffered greatly as the export price of coffee dropped 54 percent, leading to cuts in pay for agricultural workers (workers who had before the crisis earned 50 cents per day now earned only 25 cents).[19] Arturo Araujo was elected president in 1931 in the first democratic elections since the fall of the Meléndez-Quiñónez dynasty, representing the Labor Party, which he had created using inspiration from the Labor Party in England. He was largely opposed by the elite class due to his goals to seize the *latifundios,* the large estates privately owned by elites; to redistribute state land to the people; and to reduce the hours of the workday.[20] "President Araujo's failure to carry out any significant reforms forced him to reimpose repressive policies toward protests and labor organizing. As a result, many of his ardent supporters drifted to the left."[21] Araujo's failures led to his overthrow by Maximiliano Hernández Martínez, Araujo's vice president and a general in the Salvadoran army. First fraudulent elections and then repression unfolded under Martínez. This led to protests among workers, farmers, and Indigenous communities, whose growing poverty and disenfranchisement catalyzed their activism. "A cadre of ladino and indigenous leaders, with roots in the cantons, haciendas, towns, and workshops, propelled this movement forward. Often communist militants were themselves rural Indians, many of whom had been union activists on the coffee plantations for several years. Others merely shared the movement's goals: radical agrarian reform and overthrow of the regime and oligarchical rule."[22] The culmination was an uprising in January 1932, led by Augustín Farabundo Martí, early revolutionary leader and communist party founder, in conjunction with the FRTS, Chief Feliciano Ama of the Izalco tribe, and Chief Francisco "Chico" Sánchez, also of the Izalco tribe. The Salvadoran army met the insurrection head-on, carrying out a nation-wide massacre of ten to thirty thousand people—referred to as *La Matanza* (The Slaughter)—many of them people with Indigenous identities and practices. For Indigenous culture, many claim that *La Matanza* was genocidal because of the targeted killing of many Indigenous people during the massacre and how the fear afterward pervaded the local population. Indigenous people stopped wearing their traditional garb and ceased to speak Nahuatl with their children.[23] The *Matanza* left a lot of fear about communism in the population: "The memory of the uprising is the cause of the almost paranoid anti-communist fear that has gripped the nation ever since. This fear is expressed in the accusation of a communist that is launched against any reform movement, no matter how modest."[24] It also ushered in the beginning of thirteen years of authoritarian rule under General Maximiliano Martínez.

Martínez passed several laws that favored the elite class, including one that liquefied private debts, as well as creating a central reserve bank that was backed by the *cafetaleros* or coffee growers. He established a foundation that built inexpensive housing meant for people with limited resources, and the majority of them went to members of the political party that Martínez had founded in order to keep their support for his re-election. He also had an ambivalent relationship with religion and the Catholic Church. Although he did have the Church's support, he tended to tout "strange religious ideas," such as barefootedness being a healthy practice as it allowed people to better absorb the planet's benefits.[25] His ideas earned him the nickname "*el brujo*," the warlock. Martínez was re-elected in 1935 for a four-year term and again in 1939 for a six-year term. However, his attempt to extend his term past 1944 prompted a united group of military officers, civilian politicians, and businessmen to overthrow him. The first effort to oust Martínez by force failed, but soon after, a general strike that included university students and public workers, among others, finally resulted in Martínez's resignation.

General Andrés Ignacio Menéndez succeeded him; he called for free elections for the next year, 1945. General Salvador Castaneda Castro won the 1945 elections with the help of the elites, manipulating the results to ensure that the National

Worker Union party (UNT) and their candidate, Arturo Romero, did not win. Castaneda tried to prevent any retaliation against him and his conservative supporters by sending young, liberal-minded people abroad for training. Still, this measure did not deter upheaval when Castaneda tried to remain in office after his term ended; in what would become known as the Revolution of 1948, the *Juventud Militar* or Military Youth ousted Castaneda from power. Following the Revolution, a *junta* comprised of the coup leaders was established, called the Revolutionary Council. The Council remained in the presidential seat for almost two years, helping prepare the conditions for open elections in 1950. One of the leaders within the *junta*, Major Óscar Osorio, left the Council in order to make a bid in the elections as a candidate of the PRUD (Partido Revolucionario de Unificación Democrática or Revolutionary Party of Democratic Unification). He ultimately won, defeating Colonel José Menéndez of the PAR (Partido de Acción Renovadora or Renewal Action Party). Osorio's policies focused on economic development, diversification of agricultural policies, and the introduction of important public programs such as social security. He also encouraged public organization in the form of unions and collective bargaining.

Osorio's successor in 1956, Lieutenant Colonel José María Lemus, was also a member of the PRUD, and he supported many of the same policies that Osorio had in addition to enacting other liberal policies, such as granting general amnesty for political prisoners and exiles, and voiding repressive laws that were in place from past presidents. In 1957, the CGTS (Confederación General de Trabajadores Salvadoreños or General Confederation of Salvadoran Workers) was formed, which represented the people, and there was the Confederación General de Sindicatos de El Salvador or General Confederation of Salvadoran Unions, which the government formed as an alternative labor organization on the recommendation of the United States. The government opposed the CGTS, which they felt aimed to overthrow Lemus.

The CACM (Central American Common Market or Mercado Común Centroamericano) was established in 1960 on the heels of the creation of the ODECA (Organización de Estados Centroamericanos or Organization of Central American States) in 1951, which included Costa Rica, El Salvador, Guatemala, Honduras, and Nicaragua. CACM was formed in order to respond to the interests of the elite classes in Central America, as well as the interests of U.S. capital.

In 1969, the Football War, a conflict between Honduras and El Salvador, took place. Tension had been growing between the two countries for some time, particularly due to the large number of Salvadorans that had immigrated to Honduras seeking income generation opportunities—by 1969, that number was over three hundred thousand. The majority of these immigrants were there without documents. Tensions finally erupted into violence during a soccer match between the Salvadoran and Honduran national teams in San Salvador, when Honduran team members were harassed by Salvadoran fans. The Salvadoran team had received similar treatment when they were playing in Honduras. Honduras decided to expel Salvadorans from the country and persecute those who remained. El Salvador responded by launching an attack against Honduras, regardless of how this would affect the CACM. El Salvador invaded Honduras and launched air strikes against Honduran airports. Two thousand people, mainly civilians, were killed during the conflict, which lasted for four days, giving it the alternative name "the Hundred Hour War." Obviously, CACM collaboration was heavily disrupted in the wake of the conflict.

After the Football War, there was a surge in guerrilla organizations due to the increasing economic disparity that the poor people in the majority were suffering. In 1971 the UNO (Unión Nacional Opositora or National Opposition Union) was formed, a party integrating the PDC (Partido Demócrata Cristiano or Christian Democratic Party), the MNR (Movimiento Nacional Revolucionario or National Revolutionary Movement), and the UDR (Unión Democráta Nacional or National Democratic Union). UNO's candidates, José Napoleón Duarte Fuentes and Guillermo Ungo, won the 1972 elections, but the military and elites aggressively opposed this; UNO's leaders cited various counts of kidnapping and assault against the party's supporters and activists. Ultimately, Colonel Arturo Armando Molina, a candidate for the PCN (Partido de Conciliación Nacional or National Conciliation Party), was imposed as the leader on behalf of the elites. Molina enacted several economic policies in an attempt to pull the country out of the problems caused by the Football War, as well as the oil crisis in 1973 that resulted in food price hikes and decreased agricultural production. He created free trade zones for factories, which mostly favored big businesses in El Salvador since the government already did not tax them. The government also prohibited unionization in the free trade zones; coupled with a decrease in wages, the result was an increase in worker exploitation.

In 1977, PCN candidate General Carlos Humberto Romero won against the National Opposing Union using fraud and voter intimidation by government-sponsored paramilitary groups such as ORDEN (Organización Democrática Nacionalista or Democratic Nationalist Organization). This same year, Monsignor Óscar Romero was named the fourth Archbishop of San Salvador; he would eventually become an important representative of the poor and marginalized. Public unrest once again began to stir in the wake of President Romero's policies, which he called "the plan for the well-being of all" but actually resulted in increased repression, assassinations, government-sponsored kidnappings or "disappearances," and numerous paramilitary forces or death squads. Many low-income people across the country began to organize for increases in wages and better treatment from the government, which took the form of marches, demonstrations, and protests. Animated by the "preferential option for the poor," Archbishop Romero publicly began to support the rights of the poor, putting the Church in opposition to President Romero's government.

Civil War (1980 – 1992)

> As a Salvadoran and archbishop of the archdiocese of San Salvador, I have an obligation to see that faith and justice reign in my country, I ask you, if you truly want to defend human rights:
>
> - To forbid that military aid be given to the Salvadoran government;
>
> - To guarantee that your government will not intervene directly or indirectly, with military, economic, diplomatic, or other pressures, in determining the destiny of the Salvadoran people.
>
> —Letter from Archbishop Óscar A. Romero to
> President Jimmy Carter (February 17, 1980)[26]

The country's excluded majority continued to organize and unrest spread as many protests and demonstrations were held against the government's policies. They were encouraged by the victory of the Nicaraguan revolutionary forces, the Sandinistas, over their own repressive government regime in July 1979. In El Salvador, the Military Youth formed a *junta* to make several demands of the government, including: the dissolution of the ORDEN paramilitary group; an increase in salary for workers; and the formation of a commission to investigate the forced disappearances that had been occurring. But given that the *junta* did not wield any real power, the repression against the people continued, and thousands of *campesinos* were massacred or disappeared by the army. The Popular Movement grew in the face of this treatment, forming a coalition called the CRM (Coordinación Revolucionaria de Masas or Revolutionary Mass Coordination) that absorbed members from several other groups.

After the Cuban Revolution in 1954, the United States decided to use the carrot and stick approach with El Salvador. This involved promoting agrarian reform, on the one hand, while also strengthening the construction of an anti-insurgency apparatus.[27] In March 1980, U.S. President Jimmy Carter announced that he would increase military aid from the United States to El Salvador. Archbishop Romero wrote President Carter a letter, imploring him to cancel all military aid, but Carter ignored him and sent the money. President Ronald Reagan increased military aid to the Salvadoran army. By the end of the war, the United States had sent six billion dollars in aid to the Armed Forces and government of El Salvador.[28]

On March 23, 1980, Monsignor Romero spoke out against the military's actions in his Sunday homily, beseeching them to stop massacring the people. The very next day, the archbishop was assassinated while celebrating mass. This murder of a beloved and popular leader was the final straw that would spark the Salvadoran Civil War. Targeting of civilian leaders was common by the Salvadoran Armed Forces and death squads and sadly explains why 80 percent of the deaths of the civil war were carried out by the army, police, other security forces, and the death squads.

As space for civic protest closed, guerrilla groups coalesced to form the FMLN (Frente Farabundo Martí para la Liberación Nacional or Farabundo Martí National Liberation Front), named for the communist leader of the 1932 peasant uprising. The FMLN was comprised of five leftist factions: the PRTC (Partido Revolucionario de Trabajadores Centroamericanos or Revolutionary Party of the Central American Workers), the ERP (Ejército Revolucionario del Pueblo or People's Revolutionary Army), the RN (Resistencia Nacional or National Resistance), the PCS (Partido Comunista Salvadoreño or Salvadoran Communist Party), and the FPL (Fuerzas Populares de Liberación Farabundo Martí or Popular Forces of Farabundo Martí Liberation), which is the oldest of the five groups. Thirty percent of the FMLN was made up of women.[29] Although many of the early organizers and leaders of the FMLN factions had Marxist-Leninist leanings, their ideologies within the broader FMLN differed. As such, the creation of the FMLN was already characterized by ideological differences. These polarities were also held in tension with its overall desire to gain the support of more moderate citizens. The FMLN began their pushback against the military in January 1981, seizing the departments of Morazán and Chalatenango as FMLN territory. Between January and February, 168 people were killed for violating curfew by the Salvadoran Army. In March, the Salvadoran Army decided to adopt a scorched earth policy to suppress the guerrilla insurgents; they implemented wide "sweep operations" in the Cabañas department, indiscriminately killing anyone they captured. A second sweep occurred in November in the Morazán department. The Morazán operation ended in the massacre of up to a thousand unarmed citizens—this event would come to be known as the El Mozote Massacre. Rufina Amaya, the one adult survivor of the massacre, described it in the following way:

> The army had come early in the morning. They separated the men, the women, and the children. Over there, near the side entrance to the church is where they killed the men. They blindfolded them and tied their hands behind their backs. They shot them all on our church's doorstep. When they came to get us women, I managed to slip away. This tree saved my life. I hid behind it and heard the cries of my children, 'Mommy, they're killing us . . . Mommy . . . ' I had two choices: stay and die with my children or escape to tell what the Army had done.[30]

The FMLN began taking steps toward the establishment of a democratic government in 1982, calling for elections. The U.S. government, under President Ronald

Reagan, feared the FMLN would lead El Salvador down the path of communism. To that end, they began to increase military aid and to put a significant amount of money toward the elections.[31] Presidential elections were held in 1984, costing some three million dollars, making them the most expensive election in El Salvador's history.[32] José Napoleón Duarte of the PDC won with a 54 percent majority. The CIA supported Duarte's campaign, ensuring that Duarte would act on the United States' interests.[33] Human rights abuses under Duarte lessened, but still continued. By this time, nearly sixty thousand people had died during the Civil War.

Peace talks between the Salvadoran government and the FMLN began in 1987. The FMLN demanded the dissolution of all death squads and that all paramilitaries and members of the armed forces be held accountable for the atrocities they committed during the war. The Salvadoran Assembly passed an amnesty law for the release of prisoners who were being held either as suspected guerrillas or guerrilla sympathizers; four hundred political prisoners were released in accordance with this law. Amnesty was also granted to members of the army and paramilitary forces that had committed human rights atrocities.

In late 1988, Amnesty International reported that death squads had continued to kill, abuse, and kidnap citizens, despite official lip service about peace negotiations. In the presidential elections the following year, Alfredo Cristiani of ARENA, a member of one of the richest families in El Salvador, won with almost 54 percent of the vote. He made the promise to govern "for the most poor of the poor."[34] He began implementing several neoliberal policies, such as privatization of public services and companies, liberalization of prices that had once been subsidized, and the lowering of trade barriers. The end result was the rich getting richer and, contrary to his campaign motto, the poor getting poorer.

The war continued. In September 1989, the FMLN proposed to hold a dialogue with Cristiani and the government, and the Governmental Commission of Dialogue was created. They met between September 12 and 15, but nothing was settled or achieved. Another dialogue was scheduled for October, but the FMLN abstained, due to the murder of ten members of FENASTRAS (Federación Nacional de Trabajadores Salvadoreños or National Federation of Salvadoran Workers), whose headquarters had been bombed by a death squad. Then, in November 1989 the FMLN staged a "final offensive." They surrounded San Salvador in order to mount an offensive strike against the army and the government by bringing the war into the capital city of the country. The High Command of the Salvadoran Army decided to bomb the city in retaliation, with no regard to the safety of the civilian population. Another massacre occurred five days later on November 16, when the Salvadoran Army's elite Atlacatl battalion was deployed to the Universidad Centroamericana, one of three Jesuit universities in Central America, where they assassinated six Jesuit priests and two women who worked with them. This set of assassinations targeted the leadership of the university and included the UCA president and other important administrators and professors. In great part due to international pressure after the UCA massacre, President Cristiani agreed to start negotiations under the condition that the FMLN cease their military activities. There were several meetings throughout 1990, with four main objectives, as established that April: (1) to end the armed conflict peacefully; (2) to encourage democratization of the country; (3) to guarantee human rights are respected; and (4) to reunify Salvadoran society.[35] Peace was ultimately brokered between the FMLN and the Salvadoran government with support from the United Nations and the Catholic church. The Salvadoran Civil War came to an end January 16, 1992, when the Chapultepec Peace Accords were signed in Mexico. "Indeed, the accords constituted the blueprint for an extensive institutional reform process, which included, besides relatively free and fair elections, a new civilian police force, a significant reduction of the armed forces, and an overhaul of the judicial apparatus. The insurgents laid down their arms, demobilized their troops, and entered the electoral arena as a political party."[36] The Accords called for the dissolution of the National Police, of the National Guard, and of paramilitary groups, and for the creation of a new civilian police force. The FMLN became a formal political party, and another amnesty law was passed in 1993. "Considering these political developments in the mirror of the aspirations and sacrifices of revolutionary armed struggle, many former Salvadoran insurgents lamented what they saw as the postwar scramble for public resources, but few could afford not to participate in it. Hence, the experience of postinsurgent politics developed as a peculiar mix of political ascendency and disenchantment."[37] Central American sociologist Torres-Rivas sums up his analysis of the region's revolutionary movements of the 1980s by saying they didn't lead to revolutionary transformations, especially not economic transformations.[38] Citing Torres-Rivas, Sprenkels agrees with this sentiment about Salvadoran postwar revolutionary leadership in the following way: "As the former insurgents amassed postwar power, they also frequently relied on mundane or traditional political practices rather than transformative ones."[39]

Civil Society Activism and Social Movements

In the early 1930s, workers, peasants, and indigenous communities launched a popular insurrection in the western coffee growing districts against a newly installed dictatorship. The events stand as one of the largest acts of civil unrest in Latin America during the Great Depression. . . . In the late 1970s, another colossal wave of disruptive protest swept across the entire country against the longest enduring military government in the Americas, which eventually degenerated into civil war. In the late 1990s . . .

Salvadoran activists, NGOs, and public sector labor unions initiated one of the most momentous campaigns against privatization in the region.[40]

For El Salvador, much of the twentieth and twenty-first centuries have been shaped by the collective action of rural farming families, urban workers and teachers, women, students, Indigenous people, and Catholic lay ministers and the organizations they built to achieve their objectives. In response to the short-lived political opening of the 1920s, "civil society actors beg[a]n to solidify civic organizations and place demands on political authorities."[41] These efforts, in turn, created a generation of activists who joined the rebellion that was brutally repressed by General Maximiliano Hernández in 1932.

A new generation of activists and revolutionaries emerged in the 1960s and 1970s, taking advantage of political space opened by U.S.-supported reforms to dissuade a turn toward communist Cuba and of the tenets of liberation theology with its preferential option for the poor. From the early twentieth century, women's organizing emerged and has only grown over the decades. Salvadoran women's participation and leadership were a major force within the popular movement and the FMLN. And after the war ended, women's organizing, including feminist organizations, expanded rapidly; they focused on a number of issues from local development, women's rights, and also women's political participation. "With this, institutional spaces were built to solve problems related to female subordination in the National Assembly. [Also] the Parliamentary Group of Women was formed along with Municipal Offices for Women and Municipal Policies of Gender Equality."[42] To this day, Salvadoran feminists—and the organizations they run—play an increasingly important role in charting the country's development priorities.[43]

Environmental organizations have had a lot of success lately in achieving policy changes and challenging government concessions to foreign mining interests.[44] El Salvador's anti-mining movement was formally launched in 2006. It created linkages between the movement and the government, addressed a variety of concerns from the local to the national level, and worked to include a wide array of other activists and their organizations. This gave the movement a dynamism that was advantageous in building an adaptable and effective movement, which led the Salvadoran National Assembly to vote overwhelmingly in 2017 to prohibit all mining for gold and other metals, making the country the first in the world to impose a nationwide ban on metal mining.[45] Present-day organizing efforts in El Salvador continue to extend the efforts of those who come before them with a focus on addressing the effects of neoliberal policies and the deportation of Salvadoran migrants from the United States, protesting extractivist plans for mining, and calling for increased transparency and democratic practice from the Salvadoran government.

> Despite . . . appreciable advances, El Salvador's democracy remains
> weak and exhibits important continuities with past practices. Neoliberal
> policies intensified economic inequalities, and poverty reduction is
> chiefly attributable to out-migration and remittances. Social exclusion
> remains pervasive and feeds the country's gang problem. Deficient
> investigative procedures permit high levels of impunity, and PNC
> (National Civilian Police) members have been implicated in criminal
> activities, human rights violations, the torture of detainees, and death
> squads. The homicide rate has reached such alarming levels that El
> Salvador now ranks among the most violent nations in Latin America.[46]

Following the end of the war, the Salvadoran public tended to favor ARENA candidates from the right, electing four consecutive ARENA presidents until 2009, when Mauricio Funes of the FMLN party was elected. Salvador Sánchez Cerén of the FMLN, served from 2014 to 2019; before that, he was vice president to his predecessor, Mauricio Funes. Cerén was a former guerrilla leader in the Salvadoran Civil War and was the first ex-rebel to serve as El Salvador's president.

Currently, El Salvador suffers from a high crime rate from *maras* or gangs. The largest are rival groups Mara Salvatrucha (or MS-13) and Barrio 18 (also known as 18th Street). These gangs originated in Los Angeles, California, and were exported to El Salvador with the deportation of Salvadoran gang members from the United States. El Salvador's homicide rate jumped to 139 per 100,000 people in 1995 as a result of the rapid increase of gang activity. La Mano Dura ("Iron Fist") and Súper Mano Dura ("Super Iron Fist") were two government programs that were created in 2003 and 2006 respectively to combat gang-related violence, but unfortunately, they largely failed. Gang violence did decrease during the 2012 truce instituted by the government but there was an uptick in homicides when it ended in 2014. Gang violence is one of the push factors that compels Salvadorans to take on the risks of traveling from their country to the United States, often without legal documents. Many Salvadorans understand that during the journey northwards "some will be kidnapped for ransom, some will be sold into sexual slavery, some will perish in the desert, and other will perish in confined spaces."[47] Similar to Guatemala and Honduras, the remittances that Salvadorans in the United States send home on a regular basis comprise almost a quarter of the country's annual GDP.

In a surprise to many, as recent elections have moved between ARENA on the political right and the leftist F MLN, N ayib B ukele—a t hird p arty p olitician a nd marketing consultant—won the presidential elections in El Salvador in early 2019. Whether a punishment vote to the traditional two-party system and their party members, or a desire for "new ideas," this event is something to watch over the upcoming years. "Bukele was able to set up a strategy that allowed him to win in the first round an [electoral] contest in which he faced the two emblematic parties of the Postwar regime, with more experience, resources and, apparently, territorial roots."[48] While Bukele has been president, there have been many oversteps from the executive branch as well as from his majority group of legislators in the National Assembly. For example, on May 1, 2021, the National Assembly "ousted the judges of the Constitutional Court and the attorney general, and named replacements in line with their interests."[49] This action joins a list of other actions and decisions that many organizations in El Salvador, diplomats, and members of the international human rights community consider violations of the rule of law. El Salvador retains a robust civil society—a range of organizations committed to women's rights, the environment, governance and rule of law, and sustainable development. Yet, El Salvador remains a country that is divided politically and continues to experience many of the same challenges that led to the civil war in the 1970s in the first place, such as poverty and exclusion, violence, impunity, and corruption.

Recommended Reading

Almeida, Paul D. *Waves of Protest: Popular Struggle in El Salvador, 1925–2005.* Minneapolis: University of Minnesota Press, 2008.

Anastario, Mike. *Parcels: Memories of Salvadoran Migration.* Piscataway, NJ: Rutgers University Press, 2019.

Abrego, Leisy J. *Sacrificing Families: Navigating Laws, Labor, and Love Across Borders.* Stanford University Press, 2015.

Cosgrove, Serena. *Leadership from the Margins: Women and Civil Society Organizations in Argentina, Chile, and El Salvador.* Piscataway, NJ: Rutgers University Press, 2010.

Dalton, Roque. *Miguel Marmol* [English translation]. Willimantic, CT: Curbstone Books, 1995.

Danner, Mark. *The Massacre at El Mozote.* New York: Vintage, 1994.

Gould, Jeffrey L., and Aldo Lauria-Santiago. *To Rise in Darkness: Revolution, Repression, and Memory in El Salvador, 1920–1932.* Durham, NC: Duke University Press, 2008.

Moodie, Ellen. *El Salvador in the Aftermath of Peace: Crime, Uncertainty, and the Transition to Democracy.* Philadelphia: University of Pennsylvania Press, 2012.

Silber, Irina Carlota. *After Stories: Transnational Intimacies of Postwar El Salvador.* Palo Alto, CA: Stanford University Press, 2022.

Silber, Irina Carlota. *Everyday Revolutionaries: Gender, Violence, and Disillusionment in Post-War El Salvador.* Piscataway, NJ: Rutgers University Press, 2010.

Sprenkels, Ralph. *After Insurgency: Revolution and Electoral Politics in El Salvador.* Notre Dame, IN: University of Notre Dame Press, 2018.

Todd, Molly. *Beyond Displacement; Campesinos, Refugees, and Collective Action in the Salvadoran Civil War.* Madison: University of Wisconsin Press, 2010.

Tula, María Teresa, and Lynn Stephen. *Hear My Testimony: María Teresa Tula, Human Rights Activist of El Salvador.* Boston: South End Press, 1994.

Esri, CGAIR, USGS, CONANP, Esri, HERE, Garmin, FAO, NOAA, USGS

A Brief History of Honduras

INTRODUCTION

Honduras is a mountainous Central American country that is home to almost nine million people. The m ajority o f t he H onduran p opulation—ninety p ercent—is mixed race, with seven percent being Indigenous and the remaining three percent comprised of Afro-descendants and white European descendants. The Honduran economy depends mostly on the agricultural sector, particularly bananas. Implementation of the Central American Free Trade Agreement with the United States has helped in expanding the country's GDP, as the U.S. receives about 60 percent of Honduran exports.

The c ountry s uffered a U. S.-supported co up d' état in 20 09 aft er eli te fam i-lies organized against the Liberal President Manuel Zelaya, exiling him to Costa Rica. Honduras received backlash from the international community due to this upheaval. In 2012, Honduras had the highest rate of murder in its history, with 7,172 recorded murders or an average of 20 homicides per day. Since 2012, the homicide rate has decreased from 85.5 per 100,000 to 59 per 100,000 in 2016. According to the World Bank, in 2016, 66 percent of the Honduran population was living in poverty; in rural parts of the country, one in five people were making US$1.90 or less per day. In great part due to these causes, Honduras has high levels of outbound emigration. It is estimated that there are over five hundred thousand Hondurans living in the United States presently. There is a l ong h istory of U.S. military intervention and economic investment in Honduras, similar to other Central American countries.

TIMELINE OF KEY EVENTS

1502: Christopher Columbus lands in Honduras

1525: Spain begins conquest of Honduras

1539: Spain succeeds in conquest after fighting with the Indigenous population

1797: The Garifuna people—an Afro-Indigenous people from St. Vincent in the Caribbean—are exiled to Roatán, Honduras by the British.

1821: Honduras gains independence from Spain; becomes part of Mexican Empire

1823: Joins United Provinces of Central America with Costa Rica, El Salvador, Guatemala, and Nicaragua

1840: Becomes fully independent country

1932–49: General Tiburcio Carías Andino of right-wing National Party of Honduras takes power, beginning 17-year dictatorship

1954: Banana industry workers call a general strike

1963: Colonel Osvaldo López Arellano takes power after coup

1969: Football War (the Hundred Hour War) with El Salvador

1974: López resigns, allegedly receiving bribes from U.S. companies

1975: Colonel Juan Alberto Melgar Castro takes power

1978: Melgar ousted in coup; General Policarpo Paz García takes power

1980: General Paz signs peace treaty with El Salvador

1981: Roberto Suazo Córdova of Liberal Party of Honduras elected, the first civilian government in over a century

1982: *Contras* (U.S.-backed Nicaraguan counter-revolutionaries) launch operations from within Honduran territory against Nicaraguan Sandinista government

1983: Armed forces chief General Gustavo Álvarez orders detention of trade union activists and activists; death squads actions increase

1984: General Álvarez deposed

1986: José Azcona del Hoyo of the Liberal Party elected president

1988: Inter-American Court of Human Rights finds Honduran government guilty of "disappearances" of Honduran citizens between 1981 and 1984

1989: General Álvarez assassinated by left-wing guerrillas; summit of Central American presidents in El Salvador agree on demobilization of *Contras* based in Honduras

1990: Rafael Callejas becomes president, introduces neoliberal economic reforms

1992: International Court of Justice establishes new border between Honduras and El Salvador

1998: Hurricane Mitch hits the Caribbean coast, causing over 7,000 fatalities in Honduras

2003: Honduras, Guatemala, El Salvador, and Nicaragua sign free trade agreement with the U.S.

2005: Liberal Party member Manuel Zelaya elected president

2009: Zelaya ousted in internationally-condemned military coup; Honduras suspended from Organization of American States

2011: Honduras joins Open Government Partnership, a global initiative between governments and civil society organizations to promote transparency, participation, and good governance

2012: Demonstrations protest the wave of violence against journalists

2014: Juan Orlando Hernández of conservative National Party elected president

2016: Berta Cáceres, an Indigenous leader and environmental activist, assassinated

2018: Hernández re-elected for second term, despite Honduran constitution banning re-elections

January 2021: Country's constitution changed to ban abortion, supported by President Hernández

November 2021: Liberty and Refoundation Party member Xiomara Castro wins presidential election, making her Honduras' first woman president

A HISTORY OF HONDURAS

Pre-Columbian Era

> [W]e can conclude that the Valley of Naco in the period between 1300 and 1500 BCE had been converted into a multi-ethnic territory, where a probable Pipil Nahua predominance existed before the Conquest. The chontales [Náhuatl word for "foreigner"] from the 1539 document could be speakers of Maya, Lenca, or both, since we have already seen that with this name, both groups were included by the Pipil Nahua, and this was also in agreement with the indication already discussed about the three languages spoken in the Naco Valley in 1525.[1]

Honduras was home to Copán, a major city in the Mayan kingdom that flourished between 150 and 850 CE. In addition to Maya, the Lenca, Nicarao, Miskito, and Pipil Nahua peoples made up portions of the Indigenous population living in Honduras. There is evidence of bustling agricultural production with communities cultivating crops such as cotton, indigo, and agave.[2] Other products, such as honey, fish, and peppers were also traded, along with crafted products like pots and pitchers, and the trade of these items continued even through the arrival of the Spanish conquistadors.

The Nicarao and Pipil Nahua societies had many similarities, from their class divisions of nobles, "common Indians" (commonfolk), and enslaved people to their governmental system, which saw officials from noble lineages working with a council of elders.[3] There was also a hierarchical system within their religion, designating a high priest or religious leader who oversaw the other priests, all of whom lived in temples or other specially designated buildings. Many of the place names still used today in Honduras have their roots in Nahuatl.[4]

Colonization and Spanish Rule

In 1535 Andrés de Cerezeda, the acting governor and contador [accountant] of the Provincia de Higueras and Cabo de Honduras, wrote a letter to the Spanish Crown in which he described a 50 league corridor that led southward from the Central American isthmus' Atlantic coast to its Pacific coast. He recommended that a settlement be established at the corridor's midpoint, and that an interoceanic road be constructed linking the two coasts. He envisioned the settlement as the region's administrative and commercial center after the road had supplanted the Panamá crossing as the empire's primary overland conduit. Cerezeda's plan dominated the life of the Honduran corridor during the early colonial period.[5]

In 1502, Christopher Columbus made his fourth and final voyage to the region, landing on the island of Guanaja, one of Honduras' Bay Islands. Shortly after, he made it to the mainland. He called the region Honduras, meaning "depths," in reference to the region's deep coastal waters. Columbus eventually moved on from Honduras to explore other parts of Central America.

Twenty years later, in 1524, Hernán Cortés, who conquered Mexico, ordered captain Cristóbal de Olid to colonize Honduras. Olid landed in Triunfo de la Cruz and declared himself governor of the territory, establishing his own power independent of Cortés. Cortés sent his cousin, Francisco de las Casas, to re-assert his power over Olid and the colony. In addition to de las Casas, Olid was also fending off attacks from Spaniard Gil González Dávila. There are conflicting histories over whether Olid's soldiers won in the conflicts, or if de las Casas overcame them and ultimately beheaded Olid, reclaiming the territory. Cortés marched from Mexico to Honduras, and dubbed de las Casas governor of the colony in 1525.

Following conflict in 1528 over who should lead the territory, settlers in Honduras requested that Pedro de Alvarado—a conquistador who had taken part in the colonization of Mexico, Cuba, El Salvador, and Guatemala—come to Honduras to restore order. He arrived in 1536 and the situation calmed. In 1537, Francisco de Montejo was made governor, and after disagreement over who ought to be governor, Montejo moved to Chiapas, Mexico, and Alvarado replaced him as leader of Honduras.

There were many Indigenous revolts during the beginning of Spanish attempts to establish a colony. Alvarado smothered an attack led by Chief Çocamba based on the Ulúa River.[6] Lenca chief Lempira led uprisings in 1537 and 1539 "throughout Higueras and San Miguel (that) paralyzed Montejo's development efforts."[7] However, both of these uprisings were quickly stamped out by Alonso de Cáceres, one of Montejo's captains. Under Alvarado, there were many Indigenous people from Honduras' northern coast who were kidnapped and enslaved, forced to work in Spain's Caribbean territories.

Along with the slave trade, the colony of Honduras was involved in mining operations, particularly of gold and silver. In fact, the mining industry became so central to the colony that they began to bring in enslaved people from Africa; by 1545, it was estimated that the colony had two thousand enslaved Africans. Nearing the end of the sixteenth century, the silver boom that Honduras experienced diminished and gave way to an economic depression.

During this period there remained strongholds in the northern part of the region, along the Caribbean coast, where Indigenous groups continued to resist colonization. The Miskito Kingdom, in particular, fiercely defended their territory, ruled by a king. In addition to the Miskito and other Indigenous groups, the Spanish faced tensions with British forces that had begun to populate northern Honduras, which would later become British Honduras and then Belize. Tensions worsened when the Miskito king made an alliance with the English crown in 1633.[8] In 1670, the Godolphin Treaty, also called the Treaty of Madrid, established recognition for "all lands then currently occupied by the English in North America and the West Indies as their possessions," which was intended to settle territory disputes that were ongoing at the time, especially a war that had begun in 1654 over the rightful ownership of Jamaica.[9] The English claimed that this recognition included settlements in Belize and on the Mosquito Coast, particularly because of the trade relations they had already established with the Miskitos. In 1797, the British forced the Garifuna population of St. Vincent into exile on the Honduran island of Roatán. Initially comprised of 2,000 Garifuna who arrived in Roatán, today the pan-Garifuna community numbers 300,000 to 400,000, with 200,000 in Honduras.

Independence

Honduras is a particularly useful case study because it has been subject to many different forms of imperialism, ranging from the direct colonial occupation by the Spanish in the sixteenth century to the neocolonial control exercised by Britain and the United States in the nineteenth century and the regional domination of the cold war American 'sphere of influence' in the twentieth. In every case, political and especially

economic power were held by the foreign metropole, assisted by a small
cadre of local elites, and the levers of state power were twisted to the
benefit of metropolitan conquerors and businesses seeking to exploit
Honduran land and people in order to extract profits.[10]

After the creation of the United Provinces of Central America, Honduras gained
its first elected president, a lawyer named Dionisio de Herrera. Herrera's government established the first constitution. Despite their desire to work together
jointly, Honduras soon experienced social and economic tensions with the rest
of the region. General Francisco Morazán, president of the United Provinces,
made strong, but ultimately unsuccessful, attempts at keeping the five territories
together as a nation. In the end, Honduras separated from the United Provinces in
1838, becoming an independent, sovereign state. The United Provinces of Central
America later completely dissolved in 1840.

As an independent nation, the Republic of Honduras's first elected president
was Conservative General Francisco Ferrera, who had led an army to combat
president of the United Provinces and ruler of El Salvador, General Morazán.
During this post-United Provinces period, the states in the region were experiencing conflict between the Liberals and Conservatives within the countries as
well as suspicions about their neighbors. Ferrera attempted to depose the Liberal
Morazán from his seat in El Salvador, but failed.

In 1859, Honduras gained sovereignty over the Bay Islands, a group of islands
off the coast that were previously claimed by British settlers. The treaty was
contested by said settlers, who enlisted the help of William Walker, an American
who had arrived in Central America in 1855 and dubbed himself president of
Nicaragua in 1856. Walker arrived in Honduras with the expectation of receiving
support from Honduran Liberals; instead he was greeted with opposition from
both the Hondurans and the British. In 1860, Walker was put to death in front of a
firing squad in the city of Trujillo, and Honduras retained rights over the Islands.

The Bay Islands were fundamental to the burgeoning banana industry in
Honduras, which had begun to export bananas in the 1870s, setting it apart
from other Central American economies: "Unlike neighboring Guatemala and
El Salvador where a national oligarchy has enhanced its wealth through an
extensive coffee industry, Honduras first emerged in the international economy
through its foreign-owned banana enterprises which still are a leading source
of foreign exchange."[11] In 1889, the Vaccaro brothers, who were based in New
Orleans, founded the Standard Fruit and Steamship Company, which would
eventually become Dole. From there, the industry gained momentum, and the
Honduran government began making concessions for fruit companies to stimulate their growth. Soon the banana industry became so dominant that it earned

Honduras the nickname "the Banana Republic." Though the original meaning of a "banana republic" was, most literally, a country (republic) that specialized in the export of bananas, the rapid growth of the industry in Honduras became so entwined with the country's political, social, and economic development that the term soon took on new connotations: both "a country dominated by foreign interests, represented by a few companies that own large concessions" and "a country with an unstable government, usually dictatorial, in which frequent revolutions occur and has a consistent military presence in its politics."[12]

The success of the sector attracted workers from the West Indies, particularly Jamaica and the Cayman Islands, in search of work on the fruit plantations. They were well-received by the companies because "they spoke English, were more highly educated and skilled than their Honduran counterparts, and often had previous experience with the fruit industry in Jamaica and elsewhere."[13] This influx of West Indian laborers soon created tensions with the Hondurans, especially due to racial prejudice: "[F]or Honduran elites influenced by contemporary trends such as eugenics, black came to mean undesirable."[14] By the turn of the century, Honduras saw mass deportations of West Indians based on these racist fears and biases.

Twentieth Century

In the past 30 years, no chief of the Honduran armed forces has retired without having been President of Honduras. Regardless of formal status, all regimes since 1963 have in practice been civil-military regimes. Military dominance in the Honduran political system even has a constitutional basis: the 1957, 1966, and 1981 constitutions ceded progressively greater amounts of autonomy to the military.[15]

The beginning of the twentieth century also saw an increase of U.S. government intervention in the country during the so-called Banana Wars. Workers of the fruit industry throughout Central America and the Caribbean began staging protests to contest the conditions they were being subjected to. The United States had a large stake in this brewing uprising due to the fact that many of the fruit businesses were U.S.-owned; therefore, the U.S. government responded to the unrest by sending in the U.S. Marines, beginning a series of occupations and interventions that would span three decades. U.S. troops were sent into Honduras beginning in 1903. During this time, General Manuel Bonilla was serving as president. Bonilla had originally been a liberal but later converted to being a conservative; he is credited as the founder of the National Party of Honduras, Honduras' dominating conservative political party. As president, Bonilla granted many large concessions to the banana industry, giving generous tax exemptions and permits to construct roads and railways.

In 1913, the United Fruit Company created the Tela Railroad Company and the Trujillo Railroad Company, which were made possible because of the concessions from Bonilla and his successor, General Miguel Dávila. The railroad companies were granted additional land subsidies by the government, who anticipated they would construct a general national rail system in addition to the system made specifically for the fruit companies' use. However, the companies continued to expand their own interests, building railways to reach new cultivable land instead of connecting major Honduran cities. The banana industry began to wield so much power and authority over the coastal cities of Tela and Trujillo that they superseded even the local governments, thus laying the foundation of the monopoly the industry still has over the Honduran economy.

This ascendency was met with turmoil and contention; the Banana Wars persisted, and labor movements continued to organize and mobilize. The first major strike in Honduran history happened in 1917 against Cuyamel Fruit Company. Although the protest was quickly stamped out by the military, the momentum continued, and another strike occurred a year later in La Ceiba against Standard Fruit Company. A general strike was held in 1920, which earned responses from the governments of both Honduras and the United States. The first Communist party was also created around this time: "Inspired by the Bolshevik revolution in the Soviet Union, the newly formed comintern [Communist International organization], and regional leadership of Communist Parties, a small group emerged in Honduras to engage the aspirations of the working class. The railroad workers were seen as the most militant workers within that iteration of the Communist Party."[16] Seventeen coups were attempted between 1920 and 1923, clearly reflecting the general unrest and instability that was growing within Honduran society.

Conservative candidate Tiburcio Carías Andino was elected in the relatively calm presidential election of 1932, amidst the economic disaster that the Great Depression had wreaked on Honduras' banana industry. This was the beginning of a seventeen-year dictatorship, the longest continuous period of time an individual has held power in Honduras' history. Carías made moves to improve and strengthen the military, and allied himself strongly with the banana companies, as well as other Central American dictators, such as Guatemala's General Jorge Ubico and Nicaragua's Anastasio Somoza García. He outlawed the Communist Party of Honduras and censored the opposition press. He drew up new constitutions in 1936 and 1939, in order to extend his term as president until 1949. The Liberal Party attempted several failed coups against Carías and the National Party throughout his rule. In 1944, encouraged by the ousting of Ubico from Guatemala and Maximiliano Hernández Martínez from El Salvador, a group of students and women, including daughter of Liberal Party leader Policarpo Bonilla, Emma Bonilla de Larios, gathered in front of the Presidential Palace to demand Carías release political prisoners.[17] Carías complied, if only to dissipate the tension; instead, the opposition became emboldened, and another coup was attempted by a group of exiles. The coup, again, was unsuccessful. Then, in 1948, the United States, fearing even more unrest and instability in the region, petitioned Carías to allow free elections as the end of his term loomed ahead. Carías complied, and in 1949, National Party candidate Juan Manuel Gálvez took power.

In early 1954, a general strike was staged by United Fruit employees, ignited by the dismissal of the workers' union leader. Their focus was on salary issues, particularly holiday pay, as they were not receiving the extra pay for working during holidays that was designated by Honduran labor law. By May 5, about a month into the strike, over twenty-five thousand workers were protesting. J.F. Aycock, the manager of United Fruit Company, stated that he was unwilling to negotiate with workers so long as they were striking; this proved to have no effect on curbing the movement, which expanded to Standard Fruit, with eleven thousand Standard Fruit employees joining in the protesting. Workers from other industries, such as the textile and beer industries, staged solidarity strikes; teachers and students joined; and railroad workers aided in the spread of the strike: "Workers from the fincas in and around El Progreso then took over a passenger train with the support of railroad conductors and rail workers, who later joined the nascent strike movement, spreading the word to workers in all the fincas and train terminals about the strike as they passed them on the tracks."[18] On May 16, the fruit laborers outlined their demands for J.F. Aycock, including wage increases and better working conditions; significantly, the demand for improved healthcare and an eight-hour workday "reflected the fact that the workforce was becoming family-oriented, diverging from the company's assumption that it primarily consisted of single men."[19] Two days later, the strikers made gains in negotiations with Aycock and Standard Fruit, making it the first time in Honduran history that a private corporation participated in collective bargaining talks with workers. In the end, the workers did not receive all of their requests by the time they returned to work in early July, but the impact on workers' attitudes was long-lasting, encouraging unions to organize for the first time.

In 1969, the Football War, a conflict between Honduras and El Salvador, took place. Tensions had been growing between the two countries for some time, particularly due to the large number of Salvadorans who had immigrated to Honduras escaping economic disparity; by 1969, that number was over three hundred thousand. The majority of these immigrants were there without documents. The tension finally c rystalized d uring a s occer m atch b etween t he S alvadoran a nd Honduran national teams in San Salvador, when Honduran team members were harassed by Salvadoran fans; the Salvadoran team had received similar treatment when they were playing in Honduras. Honduras decided to expel many Salvadorans from the country and persecute those who remained. El Salvador responded by launching an attack against Honduras, regardless of how this would affect the Central American Common Market (CACM), an agreement established in 1951 that sought regional economic integration. El Salvador invaded Honduras and launched air strikes against Honduran airports. Two thousand people, mostly civilians, were killed during the conflict, which o nly l asted f our d ays, g iving i t the alternative name "the Hundred Hour War." CACM collaboration was heavily disrupted in the wake of the conflict.

During the 1979 Sandinista revolution in Nicaragua, Honduras became increasingly important to the United States due to its strategic location in the middle of Central America, though the United States had been active in the country throughout the century: "the U.S. hand has been heavier in Honduras than in any other Central American state, through investment, political intervention by private U.S. interests, military missions, and intergovernmental cooperation."[20] The a dministration o f U .S. P resident R onald R eagan, i n i ts quest to oust the Sandinistas and their communist ideology from Nicaragua, funded a counter-revolutionary guerrilla army called the Contras. The United States opted to use Honduras as a base for housing and training the Contra forces, from where they could infiltrate Nicaragua. When Roberto Suazo Córdova took the presidency in 1982, he, along with head of armed forces Colonel Gustavo Álvarez Martínez, formed a close relationship with the Reagan administration: "[T]he incoming government struck a perverse bargain with the Reagan administration: in exchange for geopolitical, military, and economic obedience to the United States, Honduras would be flooded w ith U .S. e conomic assistance and military 'protection.'"[21] It is estimated that between 1982 and 1983, the United States "either gave or sold over $68 million in military equipment and supplies to Honduras"; the total Honduran military budget for 1984 was reported to be $125 million.[22] The situation in the country during the Suazo-Álvarez regime was dire, due to overwhelming corruption. There w as a rumor that Suazo and Álvarez were personally receiving almost $30 million in benefits while the country itself fell into economic and political disarray, in addition to a number of disappearances, political assassinations, and political prisoners that had occurred by 1984.[23] The 1 985 p residential e lections s aw the peaceful transfer of power from Álvarez to the Liberal Party of Honduras candidate José Azcona, who was critical of U.S. support to the Nicaraguan counter-revolutionary forces.

In 1998, the Caribbean coast suffered the devastating effects of Hurricane Mitch, described by United Nations officials as "the worst natural disaster to hit the region" that century.[24] More than five thousand people died, and almost $3 billion of infrastructure was damaged. At this time, the Honduran health system was already unstable due to the constant turnover of the Ministry of Health's management. Honduras received about $415 million in aid from the United States per year, making the government and country's infrastructure incredibly reliant on U.S. support.[25] Following Hurricane Mitch, the Honduran government critically studied the structure of their health system, realizing that "screening international aid is an important feature of sustaining (our) own health infrastructure," and as a result devised a new system that would be "independently sustainable." [26]

2009 Coup and Aftermath

> The natural starting point for an analysis of the current crisis in Honduras is the kidnapping of the center-left president Manuel Zelaya Rosales on June 28, 2009. Zelaya was arrested at gunpoint and whisked in his pajamas to a U.S. military base and then to exile in Costa Rica, provoking 161 days of uninterrupted popular demonstrations that marked the launch of the *Frente Nacional de Resistencia Popular* (National Popular Resistance—FNRP).[27]

Liberal Party candidate José Manuel Zelaya Rosales won the 2005 elections with a 4 percent margin. He based his campaign around political transparency and combatting the drug trade in Honduras, which was strong given that Honduras is a major transshipment point for drugs moving from South America to the United States. Zelaya also implemented several liberal reforms, including increasing the minimum wage and joining the PetroCaribe oil alliance to reduce energy costs, especially for low-income families.[28] He also worked with regional groups that had begun organizing in the early 2000s; however, by making continued concessions to unionized workers, he began to agitate the ruling class. The tipping point was when he "tried to respond to the [workers'] movement's call for a popular assembly to rewrite the Honduran constitution."[29] The result was a coup to oust Zelaya from power.

The 2009 coup is unique from other examples seen in Honduran history in that it was ordered by the Honduran Supreme Court to be carried out, which gave the coup a "veneer of constitutional legality."[30] The internal backers of the coup included the military, members of both the right-wing National

Party and Zelaya's own left-wing Liberal Party, and the office of the attorney general, among others, and it had the support of both the middle- and business-class and the media.[31] Much of the frustration these groups felt likely stemmed from Zelaya's "verbal attacks on Honduras's 'oligarchy' and his alignment of the country with [Venezuelan socialist President] Hugo Chávez and the Bolivarian Alliance for the Peoples of Our America [an allied group of states created by Chávez and Cuban socialist President Fidel Castro]."[32] Zelaya was physically removed from office by the military in June, and exiled to Costa Rica. Head of Congress Roberto Micheletti was appointed president by natural succession. This court-sanctioned coup received immediate backlash from the international community, openly condemned by the United Nations and the Organization of American States (OAS). In fact, the OAS ejected Honduras from the organization, and most countries continued to recognize Zelaya as Honduras president.

Elections were held in November "in a climate of state terror and violent silencing of critical media and public protest."[33] National Party candidate Porfirio "Pepe" Lobo, who had run against Zelaya in 2005, won the election; on his inauguration day, "some 500,000 (1 out of every 16) Hondurans took to the streets in protest."[34] Lobo received recognition and backing from Canada and the United States. In 2011, following Pepe Lobo's 2010 inauguration, Honduras was officially reinstated into the Organization of American States.

In 2013, conservative National Party of Honduras candidate Juan Orlando Hernández, known as JOH, was elected president and inaugurated in 2014. During his term, Hernández faced multiple corruption accusations, including involvement with drug trafficking. Although the Honduran constitution only allows one-term presidencies, Hernández (illegally) sought re-election in 2017, having won the National Party of Honduras vote to be their representative. He ultimately won the election. Despite the elections being criticized as fraudulent by both Hondurans and international observers, Hernández was instated as president in 2018.

In April 2016, the Organization of American States created MACCIH (Misión de Apoyo contra la Corrupción y la Impunidad en Honduras or Mission to Support the Fight against Corruption and Impunity in Honduras). MACCIH is a fully autonomous and independent body, separate from the Honduran government, and its goal is to combat private and public corruption in an attempt to strengthen the Honduran political system through improving mechanisms of judicial investigation, control of public resources, and control of power.[35] In 2012, Honduras was dubbed the "most murderous country in the world" by a United Nations report due to rising homicide rates and common violence. Homicide rates remain one of the highest in the world outside of active war zones, according to multiple reports. Violence, gang activity, the drug trade, and poverty contribute to the emigration of Hondurans.

By 2019, roughly 3.8 million migrants had arrived in the United States from Central America, about 746,000 (19.7 percent) of whom emigrated from Honduras. Migrants who successfully establish themselves in the United States often send part of their income, called remittances, to family members back home. For example, in July 2021 alone, over US$654 million was sent in remittances to Honduras from the United States. Most recently, caravans of Central American migrants have been departing from Honduras in efforts to seek asylum in the United States, escaping the violence of their home country. People from Guatemala and El Salvador fleeing gang violence and post-war poverty have also been joining these caravans as they traverse north toward Mexico. At the border, migrants in the caravan typically have three options for how to proceed: "(1) take a number and apply for asylum in the United States; (2) stay in Tijuana indefinitely, and perhaps accept the government's offer of Mexican humanitarian visas; and (3) hire a coyote to smuggle them across the border."[36] Although the journey is difficult and fraught with dangers, this persistence to migrate in the hopes of a better life is in itself an act of resistance: "By leaving the underground, deciding to emigrate collectively and visibly, walking along federal highways and sleeping in the central squares of each town on the migration route, the exodus acquired a hypervisibility that allowed it to advance in a way in which each step in itself was a demand for dignified treatment, recognition and the right of all people, without any distinction, to seek a chance at life."[37]

Social Movements

> Social movements, and their actors, have memory. The memories social movement actors transmit from generation to generation of earlier forms of protest and resistance persist, even when every effort has been made to erase the memory of that resistance. 'Memory' is the appropriate term here rather than 'history,' because the [1954 United Fruit Company worker] strike has been erased from the official record.[38]

As a country whose development has been fraught with social, political, and economic strife, Honduras has a consistently strong history of social movements. In addition to a strong environmentalist movement, Honduras has had a consistently growing labor rights movement, which has its real beginning in 1954 with the Tela Railroad Company workers' strike, which lasted from May to July. Tela Railroad Company was, and still is, a primary subsidiary of the United Fruit Company. This pivotal strike demonstrated the workers' power: "Of the initial 30 demands submitted for negotiation on May 11, 1954, the recognition of the union as a bargaining body for the workers, and their right to organize a union, were among the greatest achievements. The strike also exposed the labor legislation of the time to be unsatisfactory."[39] In 1955, new labor laws were put into effect as a result, including the Trade Union Organizations Law, to officially recognize the organization of trade unions, and the Labor Code, to outline labor legislation and offer some social benefits to workers.[40]

Honduras is also a country with a high rate of "femicide," which is the intentional murder of women on the specific basis of their gender. Some scholars choose to use the term "feminicide" instead: "embedded in this term [feminicide] is the role the state plays in these killings. In contexts of impunity such as Honduras, the brutal killings of women denote the complicity of the state through its unwillingness or inability to provide prevention and response mechanisms."[41] In January 2021, the Honduran Congress reformed the constitution to prohibit abortion under any circumstance, including rape, one of only four Latin American countries to do so. In response, there has been a mass mobilization of women's rights activists, including the creation of the women's rights organization, Somos Muchas (We Are Many). This is only the modern continuation of a legacy of women's organizing efforts in Honduras. Other organizations include the Movimiento de Mujeres por la Paz (Women's Movement for Peace), founded in 1984 and led by Visitación Padilla; the Colectivo contra la Violencia de la Mujer (Collective Against Violence Against Women); el Centro de Estudios de la Mujer (Center for Women's Studies); el Centro de Derechos de la Mujer (Center for Women's Rights); and la Federación de Asociaciones Femeninas (the Federation of Femi-nist Associations).[42]

On a broader scale is the human rights movement, which has been mobilized particularly by state-sanctioned disappearances and other repressive actions committed by the government against the Honduran people. CODEH (Comité para la Defensa de los Derechos Humanos or Committee for the Defense of Human Rights) was formed in May 1981, and is a cornerstone to the longevity of this particular movement. A year later, in 1982, COFADEH (Comité de Familiares de Detenidos Desaparecidos de Honduras or Committee of Relatives of the Disappeared in Honduras) was formed, led by Bertha Oliva, who was married to one of the disappeared.

> Most of the water powering industrial corridors is coming from the
> ancestral rivers and wells of peasant and Indigenous communities. . . .
> If rivers are seen as exploitable sources of energy in the eyes of the
> capitalist-development complex, rivers evince a different imagination
> for the communities whose livelihoods and worldviews are intimately
> tied with them. Massive hydroelectric projects result in the violent
> displacement of peoples from their sources of material well-being,
> but also seek to cut off the lifeblood that nurtures Indigenous
> cosmovisions.[43]

Following Hurricane Mitch in 1998, there was a wave of government reforms that focused on investment in energy, mining, and tourism in an effort to recover economically from the hurricane's destruction.[44] The majority of these tourist-oriented projects push out local communities, resulting in displacement and unemployment.[45] This emphasis on tourism and extractivism relies on the unmitigated exploitation of natural resources and land, to the detriment of local human, plant, and animal populations. Salvadoran priest Andrés Tamayo led the environmental rights organization MAO (Movimiento Ambientalista de Olancho or Environmentalist Movement of Olancho) in three "Marchas por la Vida" (Marches for Life). These marches had the goal of raising national attention for the environmental movement, encouraging greater commitment for respecting life and fighting for the preservation of the land.[46] The first march was in 2003, the second in 2004, and the third and final in 2008.

In Honduras, violence has also been condoned against civil society activists, particularly Indigenous leaders and environmentalists protesting megadevelopment projects. According to a Global Witness report in 2017, since 2010 state forces have murdered more than one hundred twenty people involved in protests against projects such as dams and mines.[47] Since then, Tierra de Resistentes (Land of Resisters), a journalistic project that investigates violence against Latin American environmentalists, reported that between 2018 and 2020 at least sixty-six more Indigenous environmental activists have been murdered.[48] One of the highest profile assassinations was Berta Cáceres. Berta Cáceres was an Indigenous Lenca leader and an influential environmental activist who defended Indigenous rights. In 2015, she won the Goldman Environmental Prize for her work on a grassroots campaign that succeeded in stopping the Agua Zarca Dam from being built on the Río Gualcarque. On March 2, 2016, Cáceres was assassinated in her home, allegedly by Honduran military in collusion with Honduran business interests. The Organization of

American States and the United Nations High Commissioner for Human Rights called for investigations into her death, with Honduran President Juan Orlando Hernández stating that the investigation was a top priority. As of March 2018, nine people have been arrested for the murder of Cáceres, with the most recent being David Castillo Mejía, president of the company that was building the dam Cáceres campaigned against, who has been accused of being "an intellectual author" of the assassination. The targeting of environmentalists continues, as well as increasing signs of civil society protest throughout Honduras.[49] Garifuna communities have been targeted as well for demanding legal title to their ancestral lands. In fact, OFRANEH (Organización Fraternal Negra Hondureña or the Black Fraternal Organization of Honduras) claims that over 40 activists have been killed in recent years. Though Honduras was considered quiet in past decades compared to its neighbors with their civil conflicts (El Salvador, Guatemala, and Nicaragua) in the late twentieth century, one wonders if this is going to change in the future—and there may be bottom-up resistance coming.

In November 2021, Xiomara Castro won the presidential election in a landslide victory, making her Honduras' first woman president. Castro was a leader in the resistance movement against the 2009 coup that ousted her husband, Manuel Zelaya. She is a member of the Liberty and Refoundation Party ("Libre"), a left-wing party founded in 2011 by the National Popular Resistance Front, a coalition of leftist organizations that protested the 2009 coup. Castro has stated that she plans to promote democratic socialism during her time as president. She took office in January 2022, and many are hopeful that this will be the beginning of greater inclusion for the country.

Recommended Reading

Alvarado, Elvia. *Don't Be Afraid, Gringo: A Honduran Woman Speaks from the Heart: The Story of Elvia Alvarado*. New York City: Harper Perennial, 1989.

Amaya Amador, Ramón. *Prisión Verde*. Tegucigalpa: Editorial Universitaria, 1990 [1950].

Brondo, Keri Vacanti. *Land Grab Green Neoliberalism, Gender, and Garifuna Resistance in Honduras*. Tucson: University of Arizona Press, 2013.

Coleman, Kevin. *A Camera in the Garden of Eden: The Self-Forging of a Banana Republic*. Austin: University of Texas Press, 2016.

Frank, Dana. *The Long Honduran Night: Resistance, Terror, and the United States in the Aftermath of the Coup*. Chicago: Haymarket Books, 2018.

Loperena, Christopher. *The Ends of Paradise: Race, Extraction, and the Struggle for Black Life in Honduras*. Palo Alto, CA: Stanford University Press, 2022.

Martínez, Óscar. *A History of Violence: Living and Dying in Central America*. Brooklyn: Verso, 2016.

Morris, James. *Honduras: Caudillo Politics and Military Rulers.* Boulder: Westview Press, 1984.

Nazario, Sonia. *Enrique's Journey: The Story of a Boy's Dangerous Odyssey to Reunite with His Mother.* New York: Random House, 2007.

Pine, Adrienne. *Working Hard, Drinking Hard: On Violence and Survival in Honduras.* Berkeley: University of California Press, 2008.

Portillo Villeda, Suyapa. *Roots of Resistance: A Story of Gender, Race, and Labor on the North Coast of Honduras.* Austin: University of Texas Press, 2021.

Rowlands, Jo. *Questioning Empowerment: Working with Women in Honduras.* Oxford: Oxfam, 1997.

Soluri, John. *Banana Cultures.* Austin: University of Texas Press, 2009.

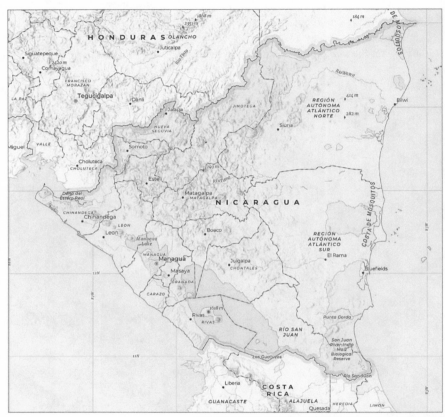

Esri, CGAIR, USGS, CONANP, Esri, HERE, Garmin, FAO, NOAA, USGS

A Brief History of Nicaragua

❋

INTRODUCTION

Nicaragua is a fiery country of volcanoes, poets, and revolutionaries. In many ways it has been and remains divided ideologically—between Liberals and Conservatives in the 1800s, and today between the Sandinista government led by president Daniel Ortega and government critics—and geographically—between the Pacific coast and the Caribbean coast. These divisions have historical roots, among them the fact that Nicaragua was colonized by the Spanish on the Pacific side and the British on the Caribbean coast. Nicaragua, maybe more than any other Central American country, has had a contentious relationship with the United States going back centuries. There is a long history of U.S. military intervention and economic investment in Nicaragua.

Interestingly, until April 2018 when widespread protests against the government began, Nicaragua was considered the safest country in Central America with the lowest homicide rate in the region. Nicaragua was even safer than Costa Rica and Panama. However, demonstrators, including students and other activists, have been protesting President Ortega's strong-arm politics and demanding respect for rule of law and human rights for a couple of years now due to corruption, lack of transparency, and increased repression of protests by the police and pro-government paramilitaries. Government repression has created a new wave of outbound migration as many Nicaraguans flee the country, most of them departing for neighboring Costa Rica. Nicaragua remains the second poorest in the Americas after Haiti. It may still be safer than its neighbors to the north, Honduras, Guatemala, and El Salvador. The Nicaragua of today—with its challenges and opportunities—is deeply informed by its history of colonization, its charged relationship with the United States, and political tensions between different Nicaraguan sectors about the best way to lead the country.

TIMELINE OF KEY EVENTS:

1502: Christopher Columbus arrives in Nicaragua

1523–24: Conquered by Spanish conquistador, Francisco Hernández de Córdoba

1538: Viceroyalty of New Spain established

1570: Southern section of New Spain claimed as part of Captaincy General of Guatemala

1610: Mt. Momotombo erupts, destroying the capital of León

1762: Battle of the Río San Juan, during the Seven Years' War

1821: Nicaragua gains independence from Spain, annexed into Mexican empire

1823: Becomes part of the United Provinces of Central America

1840: Gains full independence

1856: U.S. mercenary William Walker declares himself president of Nicaragua

1893: General José Santos Zelaya leads a revolt and takes leadership of the country

1909: U.S. deposes Zelaya

1927–33: Augusto César Sandino leads guerrilla warfare against U.S. presence

1934: Sandino assassinated on orders of General Anastasio Somoza García

1937: General Somoza elected president

1956: General Somoza assassinated, succeeded by his son Luis Somoza Debayle

1961: FSLN (Frente Sandinista de Liberación Nacional or Sandinista National Liberation Front) founded

1967: Luis Somoza dies, succeeded by his brother Anastasio Somoza

1972: Earthquake destroys much of the Nicaraguan capital, Managua

1979: FSLN ousts Somoza on July 19

1980: Somoza assassinated; FSLN government led by Daniel Ortega nationalizes much of the country's services and infrastructure

1982: The Contras, a U.S.-backed reactionary group, begin attacks against the Sandinistas from Honduras

1984: Daniel Ortega elected president; U.S. condemned by World Court for mining Nicaraguan harbors

1987–88: Talks held with the Contras; peace agreement signed

1990: Violeta Chamorro of the U.S.-backed National Opposition Union defeats FSLN in elections and becomes president

2000: FSLN wins Managua municipal elections

2004: World Bank eliminates 80 percent of the country's debt to that organization

2005: Congress approves CAFTA (Central American Free Trade Agreement), which went into effect in April 2006

2006: Ex-president Daniel Ortega re-elected

2009: Ortega changes constitution to allow himself another term in office

2011: Ortega re-elected

2016: Ortega re-elected with Rosario Murillo, his spouse, as vice president

April 2018: widespread protests against the government ignited by a lack of government response to a forest fire in a national park and proposed changes to the social security system.

November 2021: Ortega re-elected with Rosario Murillo, his spouse, as vice-president, and repression of opposition continues.

A HISTORY OF NICARAGUA

Pre-Columbian Era

> The evidence is convincing. By 1492 Indian activity throughout the Americas had modified forest extent and composition, created an expanded grasslands, and rearranged microrelief via countless artificial earthworks. Agricultural fields were common, as were houses and towns and roads and trails.[1]

According to the archaeological record, Nicaragua has been inhabited since 12,000 BCE. In pre-Columbian times, Nicaragua was home to many Indigenous groups that lived on the Pacific coast and Caribbean coast, many of whom had migrated from different parts of North and South America to Central America. By the late 1400s CE, several different Indigenous peoples related to the Aztec and the Maya lived in the country.

Before the arrival of the Spanish conquistadors, present-day Nicaragua was well-established as an agrarian society: the soil—enriched by the presence of Nicaragua's many volcanoes—supported a variety of crops, such as corn, peppers, cacao, and beans. Arable land was shared among the people that lived there. These communities came together to work the land, and to trade and distribute food in their marketplaces. At the time of the Spanish conquest in the early sixteenth century, Nicaragua was inhabited by five hundred thousand to one million Indigenous people, who occupied different parts of the country, including the Caribbean coast. On the Pacific coast, communities dedicated themselves to agricultural production, and there were a number of towns. On the Caribbean coast, there was less agricultural expansion, and coastal communities occupied temporary settlements based on the seasons.

Colonization and Spanish Rule

> With the exception of a short period in the eighteenth century, the Indian
> population has declined continuously since the sixteenth century, with the
> greatest losses being sustained during the first few decades of Spanish rule.[2]

At the turn of the sixteenth century during his third exploration of the Americas, Christopher Columbus landed on Nicaragua's Caribbean coast. It wasn't until 1522 that the Spanish began an exploration of the country in earnest, led by Gil González de Ávila; in the subsequent year, a force of Spanish conquistadors and soldiers arrived, dividing Nicaragua's fertile land into estates on the Pacific lowlands and highlands.[3] The conquistadors' focus was gold, and once they began the process of colonization in the sixteenth century, they forced many Indigenous Nicaraguans to shift from agricultural cultivation to gold mining. By the seventeenth century, much of Nicaragua's rural land was being used for cattle farming, exporting goods like beef and hides; aside from this, the colonial economy was supported by the cultivation of several cash crops, particularly cacao and indigo.[4]

The Spanish, under the leadership of Francisco Hernández de Córdoba, founded the cities of León and Granada in 1524, which remain two of the oldest colonial cities in the Americas. These two cities alternated serving as the capital of Nicaragua until 1852 when Managua—situated in between the two other cities—was officially declared the permanent capital. A series of battles between several Spanish conquistadores who wanted recognition for claiming Nicaragua's territory followed five years after the founding of Granada and León. This became known as "The War of the Captains," and concluded when some were executed; one victor was Pedro Arias Dávila, who previously had control over the Panamanian territory but gave that up to move his base to León. In 1538, during the establishment of viceroyalties throughout Mexico, Central and South America, the Viceroyalty of New Spain was created, including México and all of Central America, less Panama. There were various grabs at power and control over the country's main cities of Granada and León throughout the following centuries.

The British were active on the Caribbean coast of Nicaragua from the early nineteenth century as pirates and colonizers. This had a profound effect on the identity of the Nicaraguan Caribbean coast, and as a result many coastal inhabitants identify more with the British (as they speak English, for example) than with the Nicaraguan Pacific-side government.

Independence

> Indeed, the Nicaraguan nation of today largely inherits its lack of
> equilibrium from the confusing days of the separation from Spain and

Mexico . . . [including] [t]he latent rivalry of colonial days between the
creole city of Granada and the provincial capital, Leon.[5]

In 1821, Nicaragua was annexed into the First Mexican Empire, which lasted for
two short years. It collapsed due to lack of support, and in 1823 Nicaragua became
part of the United Provinces of Central America, a republic that included all
present-day Central American countries except for Belize and Panama. In 1840,
Nicaragua became its own, fully independent state. By this time, the multiple factions in the Nicaraguan body politic had splintered even further. Similar to the
tensions between strong-arm conquistador leaders and their control over territory
during colonial rule, the *mestizo* leaders of cities and towns often entered into conflict with each other. León and Granada mobilized armed groups to defend their
economic interests, ideological positions, and political goals. "In Nicaragua, liberal
León was primarily involved in exporting animal products such as leather and tal-
low and soon became the center for free-trading liberalism. The conservative elite
in Granada, however, had made their fortunes under the old protectionist system
and resisted change."[6] Practically stateless during its first forty years of statehood,
Nicaragua degenerated into little more than constant civil war.[7] The incapacity to
establish intra-regional national identity and a functioning state mainly related to
how "Nicaraguans became entangled in logics of mutual distrust and disbelief in
themselves which reinforced time and again vicious cycles of internal divisiveness,
civil war, and mutual annihilation."[8] In the scramble for political and economic
control during this tumultuous period, conservative and liberal elites deployed
various means and tactics to consolidate power across the country.

The cattle-farming and cash crop industries dominated Nicaragua's economy
until the introduction of coffee in the mid-nineteenth century. Many other Central American countries were experiencing a coffee boom by the 1870s, which was
followed by the development of the coffee bourgeoisie who exercised political and
economic control over their respective states.[9] In Nicaragua, the area referred to as
"the Uplands"—a southwest stretch of land from Managua-Granada to Jinotepe—
became the primary base of commercial coffee plantations. These farms received
support from the government via railroad construction and through legislation
such as the Subsidy Laws of 1879 and 1889, which gave planters a subsidy of
US$0.05 per tree planted.[10] Through the end of the nineteenth century and well
into the twentieth, Nicaragua's economy rose and fell with the price of coffee.

Nicaragua's Caribbean Coast and Foreign Relations with England and the United States

Bluefields is the most important town in Central America as far as
American interests are concerned.[11]

English pirates first established a presence on the Caribbean coast of Nicaragua in the seventeenth century. By the end of the century, piracy waned as "Britain and France finally joined with Spain to bring the lawless practice to an end," but the British presence on the Caribbean coast continued, and they extended their control over the Mosquitia, as the Caribbean coast was called.[12] The Caribbean coast of Nicaragua is the most geographically isolated part of the country as well as the poorest; yet, it has immense natural resources. The Caribbean coast is also home to at least six different ethnic groups including Afro-descendant Creoles, Afro-Indigenous Garifuna, and Miskitu, Mayagna, and Rama Indigenous groups along with *mestizos* from the Pacific coast. The Afro-descendant Creoles were the progeny of the British and Afro-descendant people who had made their way to Nicaragua. "Creole culture formed within the tiny British-dominated slave society of the Mosquito Coast in the eighteenth century, nearly 150 years before the emergence of the now-dominant Nicaraguan national culture."[13] Arriving to the Caribbean coast in the late nineteenth century from Honduras, the Garifuna are an Afro-Indigenous people originally from the Caribbean. The first Garifuna families came to the Pearl Lagoon basin, north of Bluefields, in the late nineteenth and early twentieth centuries. The social hierarchy of Nicaragua's Caribbean coast has evolved over the centuries, and its unique history emerges through Miskitu Indigenous leadership and the power struggle for control between British and Spanish colonial interests.[14] "Between 1687 and 1860 the Miskito Kingdom became a British 'protectorate.'"[15] The British relinquished their claims to this part of Nicaragua under the 1787 Treaty of Versailles.

The India rubber boom of the 1860s led to increased U.S. trading settlements on the Caribbean coast of Nicaragua in Bluefields, Pearl Lagoon, and other coastal towns. By the 1870s, the United States had replaced Great Britain in social and economic influence along the Caribbean coast of Nicaragua. U.S. companies expanded their reach by beginning to cultivate and export bananas from Bluefields. By 1894, these companies controlled 90 percent of production and had capital investments in coconuts, bananas, rubber, gold mining, transportation, and commercial enterprise, totaling somewhere between at least $2 and $10 million.[16] The Caribbean coastal city of Bluefields then became an economic hub and underwent a population boom.

The English exercised their control over the coast through the Miskitu kings until 1894 when the Nicaraguan state "reincorporated" the Mosquitia—or the Caribbean region of Nicaragua—under Nicaraguan President José Santos Zelaya as part of a negotiated settlement with the British. Afro-descendant Creoles initiated "the Overthrow," during which Nicaragua's military occupied Bluefields and the Creoles gathered 1,750 signatures to petition England for the resumption of the English Protectorate over Mosquitia, claiming: "We will be in the hands of a Government and people who have not the slightest interest, sympathy, or good feeling for the inhabitants of the Mosquito Reservation; and as our manners, customs, religion, laws, and language are not in accord, there can never be a unity."[17] Once the Nicaraguan army occupied Bluefields, riots occurred until the British military occupied the region. In July, armed Creoles began retaking the region, but the U.S. military quickly intervened to protect business interests.[18] They continued to grow their ago-export businesses on the Caribbean coast to the extent that in 1905, a U.S. consular agent commented on the importance of Bluefields for U.S. interests, a statement that exemplifies the justifications used for continual U.S. occupation, investment, and intervention in Nicaragua.[19]

The Continuation of Nicaragua's Contested Relationship with the United States

> Crucial to any understanding of the country . . . is Nicaragua's
> long, troubled relationship with the United States, which began in
> earnest with the 1848 gold rush and simultaneous Manifest Destiny-
> driven U.S. westward expansion, dramatically accentuated by an
> entrepreneurial trans-isthmian canal plan.[20]

Throughout the nineteenth century, the United States saw Central America as a potential answer to quicker maritime transportation by constructing a canal that cut through the isthmus. The question became whether to place this canal in Panama or Nicaragua. The Nicaraguan route came to the forefront of U.S. minds during the mid-century gold rush, when it was shown to be an ideal journey to the western coast of the United States compared to traveling around South America or through Panama. This rush westward caught the notice of British capitalists as well as the United States, and eventually a treaty "binding both nations to neutrality and joint control over any canal built in Central America or Panama" was drawn up in 1851.[21] By 1852, the United States had a plan underway to build a canal through Nicaragua.

Meanwhile, conflicts between the Liberals and Conservatives continued in Nicaragua. There were vicious rivalries between the economic and political elites of León and Granada, who were liberal and conservative respectively, which at times degenerated into civil war during the mid-nineteenth century. William Walker, a U.S. mercenary, took advantage of these conflicts to insert himself in Nicaraguan politics. The Liberals were searching for support abroad and signed a military contract with Walker to gain U.S. support. On May 4, 1855, Walker joined the Liberal forces with 56 volunteers. Once Walker's side won the war, he quickly usurped power and declared himself president of Nicaragua from 1855 to 1857.[22]

Walker wanted to continue expanding his power throughout Central America, which concerned Nicaragua's neighboring Central American countries and motivated them to band together against him. However, who truly challenged Walker's presidency was Cornelius Vanderbilt, owner of the Accessory Transit, a company created during the 1850s gold rush that transported prospectors in the United States from the east coast to the west coast. When Walker declared himself president, he promptly revoked the Accessory Transit's contract to use trade routes in Nicaragua and gave the rights to Vanderbilt's competitor, Morgan and Garrison. Vanderbilt was outraged and demanded that the U.S. government intervene.[23] However, the U.S. government ignored Vanderbilt's request and Vanderbilt initiated his "independent foreign policy," which consisted of hiring secret agents abroad and negotiating and conspiring with other nearby countries.[24] Costa Rica's President Juan Mora referred to Walker as "this revolutionary spirit that has been the greatest of our enemies." In total, one thousand soldiers from Costa Rica, Guatemala, Honduras, and El Salvador joined together as the Allied forces in order to fight Walker's one thousand five hundred troops in the National War. Since the U.S. government allowed Vanderbilt's rival company, Morgan and Garrison, to send ships down to Nicaragua, Vanderbilt worried they carried supplies for Walker's forces. Therefore, Vanderbilt provided the Allied army with arms and funds. The National War ended on May 1, 1857, with William Walker's surrender and return to the United States. Walker returned to Central America in 1857, 1859, and 1860. However, in 1860 Walker was captured by the British Navy and was turned over to the local Honduran authorities, who executed him.[25]

In 1893, Liberal José Santos Zelaya of Managua led a revolt and ultimately established himself as president of the country. Zelaya's rule was characterized by reforms, such as better railroad and education systems. Still, he controlled the government in an authoritative fashion, regardless of his liberal stances on modernization.

Nicaraguans begin to fight back against U.S. policies and the Somoza Regime

> Sandino declared that peace could be achieved only by the withdrawal
> of the marines, the 'replacement' of Díaz by any neutral candidate
> except Moncada, and the supervision of the coming presidential
> election by the representatives of the Latin-American republics.[26]

Born in 1895, Augusto César Sandino would become the face of Nicaraguan resistance against U.S. imperialism and national dictatorship. In 1921, at the age of twenty-six, Sandino left Nicaragua and became sensitized to the effects of U.S. involvement in Central America and was inspired to work towards the total expulsion of U.S. forces. During Sandino's time outside of Nicaragua, the country experienced a complicated election between Dr. Juan Bautista Sacasa and General Emiliano Chamorro; the latter lost, although a coup later put Chamorro in place, but the U.S. government (which backed Sacasa) stated they would not recognize Chamorro's administration and entreated him to resign. Once Chamorro resigned, the U.S. State Department put Adolfo Díaz in place as provisional president in 1912, who soon after was forced to rely on the U.S. Marines to combat a Liberal-led revolt. This resulted in over a decade of U.S. military presence in Nicaragua, eventually ending in 1925. Immediately following their departure, a violent conflict broke out between the Liberals and Conservatives known as the Constitutionalist War and became a civil war that lasted until 1927. A battalion of U.S. soldiers re-entered the country during this time, helping to create a new Nicaraguan national army called the Guardia Nacional (National Guard), whose purpose was to oversee the 1927 November presidential election. Scholars recognize that the creation of the National Guard was a combination of U.S. support and cooperation by the Nicaraguan state with long-term effects for the country.[27]

> One of the most overlooked realities of modern Nicaraguan history is that in a little less than eight years—from the eruption of civil war in late 1926 to Sandino's assassination in February 1934—the military arm of the national state, for the first time in history, successfully monopolized the country's violence-making capacities in a single institution blanketing the whole of the national territory. This upward displacement of coercive power from local-regional caudillos to the central state . . . was made possible by two driving forces: the determination of the United States to see its state-building experiment succeed, and the process of war, mainly in the mountainous northern region of Las Segovias.[28]

Sandino, who had rejected the agreement between Nicaragua and the United States and had been organizing a rebellion, did end up pushing the U.S. soldiers out of Nicaragua by waging guerrilla warfare in 1933. However, his life came to an end at the hands of General Anastasio Somoza García and the National Guard in 1934; following this, Anastasio Somoza García took over the government in 1936, starting the rule of the Somoza family dynasty that would continue until 1979.

The Somoza Dynasty

> During a familial succession unique in Latin America, backed by the gangster-like National Guard (Guardia Nacional), essentially a private army, plus dependable financial and military support from the U.S. government, the [Somoza] triad dominated Nicaragua from 1936 to 1979, monopolizing nearly every industry and natural resource in the country.[29]

The post-WWII world era saw Nicaragua's economy diversifying in order to meet changing demands; cotton, for example, became the country's second largest export, after coffee. In December 1960, the Central American Common Market (CACM) was formed, which helped stimulate Nicaragua's economy with specialization in areas like processed foods and metal manufacturing. By 1970, however, the CACM collapsed in the wake of the 1969 Football War between El Salvador and Honduras, and by the end of the 1970s, Nicaragua had the highest level of foreign debt in Central America, due to major loans for reconstruction following natural disasters. The Somoza dynasty was firmly in control of Nicaragua's economy during this period: they owned between 10 and 20 percent of the country's arable land, and much of the food processing and transportation industries. The early twentieth century strong-arm leadership model deployed by Somoza can be described as "a masked and modernized form of caudillismo."[30] Anastasio Somoza García ruled until 1956, when he was assassinated and succeeded by his son, Luis Somoza Debayle. Luis Somoza's dictatorship was much shorter compared to his father's, lasting only until 1963 when he, too, died, thus passing the presidency to the final member of the Somoza dynasty, his younger brother Anastasio Somoza Debayle.

In 1961, the Sandinista National Liberation Front (FSLN) was founded, a revolutionary group who sought to liberate Nicaragua from dictatorship and foreign (U.S.) control. The FSLN organized against the Somoza dynasty, with much of their efforts going toward ousting Anastasio Somoza, using guerrilla warfare tactics inspired by their organization's namesake, Augusto César Sandino.

In 1970, Anastasio Somoza controlled the National Guard and showed his lack of willingness to negotiate with the opposition by killing five Sandinista leaders.[31] Somoza developed a close relationship with U.S. President Richard Nixon. Somoza also allegedly gave Nixon one million dollars to fund his re-election campaign, delivered to the White House in Somoza's mother's handbag.[32] With other Central American countries remaining unaligned throughout the Cold War, Somoza's loyalty was a relief to the White House.[33] In 1972, Nixon ended the Bryan-Chamorro Treaty at the behest of Somoza, an agreement signed between the United States and Nicaragua in 1914 that granted the United States rights to build a canal in exchange for $3 million. As American investment increased in Nicaragua, Somoza and leaders within the National Guard grew wealthier.[34] This gave the Somoza regime more control over the country, and they expanded landholdings, taking land from two hundred thousand peasants for personal gain.[35]

On December 23, 1972, a 6.3 magnitude earthquake shook Nicaragua; its epicenter was twenty miles northeast of the center of Managua. The earthquake caused widespread destruction and suffering for the population of Managua: 18,000 dead, 40,000 injured, 200,000 left homeless, and 70 percent of the city in ruins.[36] The earthquake initiated a series of events which ultimately led to Somoza losing control over the country and the rise of the Sandinistas. President Nixon gave Nicaragua $32 million for reconstruction. However, the Nicaraguan Treasury received $16 million, and the other $16 million went to funding for the National Guard, which then profited from selling relief supplies.[37] The lack of disaster relief caused civil unrest and Somoza's grip began to loosen. The U.S. noticed and promptly sent six hundred soldiers from the canal zone in Panama in order to support Somoza.[38]

In 1977, Nicaraguan Archbishop Miguel Obando y Bravo sent a letter to U.S. President Jimmy Carter condemning the National Guard.[39] A small group on Capitol Hill wanted to end aid to Nicaragua; however, Nicaraguan lobbyists blocked the movement and delayed any action. Regardless, this could not prevent the suffering of Nicaraguans as the rebellion began to spread. In 1977, the United States sent $2.5 million dollars in arms for the National Guard. Somoza began bragging about his connections in Washington, D.C., which highlighted the discrepancy between Carter's commitment to human rights while simultaneously allowing Somoza to remain in power and keep the FSLN at bay.[40]

In 1979, Carter stated the United States would not support Somoza, to which Somoza replied, "Come and remove me physically." Carter reacted by cutting off any form of military and economic aid. Since the United States was no longer providing aid, Israel and Argentina sold Somoza arms, which led to increased debt for Nicaragua. Somoza asked the International Monetary Fund for a loan and the United States acquiesced to Somoza's request for a $66 million loan.[41] The trajectory changed in 1979 when ABC newsman, Bill Stewart, was dragged out of his car and killed by Somoza's National Guard. The footage was released in the United States and U.S. viewers were horrified by the violence inflicted on Stewart and Nicaragua in general. In 1979, a general strike was organized by the FSLN which successfully ousted Somoza and allowed them to take control of the Nicaraguan government on July 19, 1979. Somoza fled to Paraguay and was eventually assassinated by FSLN supporters in 1980.

Sandino Reincarnated: The Sandinista Revolution

[T]he [Sandinista] government has introduced policies that are aimed at increasing the supply of goods to the countryside, the wages paid to rural workers, and the prices paid to rural producers for their crops.[42]

The reclamation and re-creation of Nicaragua as a modern state from the ashes of the Somoza dynasty would prove difficult. The state under the revolutionary forces was to be based on "the support and participation of the general population";[43] this would demand constant effort to keep the U.S. government out of domestic affairs in order to focus on unification of Nicaragua's various ethnic groups. To achieve this, a balance needed to be struck between having an effective federal authority while maintaining the autonomy of different regions, particularly, the Caribbean coast. It also meant empowering sectors of the population who may have been marginalized in the past, such as women. "The Sandinista state represented itself as the agent of transformation and justice that would resolve existing contradictions of class, nation, and gender, and thus deliver the New Man and New Woman. However, in hinging the success of the revolution on the figure of the New Man, the state unleashed political-economic and cultural processes that (re) produced those very contradictions at every turn."[44] This critique is not just applicable to women but also to Indigenous people and Afro-descendant communities on the Caribbean coast. Promoting inclusion and granting rights was challenging for the Sandinistas for multiple reasons: first, they were fighting a proxy war with the United States through its support to counter-revolutionary forces based in Honduras and fighting in Nicaragua, and second, global ideologies about the New Man (or multicultural commitments to inclusion of ethnic minorities) conflicted with local patriarchal practices and the income-generating potential of natural resources, respectively.

The birth of a middle class also arose during this time of reformation, particularly due to governmental agrarian reform. It was the goal of the Sandinista government to dismantle the agro-export economy that they had inherited from Somoza. "The first measures had the objective of eradicating the big landholders, primarily on the Pacific coast, and nationalizing the means of production, and with that, reorganizing economic activities through cooperatives."[45] Policies geared toward improving conditions for workers in the countryside—such as increased wages and higher prices paid for crops—had the added benefit of discouraging rural migration into cities and closing the gap of inequality between rural and urban populations.[46] When the Sandinistas (FSLN) took over the government, the goal was to shift the economy's focus from private to public ownership. However, the Sandinistas continued to operate Nicaragua with a mixed economy; much of their post-Revolution efforts went to the reconstruction of the country and its infrastructure, which helped to slowly increase GDP. It proved difficult to mend what had been so horrifically broken during the Somoza dynasty. Still, Sandinista policies such as public provision of education and healthcare created a "social wage" that supplemented real cash flow and subsequently supported the average citizen.[47] During the first ten years of Sandinista government, they were also fighting a war against the counter-revolutionary forces.

The Sandinistas won almost 70 percent of the national vote in general elections in 1984, beating out the U.S.-backed Arturo Cruz. By this point, the Reagan Administration had already been supporting a reactionary group of ex-National Guard members based out of Honduras known as the Counter-Revolution or Contras, both financially and by supplying them with weapons, in order to overthrow the Sandinistas and reinstate U.S. control. This move was reported to the U.S. public as being in the best interest of the "spread of democracy," as the FSLN government maintained a socialist ideology, with ties to the USSR and Cuba. Thus, the conflict in Nicaragua was considered an "active front" in the Cold War against the spread of communism. Eventually, the Sandinistas and the Contras established a ceasefire in 1988, and the ex-Contras were allowed to reintegrate into Nicaraguan society.

Over the course of the conflict between the U.S.-supported Contras and the Sandinista Army, the Contras killed 8,000 civilians and 910 state officials.[48] Total U.S. aid approved from 1982 to 1990 amounted to $322 million for the Contras, $124 million in military assistance, and $124 for nonmilitary purposes.[49] "The costs of the eight-year Contra War on Nicaraguans were substantial: approximately 30,000 Nicaraguans killed, thousands more maimed and wounded, 350,000 internally displaced, and $9 billion in direct damages. 'By any measure,' writes Lynn Horton, 'Nicaragua's armed conflict of the 1980s took a devastating human and economic toll.'"[50] During the Sandinista Revolution (1977–79), Nicaragua experienced a sharp decrease in foreign investment and a dramatic shift in expenditures from private sector endeavors to the military budget. It is estimated that the GDP dropped 25 percent in 1979, due to loss of life and infrastructure during the Revolution.

By the end of the Sandinista government era in 1990, Nicaraguan mothers began to organize against the government because they were tired of losing so many of their children to the war. And feminists became even more active in the next era using a critical analysis of the revolutionary period: "The experiences lived by Nicaraguan feminists during the revolutionary decade (1979–1989) contributed to the recognition—although it was not fully conscious in its time—of how gender and class intersect and condition the lives of women, as an expression of the articulation of two systems of domination—the capitalist system and the patriarchal system."[51]

Sandinistas Hand Over Power

> Nicaragua has had one of Latin America's most violent political traditions, lengthy periods of dictatorial rule, and prior to 1990 had never experienced a peaceful interparty transfer of power following a free election.[52]

In 1990, the FSLN lost to the UNO (Unión Nacional Opositora or National Opposition Union), and Violeta Chamorro, the U.S.-backed candidate, became the president. One of her major contributions was to broker peace with the Contras. She also created a social pact with the FSLN in order to maintain a healthy relationship: the *Concertación* accords of 1991, which sought to avoid "political gridlock" among the traditional elites (such as the Lacayos, Chamorros, and Pellas families, who founded the Banco de América in the 1950s) and Sandinistas in the face of re-privatization.[53] In addition, she added several ex-Contras to her cabinet, along with retaining General Humberto Ortega from the previous administration, as a reflection of involving both sides in Nicaragua's political future. During the Chamorro administration, the economy was adapted to the demands of International Monetary Fund (IMF) and World Bank policies—downsizing the

public sector and military, cutting spending on social programs, attracting foreign investment, encouraging exports, and other structural adjustment policies.
Francisco Mayoraga, the Minister of Finance, created the "Plan of 100 Days," also
known as the "Mayoraga Plan," which sought to cut the national deficit and lower
inflation, and attempted to pull Nicaragua into a free market economy. However,
it ultimately damaged both the public and private sectors, who together put on
nationwide strikes against the plan.

After sixteen years of neoliberal presidents, former president Daniel Ortega
returned to power in 2006. "After 16 years out of power, Daniel Ortega, the
historic candidate of the party of the [Sandinista] revolution . . . was reelected
president in November 2006."[54]

Present Day

> Having ignored the opposition's abstention campaign, Ortega
> rules virtually unchallenged as his country continues its slide from
> competitive authoritarianism toward authoritarianism plain and
> simple. In the course of building his power since 2006, Ortega has
> raised numerous obstacles to any turn back toward democracy.[55]

In 2006, Daniel Ortega, revolutionary FSLN president and leader of the Sandinistas in the 1980s, won the presidential election again. As of 2022, he still remains
in power as the Nicaraguan president and his wife, Rosario Murillo, is the vice
president; the political rhetoric of the duo continues to focus on leftist ideals and
populist promises to the poorer sectors of the country. However, for multiple
reasons many Nicaraguans question the sincerity of his claims; one of these reasons is the land grabs associated with a failed plan to resurrect the Nicaraguan
inter-oceanic canal:

> The canal project's concessionaire, a shadowy Chinese company known
> as HKND, was to receive sovereign control over canal infrastructure and
> property for fifty years, with an option to extend these privileges for another
> fifty. The Nicaraguan government gained broad authority to expropriate
> both private property and constitutionally protected indigenous commu-
> nal property along the planned canal route between Punta Gorda on the
> Caribbean and Brito on the Pacific, but also exposed the assets of the coun-
> try's central bank to claims by HKND in the event of disputes.[56]

Ultimately, construction on the canal halted, but the proposal of this type of
mega-development project without the necessary environmental viability studies
raised the concerns of civil society organizations across the country and many

scientists as well. This initiative has been accompanied by increased state control over all aspects of civil life, including the right to protest, the right to criticize the government publicly or online, and the right to academic integrity and university autonomy for students, professors, and university administrators.[57]

Beginning in April 2018, *campesinos*, students, and other civil society activists started protesting. "This expansion of the environmental agenda is possible, especially in this century, thanks to the advances of communications and the internet."[58] The MAN (Movimiento Ambientalista Nicaragüense or Environmental Movement of Nicaragua) brings together diverse organizations including NGOs, networks, scientists, and other leaders. Initially in early 2018, protests focused on the government's poor handling of a forest fire in the Indio Maíz Biological Reserve. Then, protests escalated against a Sandinista proposal to reform the country's social security system that would reduce benefits to pensioners by 5 percent as well as increasing what people would have to pay into the system. Even though the government rescinded the proposed law, protests and government repression continued. "In both these protests, and even more in subsequent events, university students became highly visible protagonists in the ranks of the opposition" and paid the price as police and paramilitary youth targeted them for repression.[59]

Universities were closed for six months as they were unable to open their doors because they couldn't guarantee students' safety given the repressive actions of the police and pro-government paramilitary forces. Tourism dropped drastically. As the Ortega regime assumed more dictatorial powers and rule of law weakened, civil society protests were harshly repressed. Politicized and/or minoritized groups such as women, Indigenous peoples, and Afro-descendant Creoles face higher levels of exclusion; and many Nicaraguans have left their country seeking asylum in Costa Rica.[60] The repression has affected multiple groups that have been organized for decades, including students, *campesinos* in northern Nicaragua as well as Indigenous and Afro-descendant peoples on the Caribbean coast, and women. "On November 23, 2018, [Vice President] Murillo and other women government officials denounced the Nicaraguan feminist movement for sowing terror. . . . Police blocked feminists from marching in Managua and Matagalpa on November 25, the International Day for the Elimination of Violence Against Women, and the feminist leader Ana Quiros was arrested and deported the following day."[61] On the Caribbean coast where Indigenous communities and Afro-descendant groups had made progress in gaining legal ownership of their ancestral lands, which was incorporated in the 1987 constitution of Nicaragua, there is encroachment on Indigenous lands and many forms of violence are being deployed against these communities.[62] These populations are being targeted by settlers, mining companies, and agro-export interests intent on taking over their land. Between 2011 and 2020, according to the Center for Justice and Human Rights of the Atlantic Coast of Nicaragua, at least 49 Miskito were killed, 49 were injured, 46 were kidnapped, 4 were disappeared, and 1,000 were forced to flee to Honduras. These crimes were carried out with the help of soldiers and para-militaries known as "colonos" or settlers, people hired by the government or by landowners to dispossess the Indigenous people of their lands.[63] "The suffering and violence faced by the communities is not just due to the government's failure to implement the law . . . the government actually plays an active role in encouraging the colonization of the protected lands by outsiders."[64]

By the end of 2018, the repression had sown so much fear that an eerie quiet fell over the country like a dense fog. During 2019, the environment of repression involved the "criminalization of demonstrators," in which representatives of the Nicaraguan judicial system prosecuted protesters for exercising their civil rights of free speech and association, and incarcerated them, punishing them as traitors or *"golpistas"* for attempting to overthrow the government.[65] Many youth activists have either been killed, jailed, or have fled (mainly to Costa Rica). Others have gone to study at universities in Central America and beyond, or remain hiding in safe houses across the country. Today, this is the "new" normal of Nicaragua: scaring people into silence or exile through the use of selective violence and sustained harassment of activists, including many of the college students involved in the April 2018 protests. Former Sandinista and internationally recognized Nicaraguan author, Sergio Ramirez, says, "All of this brings a certain feeling of déjà vu when it comes to the entire history of Nicaragua . . . the abuses of power and the way power gathers—and structures itself—always repeat themselves. It's a kind of circular constant in Nicaragua's history throughout the whole 20th century to the present day."[66]

In 2021, the Inter-American Commission on Human Rights reported the following statistics about the repression since the April 2018 uprising: "328 fatalities in the context of the crisis and 1,614 people who were deprived of liberty; in addition, more than 136 people remain deprived of liberty; 150 students expelled; more than 405 health professionals laid off; and more than 103,600 Nicaraguan exiles."[67] The exodus of people keeps increasing. "Driven by hunger and fear thousands of Nicaraguans have left. They changed countries because they lost hope in being able to change their own country."[68]

Recommended Reading

Alegria, Claribel, and Darwin J Flakoll. *Death of Somoza*. Evanston, IL: Northwestern University Press, 1996.

Babb, Florence E. *After Revolution: Mapping Gender and Cultural Politics in Neoliberal Nicaragua*. Austin, TX: University of Texas Press, 2001.

Bellanger, Wendi, Serena Cosgrove, and Irina Carlota Silber, editors. *Higher Education at the Crossroads of State Repression and Neoliberal Reform in Nicaragua: Reflections from a University under Fire*. New York: Routledge, 2022.

Belli, Gioconda. *The Country under My Skin: A Memoir of Love and War*. New York: Anchor Press, 2003.

Chavez, Daniel. *Nicaragua and the Politics of Utopia: Development and Culture in the Modern State*. Nashville, TN: Vanderbilt University Press, 2015.

Cosgrove, Serena, José Idiáquez, Leonard Joseph Bent, and Andrew Gorvetzian. *Surviving the Americas: Garifuna Persistence from Nicaragua to New York City*. Cincinnati: University of Cincinnati Press, 2021.

Darío, Rubén. *Stories and Poems/Cuentos y poesías: A Dual Language Book*. Translated and edited by Stanley Appelbaum. Mineola, NY: Dover Publications, 2002.

Dix, Paul, and Pamela Fitzpatrick. *Nicaragua: Surviving the Legacy of U.S. Policy*. Eugene, OR: Just Sharing Press, 2011.

Gobat, Michael. *Confronting the American Dream: Nicaragua under U.S. Imperial Rule*. Durham, NC: Duke University Press, 2005.

Goett, Jennifer. *Black Autonomy: Race, Gender, and Afro-Nicaraguan Activism*. Palo Alto, CA: Stanford University Press, 2016.

Gordon, Edmund T. *Disparate Diasporas: Identity and Politics in an African Nicaraguan Community*. Austin: University of Texas Press, Austin, Institute of Latin American Studies, 1998.

Hale, Charles R. *Resistance and Contradiction: Miskitu Indians and the Nicaraguan State, 1894–1987*. Palo Alto, CA: Stanford University Press, 1994.

Jones, Sam. "Nicaragua, 'A feeling of déjà vu': Author Sergio Ramirez on ex-comrade Ortega and Nicaraguan history repeating." *The Guardian*, September 18 2021, accessed December 2, 2021, https://www.theguardian.com/world/2021/sep/18/sergio-ramirez-interview-nicaragua-ortega-novel

Kinzer, Stephen. *Blood of Brothers: Life and War in Nicaragua*. New York: Putnam, 1991.

Lancaster, Richard. *Life Is Hard: Machismo, Danger, and the Intimacy of Power in Nicaragua*. Berkeley: University of California Press, 1994.

Montoya, Rosario. *Gendered Scenarios of Revolution: Making New Men and New Women in Nicaragua, 1975–2000*. Tucson: University of Arizona Press, 2012.

Morelli, Marco, trans. and ed. *Rubén's Orphans: Anthology of Contemporary Nicaraguan Poetry*. New Hyde Park, NY: Painted Rooster Press, 2001.

Ramirez, Sergio. *A Thousand Deaths Plus One*. Translated by Leland H. Chambers. Kingston, NY: McPherson, 2009.

Rocha, José Luis. *Provocation and Protest: University Students in Nicaragua's Uprising*. Chicago: LACASA Chicago Press, 2019.

Rushdie, Salman. *The Jaguar Smile: A Nicaraguan Journey*. New York: Random House, 2008.

White, Steven. *Poets of Nicaragua: A Bilingual Anthology 1918–1979*. Greensboro, NC: Unicorn Press, 1982.

Esri, CGAIR, USGS, CONANP, Esri, HERE, Garmin, FAO, NOAA, USGS

CHAPTER SEVEN

A Brief History of Costa Rica

INTRODUCTION

Costa Rica has consistently been ranked at the top of the Happy Planet Index since 2009, which measures life expectancy, ecological footprint, equality, and overall wellbeing. The Costa Rican motto is *"pura vida,"* meaning "pure/simple life," an attitude that extends from individual households to governmental policy: the country abolished its military in 1949 and turned those funds toward education and health.

Compared with most other Central American countries, Costa Rica has had a history of relatively fair and democratic exchanges of political power, with only one major internal conflict occurring in 1948. However, Costa Rica also has a long history of discriminating against certain racial and ethnic groups in the country; for example discrimination towards the Black population, West Indian descendants who arrived in the nineteenth century to work in the banana plantations and on the Atlantic Railroad; the Indigenous population, of which there are eight major groups (Bruncas, Bribris, Cabécares, Chorotegas, Huétares, Malekus, Gnöbes, and Teribes); and the Chinese population, who also immigrated primarily for work. Costa Rica has also been the receiving country of Nicaraguans seeking employment in recent decades, as well as the destination of Nicaraguan refugees fleeing repression since 2018.

TIMELINE OF KEY EVENTS

1502: Christopher Columbus arrives, names territory Costa Rica meaning "Rich Coast"

1540: Costa Rica made part of Viceroyalty of New Spain

1821: Gains independence from Spain

1823: Becomes part of United Provinces of Central America

1838: Costa Rica leaves the United Provinces, gains full independence

1840: United Provinces disintegrate

1856: Filibuster War against William Walker, a U.S. American who attempted to rule Central America; Costa Rican troops defeat him

1874: U.S. businessman Minor Cooper Keith starts United Fruit Company

1917: Federico Tinoco ousts Alfredo González, begins 2-year dictatorship

1919: Tinoco is deposed

1921: Coto War with Panama

1948: 6-week civil war over election result dispute

1949: National Liberal Party co-founder José Figueres Ferrer elected president

2006: Public workers strike in protest over free trade deal with the U.S.

2010: First woman president, Laura Chinchilla, is elected

2010–15: Border conflicts between Costa Rica and Nicaragua over the mouth of the Rio San Juan and Isla Portillos. In 2015, the International Court of Justice confirms the sovereignty of Costa Rica over the islands.

2012: Costa Rica joins Open Government Partnership, a global initiative between governments and civil society organizations to promote transparency, participation, and good governance.

2018: Carlos Alvarado Quesada of the Citizens' Action Party elected president

A HISTORY OF COSTA RICA
Pre-Columbian Era

> Northwestern Costa Rica has been viewed as the frontier between Mesoamerican and South American spheres of cultural influence; it was dubbed the northern sector of a so-called Intermediate Area.... However, Costa Rica is better viewed as a 'buffer zone,' where cultural traits mingled and were exchanged and adapted.[1]

Archaeological evidence, such as discarded tools and fire pits, has shown that groups of hunter-gatherers arrived to the Turrialba Valley about 10,000 to 7,000 years BCE. The main Indigenous groups and cultural influences on the region were the Nahuatl to the northwest, the Chibcha in the center and south, and the Diquís, who flourished from 700 to 1530 CE. The Indigenous groups in this region were part of a cultural complex called the "Intermediate Area," as it lies between the Mesoamerican and Andean cultural areas.

While it is believed that the first peoples in the region were mainly nomadic, following prey animal migration in order to hunt them; around 5,000 BCE agriculture began to emerge, and the nomads slowly became sedentary farmers. These first peoples harvested native tubers such as yucas and sweet potatoes as well as fished and hunted. Evidence of the village communities that were established have been found all across Costa Rica, from the Isla del Caño off the Pacific coast to the Coto Colorado River Basin. One of the most famous—and mysterious—archaeological finds in this area is over three hundred large stone spheres, found on the Disquís Delta to the south. Though there is no definitive answer to the significance of these stones, it is thought that they were lined up to create a path leading to chiefs' houses.

Colonization and Spanish Rule

The reasons for Costa Rica's democratic tradition are in part at least to be found in her earlier history. The Spanish conquerors, finding a country devoid of rich deposits of gold and silver and of a large Indian population which they might exploit, had no incentive to acquire large holdings of land. As a result, Costa Rica is essentially a country of small landowners and middle-class farmers.[2]

Christopher Columbus landed on the Costa Rican Caribbean coast during his fourth voyage in 1502. The first Spanish colony was established in 1524. The Costa Rican territory was part of the Captaincy General of Guatemala, a section of the larger Viceroyalty of New Spain. Unlike many of the other areas the Spanish had conquered, Costa Rica did not have ore deposits for mining; ironically, the country was named Costa Rica ("The Rich Coast") because of initial reports about the Indigenous peoples wearing large quantities of gold jewelry. The territory did not have a large Indigenous population that the *conquistadores* could enslave because many of them succumbed to the disease and violence the Spanish brought, which meant that any settlers had to work their own land. This prevented the establishment of plantations, like had been built in most of Spain's other colonies.

Overall, Costa Rica as a colony was poor and far away from the capital in Guatemala. Consequently, the territory was largely left alone during the early colonial era; the Spanish turned their focus to other parts of the Viceroyalty with resources they were interested in exploiting. Costa Rica's relative isolation fostered a racially homogenous population in the region: "Costa Rica's homogeneous social structure . . . was composed almost exclusively of Spanish descendants (creoles and *mestizos*)."[3] Relative isolation also allowed Costa Rica the opportunity to implement a semblance of a rural democratic system thanks to not being oppressively managed by the Spanish Crown. Eventually, though, Spanish settlers discovered that Costa Rica's hills had rich volcanic soil and this, paired with a mild climate, perhaps set the stage for the development of Costa Rica as a coffee-producing country.

> Costa Rica did not inherit a *latifundio* system from colonial times,
> nor the semi-feudal social structure related to it. The Costa Rican
> peasant was free, usually very poor, and mainly engaged in subsistence
> farming. The military was not needed for mobilization of forced labor
> to enforce land expropriation [as in other Central American countries].
> Coffee production became based on hired labor and purchases of
> additional land.[4]

Costa Rica gained independence from Spain in 1821, along with Guatemala, El Salvador, Honduras, and Nicaragua.[5] In 1823, these five states formed the Federal Republic of Central America, also called the United Provinces of Central America, under General Manuel José Arce of San Salvador. In 1838, Costa Rica left the United Provinces and gained full independence. In 1840, the United Provinces dissolved entirely.

Agriculture soon became the country's main economic sector, with the coffee industry in particular experiencing rapid growth throughout the 1830s.[6] In the beginning, harvesting coffee was based on family labor due to Costa Rica's sparse population: these groups were *minifundistas*, peasants who worked small plots and farms. The scarcity of labor "impeded the appearance of the 'servitude' that abounded in the rest of Central America. Not a system of domination but a new structure was fortified in Costa Rica."[7] Soon, a coffee-based oligarchy came into existence, a "coffee aristocracy" that "searched for diverse ways to perfect political institutions and to expand its commercial economy."[8] Coffee was a "new commodity that generated significant profits (and) encouraged . . . growth of a new middle class of business leaders, lawyers and other professionals who eventually came to challenge the modernizing elite for power."[9]

In 1856, William Walker, an American filibuster, landed in Nicaragua and declared himself president. He had the plan to extend his rule into Costa Rican territory and consequently engaged Costa Ricans in battle, later called the Filibuster War. Under Commander in Chief of the Army, President Juan Rafael Mora Porras, the Costa Rican troops forced the filibusters to fall back, pushing them into Rivas, Nicaragua, where Walker and the filibusters were eventually defeated. A drummer boy by the name of Juan Santamaría was turned into a national hero after he sacrificed his life by volunteering to burn down the tower William Walker's filibusters were using as a shooting base.[10]

Justo Rufino Barrios of Guatemala attempted to reunite the United Provinces of Central America in 1885. At first, he had the support of Honduras, El Salvador, and his home country of Guatemala; later, El Salvador withdrew and allied with

Mexico in order to overthrow Barrios. Costa Rica mobilized against Guatemala, but before they could get through Honduras to the Guatemalan front, El Salvador had already defeated them, and Central America remained separate sovereign states.[11]

The presidency of Tomás Guardia, from 1870 to 1882, "put an end to the incessant coups whereby, between 1840 and 1870, competing clans within the coffee oligarchy intermittently deposed one another to gain personalistic access to the spoils of state power."[12] Guardia imposed many liberal reforms such as abolishing the death penalty and encouraging citizens to attend secondary school. His main focus was on the construction of the Atlantic Railroad. In 1871, Guardia signed a contract with U.S. entrepreneur Henry Meiggs for the construction of the railway—Meiggs was the uncle of Minor Cooper Keith, one of the founders of the United Fruit Company, who would take over the project after Meiggs' death in 1877. The Soto-Keith agreement, as it was called, "gave a vast amount of land to the railway builder and exempted his company from paying export taxes for a period of 99 years."[13] Keith also brought the banana industry in to Costa Rica, starting to export the crop in 1880.[14] Bananas, along with coffee, quickly became the dominant agricultural exports for the country.

There are records of Chinese immigrants arriving in Costa Rica as early as 1635 to trade silk and other products.[15] However, the majority of Chinese immigrants are recorded to have been brought in as laborers starting in 1847, with a large migration occurring in 1873 with the impending construction of the Atlantic Railroad.[16] Many of these laborers were brought over from Panama, where they had been working on the trans-isthmus canal.

Like the Chinese, West Indians share a similar history of immigration in Costa Rica. They were brought in to work on the railroad in the 1870s, with as many as fifty thousand West Indians making the migration to the Limón province between 1870 and 1930.[17] There are records, though, of Africans and Afro-descendants in the country from as early as 1827.[18] Following the completion of the railroad in 1890, many of these laborers stayed in the country, forming a community on the Caribbean coast in Limón. While the Costa Rican population had ambivalent feelings about the growing number of West Indians in the country, the "Costa Rican government allowed West Indian immigration to continue because the Atlantic coast region [where the province of Limón is located] was considered too unhealthy for people of European descent."[19] West Indians also tended to be favored by companies such as the United Fruit Company due to their familiarity with harvesting fruit and their ability to speak English.

Both the Chinese and West Indians faced discrimination from the broader *mestizo* population, who felt threatened by the prospect of losing their jobs to the immigrants moving in. Costa Rican president Otilio Ulate, for example, spoke on "the problem of the predomination of workers from the coloured race which prejudices the creole worker."[20] In 1862, the Costa Rican Law of Immigration was passed that "specifically prohibited Chinese and African immigration."[21] Immigration continued despite this, and in 1897, a second law attempting to stop the migration of Chinese people to the country was passed, and then a third in 1906; the immigration bans did not succeed in stopping Chinese migration.[22] Chinese migrants were also targeted for having a strong presence in the liquor industry: efforts were made to ban Chinese business owners from being able to sell liquor. Chinese merchants had to petition the Costa Rican government twice—in 1908 and in 1917—to stop this discrimination against their economic well-being.[23]

Twentieth Century

Costa Rica has been home to a stable democracy for about sixty years and has a well-educated, healthy, and relatively prosperous population. In 1950, gross domestic product (GDP) per capita in Nicaragua and Costa Rica were approximately $188 and $254 respectively (in 1950s currency) (Mitchell 1998). By 1998 gross national product (GNP) per capita had grown to $370 for Nicaragua and $2,770 for Costa Rica (Population Reference Bureau 2).[24]

In January 1917, Minister of War Federico Tinoco Granados staged a coup to usurp President Alfredo González. This was one of the few instances of violent upheaval in Costa Rica's history. Tinoco ruled with a military dictatorship until 1919, when his brother, who had aided his coup, was assassinated. Shortly after that, Tinoco resigned and fled into exile. Juan Bautista Quirós succeeded him in office.

In 1921, war broke out between Costa Rica and neighboring country Panama: "The so-called Coto War between Panama and Costa Rica in 1921 was provoked by two competing banana companies that took advantage of a border dispute in order to obtain more favorable land concessions."[25] Colonel Héctor Zúñiga Mora of Costa Rica sent out an expedition to the south of the country, and founded a caserío—essentially, a small settlement surrounded by farmland—near the border with Panama, in Pueblo Nuevo de Coto. A two-month war broke out in response to this perceived encroachment on territory. "The conflict was settled after two months of intermittent fighting, by U.S. military intervention, on terms of Costa Rican sovereignty."[26]

Rafael Ángel Calderón Guardia was elected president in 1940. He was notably focused on social issues such as poverty eradication, and aimed to enact reforms to the taxation system and expand housing for the poor. He established a minimum wage and protections for workers with the Work Code, implemented a national social security program, and instituted a healthcare program. He developed close ties with the Communist Party, which was created in 1932 and led by Manuel Mora. Succeeding Calderón Guardia was Teodoro Picado Michalski in 1944, who was backed by both Calderón Guardia, Manuel Mora, and the Archbishop of the Catholic Church.[27] Although he received some backlash, with claims of election fraud coming to the forefront, Picado's presidency was relatively calm, especially in comparison with his predecessor, who was often at odds with the Costa Rican coffee elite. The Picado administration did enact the Electoral Code of Laws in 1945, which ensures the democratic nature of elections in Costa Rica, and is still in place today.

In 1948, a forty-four-day civil war broke out in the country. Tensions regarding a contested presidential election led to the outbreak. Picado threw his support behind his predecessor and supporter, Calderón Guardia, who was running for a second term. Against him was Otilio Ulate of the National Union Party. The campaign season was tumultuous: "Assassination attempts were made on Calderón Guardia, on Picado and on Manuel Mora. There were strikes, riots and several deaths."[28] At last, when the election results came in, Ulate had won the race with a 54 percent majority. Immediately, the opposition—Picado's National Republic Party—claimed that the results were falsified, and on those grounds the congress annulled the results. Shortly after this announcement, the war began in the name of rightfully instating Ulate as president. Combatting Ulate's supporters was "a small regular army of maybe 1000 men, who were reinforced by 500 soldiers from Somoza-governed Nicaragua."[29] Nicaraguan dictator Anastasio Somoza had substantial interest in Costa Rica, and wanted to support Calderón Guardia by sending troops across the frontier.[30] Anti-communist José Figueres Ferrer, who had been exiled to México in 1942, had been waiting for his opportunity to oppose Calderón Guardia and Picado. He joined the fight, leading an armed force, the National Liberation Army, against "a Government which had allowed the Communists to infiltrate the civil service, the army, and the police."[31] The war raged on, with Figueres defeating the government troops, until Picado insisted to Manuel Mora and Calderón Guardia that they all surrender, as they were running low on supplies and support. After just over a month of fighting and with more than two thousand casualties, the Costa Rican civil war came to an end. Immediately following the war, in 1949, the government dissolved the military and outlawed the Communist Party with the Ulate-Figueres Pact.[32] In accordance with Figueres' demands, Ulate was finally declared president.[33] Figueres won the presidency under the new constitution in 1953, ushering in an age of working closely with the United Nations and the Organization of American States.[34]

Following the 1979 Sandinista Revolution, many migrants arrived to Costa Rica from Nicaragua. There were many reasons why Nicaraguans fled from their home country: some claimed ethnic persecution by the Sandinista government; some were displaced by the U.S.-backed guerrilla group, the Contras; some were afraid of being conscripted into the military; and still others left because of deteriorating economic conditions.[35] By 1989, the official registered number of Nicaraguan refugees was thirty-four thousand, with unofficial estimates including another one to two hundred thousand.[36] More than half of the Nicaraguan refugees were of the Miskito Indigenous group.[37]

Costa Rican Exceptionalism: Characteristics and Contradictions

> When international guidebook Frommer's (Greenspan 2007, p. 367) informs tourists that the country is 'called the "Switzerland of Central America" . . . a sea of tranquility in a region that has been troubled by turmoil for centuries' the ideology of exceptionalism and whiteness is metaphorically displayed to distinguish Costa Rica from its perceived inferior country neighbours and tourist competitors. The economic benefits received from tourism development, however, manifest along racial lines.[38]

"Exceptional" is a term that has often been used to describe Costa Rica, as it is seemingly singular among the Central American states given strong rule of law and good governance practices and extensive investments in education and health across the country. Costa Rica certainly appears to be exceptional, due to political choices such as demilitarization and emphasizing environmental protections, and statistics such as a 94 percent literacy rate. The nation has long cultivated an image of a "country of political virtues: peace, order, legality, harmony, prudence and neutrality in the face of the conflicts of its neighbors and a land of refuge for those fleeing from the discord that plagued their own countries."[39] However, Costa Rica's "exceptionalism" is arguably propagated by a discourse that serves nationalist ideals, one created, according to scholar Benjamín N. Narváez, by elites in the nineteenth century in order to "mask social inequalities, minimise class conflict, and forge national unity."[40]

Costa Rica's mythos of exceptionalism extends beyond socio-political uniqueness—it also purports racial homogeneity, "*la leyenda blanca*" or the "white legend," the narrative that to be Costa Rican is to be white in an inherent sense.[41] This is another claim forged to elevate Costa Rica's national identity above its regional siblings as whiteness is seen as desirable and good: "Actors in the tourism industry have sought to use whiteness and exceptionalism as 'symbolic capital' to separate the nation and give it status because of its perceived position closer to the global North in the 'global hierarchy of nations.'"[42] The story of Costa Rica as a "white, classless, peaceful democracy"[43] also serves to attract international tourists to visit its national parks and coastal vacation spots. However, to achieve this image of a safe haven in the Central American region, it has been necessary to render invisible certain groups that exist *within* Costa Rica, namely the Indigenous and Black populations; "exclusion is built into the story of Costa Rican exceptionalism."[44]

Despite having several distinct Indigenous groups, Costa Rica's perpetuation of the exceptionalism myth has contributed to the marginalization of the country's Indigenous people in the national narrative. Indigenous people were not even included in the National Census until 1950.[45] It took until 1977 for the government to adopt legislation that officially recognized Indigenous peoples and their rights, per International Labor Organization Convention 107—though this was simply a *recognition* of their fundamental rights. It would take over a decade for the government to adopt legislation that would actually protect Indigenous peoples and their rights.[46]

Present Day

> Costa Rica is a country with substantial advantages over its neighbors, the most apparent of which are its relatively stable government and economy. Over the past few decades the diversity of its flora and fauna and its inviting beaches have combined with the above factors to produce a thriving tourism sector, attracting visitors from around the world.[47]

Today, Costa Rica's main economic sector is tourism: "Costa Rica received over one million tourists in 2000, over half of whom visited at least one protected area."[48] The tourism sector employed 12 percent of Costa Rica's labor force by the late 1990s and had overtaken coffee and bananas as Costa Rica's second-leading source of foreign exchange, after microchips.[49] Costa Rica has become one of the leading countries in the region in efforts toward maintaining biodiversity, establishing protected areas on more than 25 percent of its territory.[50]

Like other countries in Central America, much of Costa Rica's tourism is because of ecotourism. Ecotourism is defined as "traveling to an undisturbed and pristine natural environment with the object of studying, admiring and enjoying the scenery with its wild plants and animals."[51] The issue that arises with the commodification of nature is how it encourages, by necessity, the development of isolated places and natural areas to be accessible to tourists, often resulting in land loss and environmental destruction. Indigenous populations are typically the most affected by these changes, as they have fewer protections to prevent development of their land. In Costa Rica, land reserves for Indigenous populations were not established until 1976; today, there are twenty-four reserves for the eight distinct groups.[52] Despite this, some Indigenous communities did not even officially receive the title to their land, making it all the easier for government and business land development interests to proceed undeterred.[53] In 1998, a Biodiversity Law was passed with the intent to "implement conservation by recognizing the economic importance of biodiversity as balanced against impacts on the rights of rural communities."[54] "Rural communities" refers to both peasant farming communities and Indigenous populations. Although this legislation was a promising step, there are still intrusions on land inhabited by these impoverished and marginalized communities, including continued deforestation and projects that endanger the water supply.

In addition to a growing environmental movement, women's organizations have been active for more than a century. The evolution of the women's movement in Costa Rica can be understood in three stages: 1. 1890–1922 the process of redefining women's roles outside of the domestic sphere; 2. 1923–52 the formation of several women's organizations and the consolidation of the movement for suffrage; and 3. 1953–85 active participation in politics.[55] During the first stage, Costa Rican women made gains such as the right to civil divorce, to manage family assets, and to exercise parental authority, as well as benefitting from the General Law of Common Education passed in 1886.[56] The second stage saw the creation of the Feminist League, the Alliance of Costa Rican Women, and the Feminist Culture League, among others. The Feminist League was at the forefront of the feminist political struggle, with their work aimed at achieving women's fundamental rights as full citizens.[57] Women gained suffrage in 1954, segueing the Costa Rican feminist movement into its third stage, where women would begin to have more active and vocal participation in politics.

In 2012, Costa Rica joined the Open Government Partnership (OGP), which was launched in 2011. The OGP brings together countries committed to open government reforms in an effort to encourage improved government effectiveness and policy-making. Costa Rica is using its membership in the OGP to "restart a process halted for 23 years to create a consultation mechanism that will allow Indigenous groups to participate in all policy making decisions that affect them, and the results of the dialogue leading to an improvement in the delivery of public services."[58]

In a parallel with the exodus following the 1979 Nicaraguan Revolution, there has been another recent increase in Nicaraguan migration, including asylum seekers fleeing across Costa Rica's borders due to the repression of the Ortega administration. Since April 2018, thousands have crossed Nicaragua's southern border into Costa Rica to escape Daniel Ortega's violent police and paramilitary forces, who have been attacking and imprisoning protestors. In comparison to the mere fifty-eight asylum applications in 2017, more than twenty-four thousand Nicaraguans officially applied for protection in Costa Rica in 2018.[59]

Recommended Reading

Bell, John Patrick. *Crisis in Costa Rica: The 1948 Revolution.* Austin: University of Texas Press, 1971.

Biesanz, Mavis Hiltunen, Richard Biesanz, and Karen Zubris Biesanz. *The Ticos: Culture and Social Change in Costa Rica.* Boulder, CO: Lynne Rheiner Press, 1989.

Cardona-Hine, Alvaro. *Flowering Thistles: An Anthology of Stories and Poetry from Four Generations of a Literary Costa Rican Family.* Self-published, CreateSpace Independent Publishing Platform, 2014.

Chomsky, Aviva. *West Indian Workers and the United Fruit Company in Costa Rica, 1870–1940.* Baton Rouge: Louisiana State University Press, 1996.

Edelman, Marc. *Peasants against Globalization: Rural Social Movements in Costa Rica.* Stanford, CA: Stanford University Press, 1999.

Evans, Sterling. *The Green Republic: A Conservation History of Costa Rica.* 1st ed. Austin: University of Texas Press, 1999.

Isla, Anna. *The "Greening" of Costa Rica: Women, Peasants, Indigenous Peoples, and the Remaking of Nature.* Toronto: University of Toronto Press, 2015.

Palmer, Steven, and Ivan Molina. *The Costa Rica Reader: History, Culture, Politics.* The Latin America Readers. Durham, NC: Duke University Press, 2004.

Ras, Barbara. *Costa Rica: A Traveler's Literary Companion.* Berkeley, CA: Whereabouts Press, 1994.

Sandoval-García, Carlos. *Threatening Others: Nicaraguans and the Formation of National Identities in Costa Rica.* Athens: Ohio University Press, 2014.

Esri, CGAIR, USGS, CONANP, Esri, HERE, Garmin, FAO, NOAA, USGS

CHAPTER EIGHT
A Brief History of Panama

INTRODUCTION

Panama is located on the land bridge that connects North and South America, bordering Colombia and Costa Rica, and has both Caribbean and Pacific Ocean coasts. The majority of the population is *mestizo* of mixed Indigenous and European descent. Around 10 percent of the country is Afro-descendant. The country has eight main Indigenous groups that, together, constitute 12 percent of the population: Ngäbe, Guna, Emberá, Buglé, Wounaan, Naso Tjërdi, Bribri, and Bokota.

Panama's economy is primarily oriented toward the financial service sector, commerce, and trade because of the Panama Canal, which itself contributes to much of Panama's economic well-being. Over the past decade, Panama has had one of the fastest growing global economies; its annual growth has been 7.2 percent, which is more than double the average for the Central American region.[1] With an annual GDP per capita of $13,645, Panama is the wealthiest Central American country.[2]

TIMELINE OF KEY EVENTS

1502: Spanish conquistador Rodrigo de Bastidas lands in Panama

1519: Panama becomes Spanish Viceroyalty of New Andalucia (later New Granada)

1821: Panama gains independence from Spain; joins confederacy of Gran Colombia with Colombia, Venezuela, Ecuador, Perú, and Bolivia

1830: Gran Colombia separates from confederacy; Panama becomes part of Colombia

1846: Panama signs treaty with U.S. to build railway across isthmus

1880s: France attempts and fails to build a canal across the isthmus

1903: Panama gains independence from Colombia; U.S. buys the right to build Panama Canal

1914: Panama Canal completed

1939: Panama ceases to be a U.S. protectorate

1968: Chief of National Guard General Omar Torrijos Herrera stages coup, imposes dictatorship

1981: Torrijos ousted

1983: Intelligence chief and U.S. CIA informant Manuel Noriega becomes head of Panama's National Guard, renames it the Panama Defense Forces

1988: Noriega charged with drug smuggling by U.S.; Noriega declares state of emergency after a failed coup

1989: Noriega claimes election results invalid and declares war following threats from U.S.; U.S. invades Panama, ousts Noriega; Noriega replaced by Guillermo Endara

1991: Parliament approves constitutional reforms such as abolition of standing army and privatization

1992: U.S. court finds Noriega guilty of drug smuggling; Noriega sentenced to 40 years in U.S. prison

1999: Mireya Moscoso becomes Panama's first female president; Panama assumes full control of the Canal

2000: Moscoso creates panel to investigates crimes committed during military governments 1968–89

2002: Moscoso creates commission to investigate corruption after civic protests against government corruption

2003: National strike over management of social security fund, more than 40 injured in clashes

2009: Ricardo Martinelli elected president

2011: Mining code reforms reversed after protests led by Indigenous groups and environmentalists

2012: Panama joins Open Government Partnership, a global initiative between governments and civil society organizations to promote transparency, participation, and good governance.

2014: Juan Carlos Varela elected president

2015: Panama Papers leaked—11.5 million documents detailing offshore account information

2018: Former president Ricardo Martinelli extradited from the U.S. to Panama amid accusations of corruption

2019: Laurenito "Nito" Cortizo of the Democratic Revolutionary Party elected president

A HISTORY OF PANAMA
Pre-Columbian Era

> The pre-Columbian Indigenous societies of Parita Bay in the Central
> Region of Panama have been considered by many specialists in
> cultural evolution to be archetypes of ranked societies. In fact, early
> anthropological definitions of chiefdoms derive from these societies
> and from the discovery of the Sitio Conte cemetery in the 1930s.[3]

The region known today as Panama was settled by several Indigenous groups, including the Monagrilo, Cueva, Chibchan, and Chocoan. Unlike many other ancient cultures, the Indigenous people of Panama did not build large cities, though it does boast being home to some of the first pottery-making peoples in the Americas. Excavation of the Spanish settlement at Panama Viejo revealed "several complete urn burials, as well as a burial of a woman who was laid on a bed of skulls and surrounded by nine more skulls," a find that predated the settlement by three hundred years and was evidence of pre-Columbian occupation one thousand five hundred years prior.[4]

Archaeological findings in the central region of the country have uncovered artifacts that speak to some of the social structures of these groups. For example, "social ranking was characterized by a strong focus on prestige goods display, elite sponsored feasting, and the burial of important individuals in deep-mound tombs at the central community."[5] Later reports from European *conquistadores* describe the use of trade routes throughout the region for inter-tribal exchanges, further evidenced by some of the burial objects that have been excavated: certain ceremonial figurines and jewelries suggest a trade relationship with metal-using cultures based in Colombia, and perhaps as far as Mexico.

Colonization, Spanish Rule, & Gran Colombia

> Beginning in the sixteenth century, the Spanish used this route [the
> natural Panama Canal from the Atlantic to the Pacific] to supply
> Panama City and move gold and silver from the city to galleons in the
> Caribbean.[6]

Spanish conquistador Rodrigo de Bastidas landed on the Isthmus of Panama in 1501 during his voyage along the eastern coast of the Americas. The following year, Christopher Columbus, an Italian navigator funded by the Spanish crown, explored the region on his fourth voyage. By 1509, the Spanish were colonizing the region, with the first permanent settlement established in 1510. The isthmus was used by the Spanish for transporting trade goods from galleons in the Caribbean to

Panama City, which lent itself to being a target for pirating and sacking. "In 1671, famed English privateer Captain Henry Morgan took the largest pirate fleet in history to sack [Panama City, the capital]."[7] So devastating was Morgan's attack that the Spanish rebuilt the capital city "on a more easily defensible rocky promontory eight kilometers down the coast from the original site," where it still stands today.[8]

The Viceroyalty of New Andalucia, later renamed New Granada, was established in 1717, and included the Isthmus of Panama, as well as present-day Colombia, Ecuador, and Venezuela. The capital of New Granada was Santa Fe de Bogotá. Issues arose due to Bogotá's distance and consequent inability to maintain a strong authority over the territory; challenges to Bogotá's authority were made by the Viceroyalty of Perú, as well as by Panama. Tensions between Bogotá and Panama persisted until 1819, when Gran Colombia was established. Gran Colombia consisted of present-day Colombia, Venezuela, Ecuador, northern Peru, western Guyana, and northwest Brazil. Its first president was Venezuelan military leader Simón Bolívar. Panama gained independence from Spain in 1821, and was promptly annexed into Gran Colombia that same year.

Gran Colombia dissolved a mere ten years later in 1830. However, even following the collapse of Gran Colombia, Panama remained a department of the country of Colombia, together forming New Granada once again. In the mid-nineteenth century, New Granada and the United States struck a deal to construct the first transoceanic railway and give "U.S. citizens and cargo the right to free passage through the isthmus."[9] This railway was pivotal to the Gold Rush period in the United States, as it allowed quick transportation of gold from the west coast to the northeast. Construction began in 1850 and was completed by 1855.[10] In 1882, the French-owned New Panama Canal Company attempted to construct their own canal across the isthmus. However, due to engineering challenges that could not surmount the environment's geography, as well as many of the workers falling ill with disease and ultimately dying, the project was declared a failure by 1889.

Independence and the Panama Canal

Panama acquired its independence from Spain in 1821, beginning an ill-fated 80-year period of subordination to distant Bogota—first as part of Simon Bolivar's Gran Colombia, then as a state of New Granada and, finally, as a restless appendage of the Republic of Colombia.[11]

Prior to Panamanian secession, the United States signed a treaty with Colombia, called the Hay-Herran Treaty, first proposed in 1901 and signed in 1903. The treaty "authorized the United States to cut a canal across the Isthmus of Panama, then a part of Colombia, and it granted the United States for the period of one hundred years, subject to renewal by the United States as long as it might desire to do so, a zone from ocean to ocean through which the canal should run."[12] However, the Colombian Senate rejected some of the language in the treaty, which eventually led to U.S. support for Panamanian rebellion and secession: "When Colombia balked at U.S. terms for a canal treaty, the United States first sent Marines to occupy the Panama Railroad, and then prevented the Colombian government from halting Panama's secession."[13]

Panama remained a department of Colombia until 1903, when it declared its independence and was officially separated from the South American nation. This separation was spurred by tensions between Colombia and the United States, as the United States had made bids for the territorial rights to Panama's Canal Zone, which Colombia had refused. This led the United States "to circumvent the authority of the government of Colombia. . . . The United States encouraged and supported Panamanians to declare their independence in 1903, motivated by the hope of exercising direct influence" over the country, particularly the Canal Zone.[14]

The United States bought the assets from the failed French New Panama Canal Company to get the project initiated; they also purchased rights to the Canal Zone from the Panamanian government for $10 million.[15] Over the course of its construction, over seventy-five thousand people worked on the Canal. Many of these were laborers from the West Indies while others were from European countries, particularly Italy and Spain. After just over a decade of construction, at a cost of approximately US$387 million, the Panama Canal officially opened in August 1914.[16]

In 1921, the United States and Colombia signed a treaty "to remove all the misunderstandings growing out of the political events in Panama in November 1903," as well as to "define and regulate [the U.S. and Colombia's] rights and interests in respect of the interoceanic canal."[17] The treaty additionally called for Colombia to recognize Panama as an independent nation and have its borders officially defined; this recognition would allow the United States and Colombia to be "in a position to meet as equals and to arrange their business upon a footing of equality, as is the case with other nations."[18]

Twentieth Century

Panama's history is very different from that of the stereotypical Central American polity lurching from one military coup to the next. From the time of its founding as an independent state in 1904 up until 1968, it was an imperfect but evolving democracy. Its first military coup in 1968 marred a record of civilian political control that was unique in its region.[19]

Although the U.S. and Panamanian governments had seemingly come to an understanding regarding the Canal, eventually Panama requested that negotiations be re-opened. In 1933, president Harmodio Arias travelled to the United States in order to discuss a new treaty in person. He was focused on mitigating the impact of the global economic depression by implementing a moratorium on the national debt and a reduction in civil service salaries, and by creating a savings bank. However, these were only stopgap solutions and didn't fully address the issues caused by the depression, which the president was aware of: "Arias recognized that Panama's economy was inextricably bound up with that of the Canal Zone. Only by [gaining control over] a greater share in the benefits of the canal could Panama solve her economic problems."[20] Arias originally proposed more participation and opportunity for Panamanian merchants in the Zone, and for U.S. subsidiary business activities related to the Panama Railroad—such as hotels in the area—to end.

Between 1933, when Arias visited the United States, and 1936, the United States and Panama drafted a mutually beneficial agreement. The Hull-Alfaro Treaty was signed in 1936 and included the following agreements: "1) to end the Panamanian protectorate; 2) to recognize Panama's rights to a larger share of canal prosperity; 3) to increase the annuity from $250,000 to $436,000 dollars; 4) to recognize a joint commitment to canal defense; 5) to uphold the right of transit across the Zone for Panamanian citizens; and 6) to abrogate the treaty stipulation of intervention in Panama City and Colon."[21]

In 1968, Dr. Arnulfo Arias Madrid was elected as president for the third time; he had been previously ousted by the Panamanian military two times before, and after only ten days in office, he was ousted once more. The chief of the National Guard, Colonel Omar Torrijos, with the help of Major Boris Martínez, led a coup that "nullified controversial election results that had eventually led to Arnulfo Arias being sworn in as president of Panama."[22] This coup received the support of the United States, given its issues with Arias—he had "been perceived in Washington as pro-Axis during WWII and as a controversial, populist political figure that seemed to generate political turmoil." The United States thus believed that the new military regime of Torrijos would maintain political stability and a regime that would follow U.S. interests.[23]

Although Torrijos led a corrupt government, he was also known for his socialist programs that were beneficial to marginalized populations: "Under a military corporatism model he furthered political participation of traditionally disenfranchised groups, fostered economic development by the creation of agricultural settlements on 'underutilized' lands, and promoted hierarchical leadership entities and community settlements among the country's Indigenous populations."[24] He also re-visited the Canal agreement with the United States, wanting to update it from its 1936 revision, and initiated talks in 1971. But, "[b]y the end of 1972 the talks had collapsed, both sides unwilling to accept what had been agreed to previously," especially with Torrijos' staunch nationalist position, with which the United States refused to agree.[25] Then, in 1977, the first of the two Torrijos-Carter Treaties was signed, which allowed for the "gradual return of the canal and the Canal Zone to Panamanian sovereignty."[26] It also converted the fourteen U.S. military bases that were placed in the Canal Zone into places for civilian use.[27] However, before any of this happened, "the Carter administration . . . [was] concerned about the fact that the U.S. government had negotiated a new treaty with a repressive military regime. Therefore, General Torrijos was persuaded to agree to a restoration of democracy once the treaties were signed, ratified, and implemented."[28] Torrijos died in a plane crash in 1981 that has been suspected to be planned rather than accidental, an assassination by some unknown party.

Noriega and the 1989 U.S. Invasion

The December invasion represented the culmination of over two and a half years of acute political crisis within Panama and 22 months of high-level U.S. efforts to remove General Noriega from power. In the process, Panama's economy was devastated, long existing class and racial divisions in its society were exacerbated, and traditional norms of political behavior, which had made Panama a relatively non-violent nation by regional standards, were destroyed.[29]

Even after his death, Torrijos' legacy of a military government persisted, with the Panama Defense Forces (PDF) continuing to control the political sphere behind the guise of civilian rule. In 1983, "General Manuel Noriega took control of Panama's armed forces . . . after cunningly working his way through three other higher ranking officers."[30] Due to his high military ranking, Noriega became the de facto leader of the Panamanian government. Noriega was heavily involved with narco-trafficking: his rule has been called a "narco-military regime," and he referred to himself as a "kingpin."[31] This made him particularly difficult to negotiate with due to his entanglement with the Medellin drug cartel based in Colombia: "The real threat to him is not the United States or the other countries that oppose him. It is not the indictments. It is the Medellin drug cartel. It was reported that in 1987, when Noriega was believed to be talking to the United States about his possible departure, a Colombian drug lord sent him a tiny coffin with his name engraved on it. There is no negotiating with Medellin. Noriega has no possible option but to cling desperately to power."[32] In May 1989, national elections were held, and

Noriega ran against Guillermo Endara, the leader of the Democratic Alliance of Civic Opposition, a group that opposed Noriega. Unfortunately, the Noriega government annulled the election results when it was revealed Endara had won, claiming that there was U.S. interference and other forms of voter fraud.

Following this, the United States became intent on removing Noriega from power. Their attempts to achieve this were many and multileveled:

> The U.S. government carried out a series of escalating actions against the Noriega regime, designed to pressure the general into stepping down from power. First, information was leaked to the press and to the U.S. Congress. Second, U.S. officials negotiated with Noriega for his exit from power, offering him safety and money. Next, the general was indicted, in hopes that playing hardball would encourage him to concede. Then, Washington once again attempted to broker a deal with Noriega. Once he refused, economic sanctions at ever-increasing magnitude were levied against the Noriega regime, in hopes that the Panamanian people would take to the streets and undermine the regime.[33]

They also attempted to stage a coup to oust Noriega, but that also proved to be futile.[34] Finally, when all of these approaches failed to have any impact on Noriega, the United States decided that an actual military invasion was their only remaining option in order to stop Noriega. Thus, in December 1989, the Bush administration authorized an operation—dubbed Operation Just Cause—where U.S. forces would "apprehend the general, dissolve the PDF and put in power the pro-U.S. government that was elected in the May 1989 elections."[35] The U.S. troops achieved their mission, extracting Noriega within a week.

The estimated civilian death toll of this operation is six hundred fifty, with hundreds more wounded and displaced.[36] The invasion financially gouged the country, with property losses due to damage and looting estimated at nearly $2 billion; these losses resulted in a 25 percent increase in unemployment.[37] All of this cost combined with the $5.5 billion debt from Noriega's rule devastated Panama's economy. The country also had to contend with a restructuring of their police and military, given that at the time of the invasion, the military's forces were upward of fourteen thousand. There was a desire to decrease the force's numbers significantly for fear of the nation returning to the situation where it was "not a country with an army but an army with a country."[38]

Since the invasion, Panama has been recovering politically and economically. Some view the 1989 intervention as somewhat positive: "Panamanians attribute their democratic era to the period post the U.S. invasion, with its independence confirmed by the U.S. departure on the final day of 1999,"[39] with the signing and ratification of the second Torrijos-Carter Treaty, which officially gave over control of the Canal to Panama.

Social Movements

> As in many other Latin American countries, Panamanian-style racism denies the very existence of racism. Instead, it characterizes Panamanian society as a perfect 'melting pot' of Spanish-speakers, in which white people, Indigenous people, and Black people of colonial origin merge without distinction into a single nation. . . . The notion of a racial melting pot . . . promotes racial mixing and ambiguity, and minimizes the presence of the Black population in the country.[40]

As is an unfortunately common theme throughout much of Central America, the Afro-descendant population in Panama faces discrimination. What discrimination already existed was amplified following the 1989 U.S. invasion and the subsequent adoption of neoliberal policies to further align Panama with U.S. interests—under Pérez Balladares, unemployment was at 13 percent, with the rates of poverty and *extreme* poverty at 38 percent and 20 percent respectively.[41] Because Afro-Panamanians experience higher rates of unemployment and poverty compared to the national average, they suffered the brunt of such reforms. In response to this, in 1995, MODESCO (Movimiento de Desempleados de Colón or Colón Unemployed Movement) protested against these labor reforms, demanding the creation of temporary government jobs in an effort to alleviate some of the Colón province's poverty. MODESCO was predominantly made up of Afro-Panamanian men and women, and although they did not organize specifically around racial issues, their lived experiences as Black Panamanians living on or below the poverty line certainly intersected. This mobilization of Panama's Afro-descendant population has continued into the twenty-first century: at a meeting in Costa Rica in 2004, Panama's delegates outlined a "Plan of Action for the Advocacy of Afro-Panamanians" which sought to achieve "authentic equality in the face of the law and society for Afro-descendant men and women, as well as getting state institutions to guarantee their social inclusion."[42] The following year, 2005, Black movement groups were successful in pressuring the Torrijos government to create a Special Commission for the Inclusion of the Black Ethnicity, which would eventually evolve into the National Council for the Black Ethnicity in 2007. The National Assembly also approved the right for Panamanians abroad to vote, which had been a goal of Panamanians in the diaspora for over thirty years.[43]

Another ethnic group that faces marginalization in Panama are Chinese Panamanians. Panama has the largest Chinese population in the Central American region but this group is still a considerable minority, estimated to be between one hundred fifty and two hundred thousand people, or about 4 percent of Panama's total population. Chinese people began immigrating to Panama in the 1850s as contract laborers for the trans-Panama railroad. The 1980s saw a large increase in Chinese immigration following China's post-Maoist reformations that eased travel restrictions. In July 1990, police raided the homes of Chinese immigrants in three cities, claiming they were suspected to be undocumented. The consequent outrage led to a mobilization of the Chinese community, with major organizational efforts coming from the Chinese Panamanian Association, which not only began a petition among ethnic Chinese to protest inhumane treatment of Chinese immigrants, but also directly petitioned President Guillermo Endara to formally investigate the raids.[44] Many Chinese shopkeepers also organized their own nationwide strike, closing their shops and effectively denying many rural communities throughout the country access to their usual source of food and household items. The result was the formation of a Special Commission, which led to the re-documentation of Chinese immigrants who had had their rights stripped.

As in much of Central America, extractivism—the systemic identification and extraction of valuable natural resources on a mass scale for capital benefit—is a core issue to the environmental movement in Panama. Extractivist projects particularly impact Indigenous communities, which largely occupy land rich in mineral, petroleum, and lumber reserves.[45] Between the mid-twentieth century and the early twenty-first century, six *comarcas* have been established, which are regions occupied by substantive Indigenous populations, demarcated and officially recognized by the government. Four of the *comarcas* are large enough to be functionally equivalent to provinces: Emberá-Wounaan, Guna Yala, Naso Tjër Di, and Ngäbe-Buglé. The remaining two—Kuna de Madugandí and Kuna de Wargandí—are subdivisions to the Panamá and Darién provinces, respectively. The Indigenous populations legally possess exclusive land rights within their *comarcas*, as well as significant administrative autonomy. This grants the Indigenous people important legal standing to defend themselves against pressures from the Panamanian government. For example, in 2011 and 2012, hundreds of Indigenous Ngäbe protested reforms to Panama's mining law that would allow foreign enterprises to invest in the country's mines. The Cerro Colorado, one of the world's largest copper deposits, is located on Ngäbe land. Ultimately, they were successful in convincing the government to reverse the reforms.[46] However, despite this win, the government moved forward with a related project: the construction of a hydroelectric dam, the Barro Blanco, which was presumably intended to provide electricity for the Cerro Colorado mine. The Ngäbe protested this project, as well, by blocking the Pan-American highway. They were repressed by the National Border Service and consequently several Ngäbe were killed, as well as suffering the loss of religiously significant artifacts that existed in the river on their land, which were completely destroyed by the water from the dam.[47] The movement for protection of Indigenous lands continues to be a fight, especially as the government persistently pushes for development of roads, mines, and other construction projects to appease and attract foreign investors.

Present Day

Economic growth rates in Panama for much of the last decade have been between 5–10 percent (World Bank, 2012) attracting tourism and investment. The country's high growth rates, political stability, dollarized economy, and historically prominent use of the English language have attracted investment, particularly in the forms of infrastructure development, retiree recruitment, lifestyle migration, and tourism. International tourist arrivals almost tripled between 2000 and 2010 (ibid.) and tourism growth rates have been 15 percent in the last two years (Gacs, 2012).[48]

In 1999, the country's first female president, Mireya Moscoso, was elected. She focused on strengthening social programs, particularly education and child development. In 2002, she created a commission to investigate political corruption and crimes committed by government administrations between 1968 and 1989.

Aside from the Canal, Panama's economy also generates a large portion of its revenue from the flourishing banking sector. In fact, in recent times, "the Canal's significance has dwindled gradually compared to banking, which now employs more people in Panama (12,800) and generates a larger share of its GDP (11% in 2000, compared to 2.5% in 1960 and 4.1% in 1970)."[49] This has been encouraged by the government reworking the tax system to benefit foreign investors, including offshore business being exempt from national tax and overall reduction in tariffs and quotas. Overall, Panama's banks "generate around $180 million annually in net external interest earnings."[50]

In 2015, an anonymous source leaked 11.5 million documents that disclosed information on nearly 215,000 offshore entities. "The Panama Papers" implicated many public officials in being involved with shell corporations that were being used for illegal actions such as fraud and tax evasion; among these public officials were United Arab Emirates president Khalifa bin Zayed Al Nahyan and Prime Minister of Iceland Sigmundur Davíð Gunnlaugsson. The documents were called the Panama Papers because they were leaked from Mossack Fonseca, a corporate service provider based in Panama. Although the leak had a global impact, the fact that it was connected directly to Panama as the provider's homebase added to the narrative of Panama as a fiscal paradise, one that Panamanian officials publicly refuted and attempted to move away from.

In 2019, Laurentino Cortizo of the center-left Democratic Revolutionary Party was elected president, beating out conservative Democratic Change Party candidate Romulo Roux by just 2 percent of the vote. Cortizo previously served as Minister of Agricultural Development under Martin Torrijos, but resigned in 2006 because he did not support the concessions Torrijos made during negotiations for the U.S.-Panama Free Trade Agreement. He campaigned on promises to address the wealth disparity and inequality in the country, making particular promises to the Indigenous Ngäbe-Buglé people to build a University of Panama in their *comarca* as well as other health clinics and schools.

Recommended Reading

Biesanz, John, and Mavis Hiltunen Biesanz. *The People of Panama*. New York: Columbia University Press, 1955.

Delgado, James P, Tomás Mendizábal, Frederick H. Hanselmann, and Dominique Rissolo. *The Maritime Landscape of the Isthmus of Panama*. Gainesville: University Press of Florida, 2016.

González, María Victoria. *La invasión a Panamá: Un relato, un testimonio*. Panama: Ríos Editores, 1992.

Koster, Richard M., and Sánchez, Guillermo. *In the Time of the Tyrants: Panama, 1968–1990*. New York: W.W. Norton, 1990.

McCullough, David G. *The Path between the Seas: The Creation of the Panama Canal, 1870–1914. A Touchstone Book*. New York: Simon and Schuster, 1977.

Parker, Matthew. *The Panama Fever: The Epic Story of the Building of the Panama Canal*. New York: Anchor Press, 2009.

Ropp, Steve C. *Panamanian Politics: From Guarded Nation to National Guard*. Politics in Latin America. New York: Praeger, 1982.

Tice, Karin E. *Kuna Crafts, Gender, and the Global Economy*. Austin: University of Texas Press, 1995.

Zien, Katherine. *Sovereign Acts: Performing Race, Space, and Belonging in Panama and the Canal Zone*. New Brunswick: Rutgers University Press, 2017.

Zimbalist, Andrew, and John Weeks. *Panama at the Crossroads: Economic Development and Political Change in the Twentieth Century*. Berkeley, CA: University of California Press, 1991.

Thinking in Historical Perspective about Central America Today

INTRODUCTION

Central America is a small region, but it has a global impact for multiple reasons. It is strategically located between North America and South America. Anyone wishing to travel to the Pacific from the Caribbean or Atlantic Ocean can do it much more quickly using the Panama Canal or traveling overland across Central America. For centuries, Central America has been involved in vigorous regional trade and international trade as well providing inputs for the global textile industry and supplying agro-exports such as sugar, coffee, bananas, and palm oil around the world. Central America bears the imprint of centuries of colonization and neocolonial efforts. European colonial powers from the sixteenth century on, and territorial and neocolonial policies of the U.S. from the nineteenth century on, have affected the region's economies, politics, and social affairs, and often not for the best—if by best we mean, generating wealth and enfranchisement for the majority of the population. Being a connector region joining North and South America, Central America also suffers from the problems of neighboring regions. Drugs from South America destined to be sold and consumed in North America often get moved through Central America. Central America is often caught in the middle as more powerful neighboring countries or interests exert pressure or apply demands. These are just some of the reasons why it's important to know more about the history of Central America because this history is also connected to other histories, particularly the economic and political developments of Europe and countries along the Americas, including the United States. If you want to understand the history of U.S. foreign policy better, study the history of Central America. If you want to understand the effects of colonization of European powers, study Central America.

The purpose of this conclusion is to highlight four intertwined historical themes with present-day manifestations that connect Central America to the world, and vice versa. The following sections, each of which open with quotes from Central American scholars analyzing today's current situation, examine the present-day legacies of historical events, movements, and trends. We begin with the leadership imprint of Central American *caudillo* or strong-arm leaders. Second, we examine the centuries-long relationship between the United States and Central America, with an eye toward the long-term effects of U.S. interventionism from the mid-nineteenth century to the present. Third, the effervescence of Central American social movements shows how much Central Americans challenge elite exploitation and foreign intervention, confirming the powerful potential of leadership from the margins to effect change today. And finally, we explore Central American migration; in addition to outbound migration in which Central Americans leave the region for other parts of the world, often the United States, this section will also examine migration within the region. The goal of this conclusion is to summarize key themes and open a discussion for continued thought and reflection past the actual pages of this book.

LOCAL *CAUDILLISTA* MODELS OF LEADERSHIP AND THE AUTHORITARIAN TURN

> Power in Central America manifested itself as two forces:
> political monopoly and bureaucratic arbitrariness.[1]

Many historians claim that the Spanish model of colonization took advantage of autochthonous or local models of leadership in place before the arrival of colonial representatives, in which Spanish *conquistadores* respected local leaders if they paid tribute and provided labor. This practice led to a *mestizo* model of strong-arm leadership after independence informed by self- and class-interests, which, in turn, contributed to tensions between fiercely independent local leaders and the authoritarian treatment of much of the population or anyone who challenged the status quo. Whether during the short-lived attempt to unify Central America under the federal republic or during the early state-building efforts of the individual countries, plans to establish institutions that served the interests of the majority of inhabitants were stymied by *caudillo* leaders. As described in the introduction to this book, *caudillo* means a strong-arm leader who has amassed enough wealth to hire mercenaries to protect his interests. Throughout early state building, *caudillo*-type leaders often had a sphere of influence located in particular cities or areas, which they would defend with local armies. This pattern greatly impeded state development throughout the nineteenth century as manifested by the fighting between Conservatives and Liberals and followed by multiple examples of strong-arm leadership throughout the twentieth century and in some cases into the twenty-first century.

Examples from the early twentieth century include strong-arm leaders such as Anastasio Somoza García a Nicaraguan who created a forty-three-year dynasty in which power passed between family members for a couple of generations, and in El Salvador, members of the Meléndez family dynasty held executive power from 1913–27. "In Guatemala, Rafael Carrera rose to power beginning in 1837, toppled Morazán in 1840, and dominated Guatemala until his death in 1865. Other *caudillos* followed, most notably Justo Rufino Barrios from 1871 to 1885, Manuel Estrada Cabrera from 1898 to 1920, and Jorge Ubico from 1931 to 1944."[2] There was General Tiburcio Carías Andino who ruled Honduras from 1932–49. In these cases, the leaders created armed forces they used to quell dissent and protect their interests and the interests of their cronies. But they also used paramilitary groups to carry out repression and keep order. This strategy included the Camisas Azules (Blue Shirts) in Somoza's Nicaragua who were apparently modeled on Hitler's Brown Shirts, or the death squads of repressive governments of the late twentieth century such as that of El Salvador during the civil war (1980–92) in which the Salvadoran Armed forces along with other security forces and the death squads were assigned responsibility for 95 percent of the seventy thousand deaths during the conflict with the guerrilla forces of the Farabundo Martí Liberation Front or FMLN.[3]

A present-day example of this authoritarian leadership model and the use of threats and repression are typified by former revolutionary Daniel Ortega in Nicaragua. Ortega has held power in Nicaragua since 2007 and uses the Sandinista Youth and other young and disenfranchised paramilitary groups to supplement the police in silencing the opposition. Another example includes Salvadoran president Nayib Bukele who uses populist, strong-arm techniques to maintain power. For example, he sent the police into the National Assembly (Congress) to force them to approve his hard-on-crime plan in February 2020.[4] The *Economist* refers to these examples as "democratic regression" and also describes examples from Guatemala and Honduras. Honduras and Guatemala each have histories of state violence and face grave challenges to democracy as well. Guatemala, on the one hand, continues to face governance and transparency challenges exemplified by the government's 2019 decision to disband CICIG, the United Nations sponsored-anti-corruption unit. "'Over the past two years military men, corrupt officials and criminals have only become more powerful,' says Carmen Rosa de León, who heads the Institute for Sustainable Development, a Guatemalan think-tank. . . . Drug money has started to seep into the state, too. Ms. de León's organisation has connected 38 lawmakers to drug-traffickers."[5] In Honduras, one of the principal problems is the criminality of the state. Government leaders are connected to the drug trade as well as complicit with private investors and official security forces and paramilitary groups in the intimidation, disappearance, and assassination of activists seeking to bring attention to the potential impacts of mega-development projects or the expansion of infrastructure development for tourism.

IMPACT OF U.S. FOREIGN POLICY, U.S. CAPITAL, AND TERRITORIAL EXPANSIONISM

> Under these new geopolitical coordinates [militarization, securitization, etc.], any alternative social project needs to consider the widening of geographical boundaries. Even though Central America has promise and possibility for many, this won't happen without keeping in mind that the region is circumscribed by a growing space of control, surveillance, and repression.[6]

Many of the strong-arm leaders of Central America from the twentieth century benefited from protections and support from the United States. From the expansion of the United States "from sea to shining sea," the Monroe Doctrine instituted a framework that justified the imposition of U.S. foreign policy and varied U.S. economic interests over political and economic agendas throughout Central America. This combination of paternalism and self-interest led U.S. presidents and private business interests to involve themselves in the running of countries as well as to make major economic investments serving foreign stockholders. These actions were implemented via development and aid packages, diplomacy, military intervention, military assistance, meddling, and economic investment. From William Walker in the mid-nineteenth century to military intervention in the early twentieth century to the structural adjustment policies imposed on the region in the late twentieth and twenty-first centuries, local elites saw that if they profit-shared with these interests, they would have the capital and military might to quell pushback.

From the Cold War through the end of the twentieth century, U.S. foreign policy was particularly disastrous for the majority of Central Americans as it had a double-pronged economic and political impact on the region. There are multiple examples of the United States toppling democratically elected leaders, such as Jacobo Árbenz in Guatemala, and supporting authoritarian strong-arm leaders with U.S. troops and military aid, such as Anastasio Somoza García and his descendants in Nicaragua. Then there were decades of safeguarding U.S. economic interests by using force and diplomacy to overturn agrarian reform laws or repress movements for worker rights across the region. The United Fruit

Company received support from the U.S. government to protect their interests across the region, and by "1915, the company owned over a million acres of land in the Caribbean and Central America, including 252,000 acres in Costa Rica, 141,000 acres in Guatemala, 62,000 acres in Honduras, and 193,000 acres in Nicaragua."[7] The United States systematically contributed to dependence and weak state institutions across the region.

Today, the United States continues to undermine regional security and integration and more inclusive forms of economic development through foreign policies against drugs and terrorism—which in turn have further militarized the region—as well as through pressures to adopt free-trade agreements, which have contributed to increased poverty, outbound migration, and regional disintegration. This long history of foreign policies, up to the present day, that preference U.S. interests over Central American interests have contributed to the challenges that the region faces. Tensions between Central American countries have been exacerbated by migration flows, often fomented by U.S. foreign policy and military aid. Regional tensions mean that the Central American Court of Justice is unable to resolve border conflicts, many of which have existed between countries back to the nineteenth century, and the challenges to regional economic development which have been hampered by CAFTA, the Central America Free Trade Agreement, which has displaced efforts to generate trade within the region and favored the interests of the United States.[8] Diplomacy and aid could be deployed very differently, and the United States could play a very different role. "A positive first in U.S. foreign policy toward the region would be to hold deeply corrupt governments truly accountable for their actions. Likewise, a just response to the situation at the border can start by understanding that corruption, inequality, and human rights violations abroad are not accidents but the result of deliberate choices by those in power and the tacit support of their allies. . . . Lastly, assistance should focus on those most vulnerable to abuse by those in power, including women, unemployed youth, and Indigenous populations."[9]

Economic development in the region has seldom had the long-term interests of inclusive local economies in mind; rather it has contributed to an extractive, agro-export model that involved extensive foreign ownership of land and production. This enclave model shaped economic development in Costa Rica, the Nicaraguan Caribbean coast, Honduras, and Guatemala. From the nineteenth century onward, this model was replicated over the next hundred and fifty years with long-term impacts for the region and individual countries. Today, these practices have morphed into extraction-based companies that gain mining concessions from Central American governments to extract minerals and other metals. "The presence of extractive companies from Canada and the United States are a constant in the region, but companies from Europe and China, more and more, are appearing."[10]

These policies and investments have created repercussions across the region, particularly in the development of social movements that contested the status quo as well as in international solidarity efforts protesting U.S. interventionism and supporting local popular and revolutionary movements. As early as the 1920s, there were organized anti-imperial and anti-interventionist activists leading protests across the United States demanding the withdrawal of the U.S. Marines from Nicaragua; the Marines supported strong-arm leader Anastasio Somoza García and the Nicaragua National Guard in their fight against General Augusto César Sandino and his guerrilla army.

CENTRAL AMERICAN SOCIAL MOVEMENTS

> Emergent movements are radical in a new way because their struggles
> have the objective of transforming the quotidian realities of people
> here and today and not necessarily in some distant future....
> Emancipation starts today or never.[11]

From the earliest years of colonization to today, Central America has been the home of a polyphony of movements by disenfranchised and marginalized groups throughout its history. Every epoch has had multiple examples of resistance against colonization, inequality and poverty, and exclusions such as racism, sexism, and homophobia. There are many examples of Indigenous resistance against Spanish and British colonization exemplified by frequent uprisings. During early state-building efforts, t here w ere m ultiple e xamples o f r esistance t o e lite r ule. There was also a lot of what can be called persistence in which Indigenous groups simply moved to remoter and remoter areas to escape *mestizo* leaders. Throughout the twentieth century there were liberation theologians and Christian-base communities, union organizing efforts, communists and socialists, and feminists, who challenged repression and elite rule, and organized groups in their respective countries to demand change. There were also popular movements and armed guerrilla efforts to overthrow authoritarian governments which, in turn, created new opportunities for protest and social change.

The new revolutionary man or "hombre nuevo revolucionario" was part of the organizing of the 1970s and 1980s, which mobilized workers and farmers along fairly patriarchal and heteronormative lines.[12] "Born in the crucible of the armed struggle against the forces of oppression, the New Man was a heroic, class-conscious revolutionary willing to sacrifice himself for the liberation of the poor and exploited, whose interests he presumably represented. Given Latin America's historical subordination to the United States, the New Man was also, inevitably, an unbending anti-imperialist and (inter)nationalist."[13] The New Man became less compelling in the twenty-first century for those who asked themselves "what is the point of a revolutionary party if the revolution isn't possible."[14] After the civil wars of the late twentieth century, many former revolutionaries chose jobs in the public sector or civil society organizations. This professional focus on carrying out palliative efforts, however, led to turning away from creating alternative models.[15] Many young activists became disillusioned with the top-down collective action of the 1970s and 1980s and sought new approaches. This has led to new social movements in the postwar years of the late twentieth and early twenty-first centuries across the region. Today movements aren't just concerned with economic and class interests but a variety of social and cultural issues connected to quality of life, subjective life experiences, and quotidian manifestations of power in public and private spheres. "The emphasis today can be found in the actions of civil resistance, generally non-violent and less disruptive."[16] Movements today include community organizing efforts, environmental movements, Indigenous and Afro-descendant struggles for ancestral lands and natural resources, and movements for the rights of women, people with nonbinary identities, and gay rights, to mention a few. "These new movements have become places of identity production that resist normalization and challenge totalitarian power and universalizing narratives. This has created a politicization of other areas of life that didn't used to be considered part of political action."[17]

Indigenous peoples and Afro-descendant groups have also been active in the twenty-first century demanding inclusion and respect for ancestral lands. After the civil wars, there were a number of international landmark cases that granted Indigenous communities in Guatemala, Honduras, and Nicaragua rights to ancestral land. These achievements were the combination of sustained activism by Indigenous communities and interestingly also benefited from conditionalities on neoliberal international aid packages in which Central American states were required to recognize the land demands of Indigenous groups. Hale raises the questions "will the subjugated knowledge and practices be articulated with the dominant, and neutralised? Or will they occupy the space opened from above while resisting its built-in logic, connect with others, toward 'transformative' cultural-political alternatives that still cannot even be fully imagined?" in his analysis of the effects of this type of multiculturalism for the Indigenous Maya of Guatemala.[18] Today, many of these same Indigenous, Afro-Indigenous, and Afro-descendant communities in Guatemala and across Central America are challenging extractivist efforts to open mines and build mega-development projects without satisfactory environmental feasibility studies or mitigation plans. In Honduras, the Afro-Indigenous group, the Garifuna, are challenging the land development schemes of national elites and foreign investors. Sadly, though, these activists are subject to repressive measures when protests come up against national interests. Central America remains one of the most dangerous places to be an environmental defender.

OUTBOUND MIGRATION

> Central Americans are punished for wanting to work where they weren't born.[19]

Histories of colonial and neocolonial interventions, twentieth century internal conflict and civil wars, and twenty-first-century violences contribute to high levels of outbound emigration for some Central American countries. "More violence, more migration" is the tenet that sociologist José Luis Rocha uses to explain how emigration has grown over the past twenty years "spurred by economic reasons, by the political instability that in Honduras deepened after the coup d'état of 2009 and by the multiple violences that took place in [the Northern Triangle]: among others, those led by the powerful transnational gangs called 'maras,' the persecution of indigenous and environmental activists, and the hitmen at the service of drug traffickers and those profiting from land grabs for tourism, mining, hydroelectric projects, real estate projects, and [other] speculative [projects]."[20] Also, immigration policies in receptor countries can create additional problems for Central Americans who may be fleeing political threats or gang violence. For example, U.S. immigration policies informed by cold-war rhetoric made it easier for Nicaraguans fleeing the Sandinista government of the 1980s than political refugees fleeing U.S. supported authoritarian regimes such as Guatemala, El Salvador, and Honduras.[21] These cold-war policies have present-day impacts as exemplified by how Hondurans are more likely to be deported and have less access to residency.

Interestingly, not all Central Americans who face deprivation, threat of violence, and poverty in their own countries want to leave for the United States. Nicaragua is an interesting case: emigration is on the rise but not at the levels of the three countries to its north. Recent political violence has increased outbound migration northwards, but the real increase has been from Nicaragua to Costa Rica, taking advantage of the long tradition of south-south, seasonal migration to Costa Rica for participation in agro-export harvests and service work such as domestic service and other jobs in the service sector. "In Nicaragua, for example, many are choosing to go to Costa Rica where the government has a more welcoming policy than the United States practices towards its Central American neighbors. Nicaraguan migration to Costa Rica is a major case of South-to-South migration in Latin America. It takes place in Central America, a region where migration—both intraregional and extraregional—is a structural dimension of everyday life."[22] As of 2021, 86 percent of asylum seekers in Costa Rica are Nicaraguan compared to only a tiny share in previous years.[23] The COVID-19 pandemic has also affected the region, particularly Central Americans and others moving through the region to other countries. Though migration statistics dropped significantly in 2020 due to border closures and public health policies, Central American migration has increased drastically since then.

Central American migration is a complex issue, but political leaders and policy makers in Central America and other countries, especially the United States, must stop shying away from examining the root causes such as "state-sponsored violence, the persecution of human rights defenders and activists, U.S. intervention, the negative effects of neoliberalism and megaprojects, and historical land inequality."[24] There are no easy solutions to these interconnected issues that exacerbate the effects of poverty, exclusion, climate change, food insecurity, crime, and corruption in Central America, but a good place to start might be with a close reading of history and critical reflection about how participation, equity, and inclusion can be supported across the region. "The United States does not need harsh immigration laws that criminalize Indigenous peoples, migrants, and asylum seekers. Rather, there needs to be serious attention to local and community-led initiatives that seek to tackle the historical and structural inequalities . . . [that] have caused centuries of territorial dispossession."[25]

History of Natural Disasters in Central America

By Faye White

YEAR	COUNTRY	NAME/TYPE	DAMAGE
2020	Belize, Costa Rica, El Salvador, Guatemala, Honduras, Nicaragua, Panamá	Hurricane Eta	Category 4 Hurricane that left 172 dead.
2018	Guatemala	Fuego Volcano	Deadliest eruption in Guatemala. It left little evacuation time and led to the deaths of almost 200 people. Largest eruption of the volcano in 44 years.
2015	Guatemala	Landslide	Heavy rains led to a massive landslide in El Cambray Dos. Over 280 people were killed and most of the village was leveled.
2010	Guatemala, Nicaragua, El Salvador, Honduras	Tropical storm Agatha	204 deaths, $1.1 billion in damages. Triggered mudslides and in Guatemala, a massive sinkhole. Guatemala was the most affected country and had the most fatalities.
2009	Nicaragua	Hurricane Ida	Ida killed 199 people, displaced 15,000, and damaged 2,350 homes.
2007	El Salvador, Guatemala, Honduras, Nicaragua	Hurricane Felix	170 mph winds, 189 deaths.

YEAR	COUNTRY	NAME/TYPE	DAMAGE
2005	Costa Rica, Nicaragua, Honduras, El Salvador, Belize, Guatemala	Hurricane Stan	The most affected country was Guatemala which suffered 1,500 fatalities.
2001	El Salvador	Earthquake	A 7.7 earthquake that caused 844 deaths and 5,565 injuries. 108,261 houses were destroyed and 150,000 buildings were damaged. The earthquake was accompanied by destructive landslides that increased the death toll as well as thousands of aftershocks.
2000	Belize	Hurricane Keith	Category 4 Hurricane with winds up to 155 mph.
1998	Nicaragua	Cristobal Volcano	Eruption and mudslide caused 1,620 deaths.
1998	Honduras, Belize, Guatemala	Hurricane Mitch	Winds up to 180 mph. Death toll of more than 11,000.
1996	Panama, Nicaragua, Guatemala, El Salvador	Hurricane Cesar-Douglas	Around 100 people were killed in the affected Central American countries.
1993	Costa Rica, Nicaragua, Honduras, El Salvador, Guatemala, Belize	Hurricane Gert	116 deaths.
1992	Nicaragua	León Earthquake and tsunami	A 7.2 earthquake triggered a tsunami. 116 were killed.
1991	Costa Rica	Limón Earthquake	Strongest recorded earthquake in the country's history, 7.7. Caused flooding and 125 deaths.
1988	Nicaragua, El Salvador, Guatemala	Hurricane Joan	148 deaths in Nicaragua.
1986	El Salvador	Earthquake	1,000 were killed.
1982	Honduras, Nicaragua	Aletta tropical storm	Tropical storm Aletta caused 308 deaths.

YEAR	COUNTRY	NAME/TYPE	DAMAGE
1982	Guatemala, El Salvador	Flooding and mudslides	Estimated 1,200 deaths. Destruction of El Salvador's cotton, coffee, and corn crops.
1976	Guatemala	Earthquake	7.5 earthquake that struck while people were sleeping. 23,000 were killed.
1974	Nicaragua, Honduras, Belize, El Salvador, Guatemala	Hurricane Fifi	Third deadliest Atlantic Hurricane which killed 7,000 people.
1973	Honduras	Landslide	2,800 killed.
1972	Nicaragua	Earthquake	6.3 earthquake that caused the destruction of most of Managua. 10,000 people were killed.
1965	El Salvador	Earthquake	125 dead.
1961	Belize	Hurricane Hattie	The eye of Hurricane Hattie killed 307 in Belize City as it passed between Belize City and Dengriga. Hurricane winds reached 115 mph with 200 mph gusts. The hurricane caused the People's United Party (PUP) to relocate their capital to Belmopan.
1955	Belize	Hurricane Janet	Hurricane winds reached up to 170 mph. Sixteen people were killed and 20,000 were left homeless.
1951	El Salvador	Earthquake	At least 400 dead.
1949	Guatemala	Floods	Death toll estimates 1,000-40,000.
1943	Nicaragua	Mazatlan Hurricane	106 deaths.
1936	El Salvador	Earthquake	200 deaths.
1931	Nicaragua	Earthquake	6.1 magnitude earthquake that sparked a devastating fire. Estimated 1,000-2,450 deaths.
1931	Belize	Hurricane	Deadliest hurricane in the country's history. It killed 2,500 people.

YEAR	COUNTRY	NAME/TYPE	DAMAGE
1919	El Salvador	Earthquake	100 deaths.
1917	Guatemala	Earthquake	5.6 earthquake that caused 250 deaths.
1910	Costa Rica	Earthquake	700 deaths.
1902	Guatemala	Santa Maria Volcanic eruption	First recorded eruption. Locals did not recognize warning signs; estimated 6,000 deaths. Indigenous people forced to work for free while criollos were given lands stolen from native communities to compensate for their losses.
1885	Nicaragua	Earthquake	Extensive damage to León, Chinandega, and Managua.
1882	Panama	Tsunami	Estimated 100 deaths.
1859	Guatemala	Earthquake and eruption	One of the strongest earthquakes in Central America. Izalco volcano erupted.
1773	Guatemala	Earthquake	7.5 earthquake that left estimates of 500-600 dead.
1663	Nicaragua	Earthquake	Earthquake caused the destruction of León and affected other nearby areas with multiple landslides.
1648	Nicaragua	Earthquake	Extensive damage to the capital, León.
1609	Nicaragua	Momotombo Volcanic eruption	Destruction of capital, León.
1541	Guatemala	Eruption	Damage to the capital from flooding mud from Agua volcano.

Bibliography

Adomat, Friederike, and Eberhard Gischler. "Assessing the suitability of Holocene environments along the Central Belize Coast, Central America, for the reconstruction of hurricane records." *International Journal of Earth Sciences*, March 26, 2016. https://www.researchgate.net/publication/299444566_Assessing_the_suitability_of_Holocene_environments_along_the_central_Belize_coast_Central_America_for_the_reconstruction_of_hurricane_records

Alonso-Henar, Jorge, Walter Montero, José J. Martínez-Díaz, José A. Álvarez-Gómez, Juan M. Insua-Arévalo, and Wilfredo Rojas. "The Aguacaliente Fault, source of the Cartago 1910 destructive earthquake (Costa Rica)." *Terra Nova*. April 1, 2013. https://pubs.geoscienceworld.org/ssa/bssa/article-abstract/30/4/377/101128/The-Salvador-earthquakes-of-December-1936

Central American Actuarial Association. "The Experience of Earthquake Risk in Central America." Accessed November 1, 2021. https://www.casact.org/sites/default/files/database/astin_vol9no3_306.pdf

Charvériat, Céline. "Natural Disasters in Latin America and the Caribbean: An Overview of Risk." Inter-American Development Bank. October, 2021.https://www.preventionweb.net/files/2544_ENVNatDisastLACeline.pdf

Global Volcanism Program. "Report on San Cristobal (Nicaragua)." *Bulletin of the Global Volcanism Network*, Smithsonian Institution. October 1998. https://doi.org/10.5479/si.GVP.BGVN199810-344020

Kornei, Katherine. "Eruption in El Salvador Was One of the Holocene's Largest." American Geophysical Union. June 5, 2019. https://eos.org/articles/eruption-in-el-salvador-was-one-of-the-holocenes-largest

Landsea, Christopher W., Roger Pielke, and Jose Rubiera. "Hurricane Vulnerability in Latin America and The Caribbean: Normalized Damage and Loss Potentials." *Natural Hazards Review*. August 2003. https://www.researchgate.net/publication/237461297_HurricaneVulnerability_in_Latin_America_and_The_Caribbean_Normalized_Damage_and_Loss_Potentials

Levin, S. Benedict. "The Salvador earthquakes of December, 1936*." *Bulletin of the Seismological Society of America*. October 1, 1940. https://pubs.geoscienceworld.org/ssa/bssa/article-abstract/30/4/377/101128/The-Salvador-earthquakes-of-December-1936?redirectedFrom=fulltext

Pan American Health Organization. "A World Safe From Natural Disasters." 1994. https://iris.paho.org/bitstream/handle/10665.2/34151/9275121141-eng.pdf

United Nations Office for the Coordination of Humanitarian Affairs (OCHA). "Central America: Hurricanes Eta & Iota - 6-months Operation Update (MDR43007)." June 22, 2021. https://reliefweb.int/report/guatemala/central-america-hurricanes-eta-iota-6-months-operation-update-mdr43007

U.S. Geological Survey. "Today in Earthquake History." Accessed November 1, 2021. https://earthquake.usgs.gov/learn/today/index.php?month=5&day=3

World Bank. "Disaster Risk Management in Latin America and the Caribbean Region: GFDRR Country Notes." Accessed November 1, 2021. https://dipecholac.net/docs/files/521-drm-lac-countryprograms.pdf

NOTES

CHAPTER ONE: IMAGINING CENTRAL AMERICA

1. John A. Booth, Christine J. Wade, and Thomas W. Walker, *Understanding Central America: Global Forces, Rebellion, and Change* (Boulder: Westview Press, 2015), 34.
2. Edelberto Torres-Rivas, *History and Society in Central America* (Austin: University of Texas Press, 1993), 3–4.
3. Ibid., 1–2.
4. Robert Patch, *Indians and the Political Economy of Colonial Central America, 1670–1810* (Norman: University of Oklahoma Press, 2013), 138.
5. Joan Martínez-Alier, "Conflictos ambientales en Centroamérica y las Antillas: Un rápido toxic tour," *Ecología Política*, 60 (2020): 53; "son los temas principales de la ecología política de la región: las fronteras de la extracción minera de oro, cobre, níquel, carbón; energía hidroeléctrica; plantaciones y extracción de biomasa; infraestructuras; compañías transnacionales; conflictos transfronterizos; el racismo anti-indígena y la nueva resistencia indígena y afroamericana; los abundantes asesinatos de activistas; las vinculaciones internacionales de los movimientos activistas . . . "
6. Ibid., 148.
7. Torres-Rivas, *History and Society in Central America,* 122.
8. Patch, *Indians and the Political Economy of Colonial Central America, 1670–1810*; Ralph Lee Woodward, *Central America, A Nation Divided*, 3rd ed. (New York: Oxford University Press, 1999).
9. Aviva Chomsky, *Central America's Forgotten History: Revolution, Violence, and the Roots of Migration* (Boston: Beacon Press, 2021), 13–14.
10. Christopher H. Lutz, *Santiago de Guatemala, 1541–1773: City, Caste, and the Colonial Experience* (Norman: University of Oklahoma Press, 1994), 127.
11. William M. Denevan, ed., *The Native Population of the Americas in 1492* (Madison: University of Wisconsin Press, 1992), xvii–xxix.
12. Patch, *Indians and the Political Economy of Colonial Central America, 1670–1810,* 80.
13. W. George Lovell and Christopher H. Lutz, "The Historical Demography of Colonial Central America," *Yearbook (Conference of Latin Americanist Geographers)* 17/18 (1990): 129.
14. Torres-Rivas, *History and Society in Central America,* 3.
15. Héctor Pérez-Brignoli, *El laberinto centroamericano: Los hilos de la historia* (San José, Costa Rica: Centro de Investigaciones Históricas de América Central, 2017), 33.
16. Serena Cosgrove, *Leadership from the Margins: Women and Civil Society Organizations in Argentina, Chile, and El Salvador* (Piscataway, NJ: Rutgers University Press, 2010), 76.
17. Denevan, *The Native Population of the Americas in 1492,* xvii–xxix.
18. Ibid.; Linda A. Newson, "The Demographic Impact of Colonization," in *The Cambridge Economic History of Latin America*, ed. Victor Bulmer-Thomas, John Coatsworth, and Roberto Cortes-Conde, (Cambridge: Cambridge University Press, 2005), 143.

19. Sylvia Sellers-García, *Distance and Documents at the Spanish Empire's Periphery* (Redwood City: Stanford University Press, 2013), 8.

20. Ibid., 143.

21. Torres-Rivas, *History and Society in Central America*, 125.

22. BELIZE, https://www.cia.gov/the-world-factbook/countries/belize/#people-and -society; http://sib.org.bz/census-data/
GUATEMALA, https://www.cia.gov/the-world-factbook/countries/guatemala/ #people-and-society; https://www.censopoblacion.gt/explorador
EL SALVADOR, https://www.cia.gov/the-world-factbook/countries/el-salvador/ #people-and-society; http://www.digestyc.gob.sv/index.php/temas/des/poblacion-y -estadisticas-demograficas/censo-de-poblacion-y-vivienda/poblacion-censos.html
HONDURAS, https://www.cia.gov/the-world-factbook/countries/honduras/#people -and-society; https://www.ine.gob.hn/publicaciones/Censos/Censo_2013/06Tomo -VI-Grupos-Poblacionales/cuadros.html
NICARAGUA, https://www.cia.gov/the-world-factbook/countries/nicaragua/#people -and-society; https://www.inide.gob.ni/Home/Compendios
COSTA RICA, https://www.cia.gov/the-world-factbook/countries/costa-rica/#people -and-society; https://www.inec.cr/poblacion/temas-especiales-de-poblacion
PANAMA, https://www.cia.gov/the-world-factbook/countries/panama/#people-and -society; https://www.inec.gob.pa/publicaciones/Default3.aspx?ID_PUBLICACION =360&ID_CATEGORIA=13&ID_SUBCATEGORIA=59

23. Christopher H. Lutz, *Santiago de Guatemala, 1541–1773*, and Sellers-García, *Distance and Documents at the Spanish Empire's Periphery*, 8–9, for Guatemala; Germán Romero Vargas, *Las estructuras sociales de Nicaragua en el siglo XVIII* (Managua: Vanguardia, 1988), and Germán Romero Vargas, *Las sociedades del Atlántico en Nicaragua en los siglos XVII y XVIII* (Managua: Fondo de Promoción Cultural-BANIC, 1995), for Nicaragua.

24. Lowell Gudmundson and Justin Wolfe, *Blacks and Blackness in Central America: Between Race and Place* (Durham, NC: Duke University Press, 2010), 2.

25. Jeffrey L. Gould and Aldo Lauria-Santiago define *mestizaje* as "a nation-building myth of race mixture and a cultural process of 'deindianization,' [that] has contributed substantially to Central American . . . nationalist ideologies and played a key role in shaping contemporary political culture." *To Rise in Darkness: Revolution, Repression, and Memory in El Salvador, 1920–1932* (Durham, NC: Duke University Press, 2008), xv.

26. Ibid., 4.

27. Ibid., 19.

28. Lynn V. Foster, *A Brief History of Central America*, 2nd ed. (New York: Checkmark Books, 2007), 71.

29. Newson, "The Demographic Impact of Colonization," 153.

30. Ibid.

31. Chomsky, *Central America's Forgotten History*, 7.

32. H. Glenn Penny, "Latin American Connections: Recent Work on German Interactions with Latin America," in *Central European History* 46 (2013): 362.

33. Torres-Rivas, *History and Society in Central America*, 27.

34. Ibid.

35. David Díaz Arias and Ronny J. Viales, "Sociedad imaginada: El ideario político de la integración excluyente en Centroamérica: 1821–1870," 208.

36. In Guatemala, this growing segment of the population is referred to as *ladinos*, which probably has its roots in the early Spanish colonial term "ladino," a term used to describe an Indigenous person who spoke Spanish (Patch, *Indians and the Political Economy of Colonial Central America, 1670–1810*).

37. Cited in Gould and Lauria-Santiago, *To Rise in Darkness: Revolution, Repression, and Memory in El Salvador, 1920–1932*, 7.

38. See Jeffrey Gould, "Gender, Politics, and the Triumph of *Mestizaje* in Early 20th Century Nicaragua," *Journal of Latin American Anthropology* 2, no. 1 (1996): 4–33 for Nicaragua, and Diane M. Nelson, "Perpetual Creation and Decomposition: Bodies, Gender, and Desire in the Assumptions of a Guatemalan Discourse of *Mestizaje*," *Journal of Latin American Anthropology* 4, no. 1 (1998): 74–111 for Guatemala.

39. Torres-Rivas, *History and Society in Central America*, 28.

40. Ralph Lee Woodward, *Rafael Carrera and the Emergence of the Republic of Guatemala, 1821–1871* (Athens: University of Georgia Press, 1993), xiii.

41. Ralph Lee Woodward, "The Rise and Decline of Liberalism in Central America: Historical Perspectives on the Contemporary Crisis," *Journal of Interamerican Studies and World Affairs* 26, no. 3 (1984): 292, https://doi:10.2307/165672.

42. Arias and Viales, "Sociedad imaginada: El ideario político de la integración excluyente en Centroamérica: 1821–1870," 217; "En definitiva, en sus intentos por producir gobiernos buenos, los primeros liberales centroamericanos chocaron con las estructuras coloniales que pretendían cambiar y, pronto, se percataron de que el futuro que podían imaginar, dependía no solo de los buenos deseos, sino de producir Estados sobre bases sumamente desiguales. Los grupos 'conservadores' vieron en aquellos ideales liberales, los orígenes del mal gobierno y soñaron e insistieron en volver al 'orden' colonial, consiguiendo que las masas populares los apoyaran en varias ocasiones . . ."

43. Víctor Acuña Ortega, "Centroamérica: Raíces autoritarias y brotes democráticos," *Envío* 170 (1996): 3.

44. Ibid., 6.

45. Pérez-Brignoli, *El laberinto centroamericano*, 35.

46. Torres-Rivas, *History and Society in Central America*, 9.

47. Ibid., 3.

48. Jordana Dym, *From Sovereign Villages to National States: City, State, and Federation in Central America, 1759–1839* (Albuquerque: University of New Mexico Press, 2006), 261.

49. Woodward, *Central America, A Nation Divided*, 112.

50. Ibid., 91.

51. Jordana Dym and Christophe Belaubre, *Politics, Economy, and Society in Bourbon Central America, 1759–1821* (Boulder: University Press of Colorado, 2007), 267.

52. Gudmundson and Lindo-Fuentes, *Central America, 1821–1871: Liberalism before Liberal Reform*, 86.

53. Woodward, *Central America, A Nation Divided*, 292.

54. Ibid., 92.

55. Ibid., 92–93.

56. Gudmundson and Lindo-Fuentes, *Central America, 1821–1871: Liberalism before Liberal Reform*, 88.
57. Ibid., 90.
58. Gudmundson and Lindo-Fuentes, *Central America, 1821–1871: Liberalism before Liberal Reform*, 83.
59. Acuña Ortega, "Centroamérica: Raíces autoritarias y brotes democráticos," 4; "haya persistido una cultura política basada en el despotismo, el militarismo, la alienación y la deferencia."
60. Torres-Rivas, *History and Society in Central America*, 13.
61. Ibid., 47.
62. Ibid., 20.
63. Chomsky, *Central America's Forgotten History*, 31.
64. Alberto Martín Álvarez, "Desafiando la hegemonía neoliberal: Ideologías de cambio radical en la Centroamérica de posguerra," *Historia Actual Online*, 25 (2011): 113.
65. Nora Hamilton and Norma Stoltz Chinchilla, "Central American Migration: A Framework for Analysis," *Latin American Research Review* 26, no. 1 (1991): 105.
66. Torres-Rivas, *History and Society in Central America*, 61.
67. Mariel Aguilar-Støen, "Beyond Transnational Corporations, Food and Biofuels: The Role of Extractivism and Agribusiness in Land Grabbing in Central America," *Forum for Development Studies* 43, no. 1 (2016): 155–75.
68. Pew Research Center, "Religion in Latin America: Widespread Change in a Historically Catholic Region," November 13, 2014, https://www.pewforum.org/2014/11/13/religion-in-latin-america/
69. Marta Tienda and Susana M. Sánchez, "Latin American Immigration to the United States," *Daedalus* 142, no. 3 (2013): 48–64.
70. Hamilton and Chinchilla, "Central American Migration: A Framework for Analysis," 81.
71. Chomsky, *Central America's Forgotten History*, 219.
72. Hamilton and Chinchilla, "Central American Migration: A Framework for Analysis," 57.
73. Allison O'Connor, Jeanne Batalova, and Jessica Bolter, "Central American Immigrants in the United States," *Migration Policy Institute*, August 15, 2019: 1, accessed January 31, 2022, https://www.migrationpolicy.org/article/central-american-immigrants-united-states-2017
74. José Luis Rocha, "Tres años de represión y exilio de los nicaragüenses: 2018–2021," CETRI, November 12, 2021: 2, accessed November 23, 2021, https://www.cetri.be/Tres-anos-de-represion-y-exilio-de. "Los últimos datos disponibles en el U.S. Census Bureau (2019, 2019a) señalan que en Estados Unidos viven 257,343 personas nacidas en Nicaragua, 745,838 nacidas en Honduras, 1,111,495 nacidas en Guatemala y 1,412,101 nacidas en El Salvador. A esta población hay que sumar sus descendientes, migrantes de segunda y tercera generación, hasta totalizar 429,501 nicaragüenses, 1,083,540 hondureños, 1,683,093 guatemaltecos y 2,311,574 salvadoreños por su origen. Esta migración ha sido alimentada por camadas de tamaño creciente, cuyo saldo queda reflejado en esas cifras."
75. Jie Zong and Jeanne Batalova, "Central American Immigrants in the United States," *Migration Policy Institute*, September 2, 2015, accessed January 24, 2022, https://

www.migrationpolicy.org/article/central-american-immigrants-united-states-2013.

76. Hamilton and Chinchilla, "Central American Migration: A Framework for Analysis," 99.

77. Steven A. Camarota and Karen Zeigler, *Central American Immigrant Population Increased Nearly 28-Fold since 1970*, November 1, 2018, https://cis.org/Report/Central-American-Immigrant-Population-Increased-Nearly-28Fold-1970; Manuel Orozco, *Recent Trends in Central American Migration*, 2018, https://www.thedialogue.org/wp-content/uploads/2018/05/Recent-Trends-in-Central-American-Migration-1.pdf; Jie Zong and Jeanne Batalova, "Central American Immigrants in the United States," *Migration Policy Institute*, September 2, 2015, accessed January 24, 2022, https://www.migrationpolicy.org/article/central-american-immigrants-united-states-2013.

78. Allison O'Connor, Jeanne Batalova, and Jessica Bolter, "Central American Immigrants in the United States," Migration Policy Institute, August 15, 2019, accessed January 31, 2022, https://www.migrationpolicy.org/article/central-american-immigrants-united-states-2017.

79. Chomsky, *Central America's Forgotten History*, 225.

80. Chomsky, *Central America's Forgotten History*.

81. Kevin Casas-Zamora, "The Travails of Development and Democratic Governance in Central America," policy paper, *Foreign Policy at Brookings*, number 28 (June 2011): 21.

82. Education Policy and Data Center, *Violence Threatens Educational Gains in Central America*, accessed October 19, 2019, https://www.epdc.org/epdc-data-points/violence-threatens-educational-gains-central-america

83. Global Impunity Dimensions, GII-2017 Global Impunity Index, August 2017, https://www.udlap.mx/cesij/files/IGI-2017_eng.pdf

84. Transparency International, *Corruption Perceptions Index 2018*, 2018, https://www.transparency.org/cpi2018

85. World Justice Project, *Rule of Law Index 2014 Report*, https://worldjusticeproject.org/sites/default/files/documents/RuleofLawIndex2014.pdf; World Justice Project, *Rule of Law Index 2015 Report*, https://worldjusticeproject.org/sites/default/files/documents/roli_2015_0.pdf; World Justice Project, *Rule of Law Index 2016 Report*, https://worldjusticeproject.org/sites/default/files/documents/RoLI_Final-Digital_0.pdf; World Justice Project, *Rule of Law Index 2017–2018 Report*, https://worldjusticeproject.org/sites/default/files/documents/WJP-ROLI-2018-June-Online-Edition_0.pdf; World Justice Project, *Rule of Law Index 2019 Report*. https://worldjusticeproject.org/sites/default/files/documents/WJP_RuleofLawIndex_2019_Website_reduced.pdf

CHAPTER TWO: A BRIEF HISTORY OF BELIZE

1. Norman Hammond, "The Prehistory of Belize," *Journal of Field Archaeology* 9, no. 3 (1982): 1.

2. Melissa A. Johnson, "The Making of Race and Place in Nineteenth-Century British Honduras," *Environmental History* 8, no. 4 (2003): 600.

3. Nancy Lundgren, "Children, Race, and Inequality: The Colonial Legacy in Belize," *Journal of Black Studies* 23, no.1 (1992): 100.

4. Matthew Lange, James Mahoney, and Matthias Vom Hau, "Colonialism and Development: A Comparative Analysis of Spanish and British Colonies," *American Journal of Sociology* 111, no. 5 (2006): 1427, https://doi.org/10.1086/499510
5. Lundgren, "Children, Race, and Inequality," 93.
6. John C. Everitt, "The Torch is Passed: Neocolonialism in Belize," *Caribbean Quarterly* 33, no. 3/4 (1987): 44.
7. Elisabeth Cunin and Odile Hoffmann, "From Colonial Domination to the Making of the Nation: Ethno-Racial Categories in Censuses and Reports and their Political Uses in Belize, 19th–20th Centuries," *Caribbean Studies* 4, no.2 (2013): 44.
8. Alma H. Young and Dennis H. Young, "The Impact of the Anglo-Guatemalan Dispute on the Internal Politics of Belize," *Latin American Perspectives* 15, no. 2 (1988): 21.
9. Mark Moberg, "Structural Adjustment and Rural Development: Inferences from a Belizean Village," *The Journal of Developing Areas* 27, no.1 (1992): 4.
10. Annita Montoute, "CARICOM's External Engagements: Prospects and Challenges for Caribbean Regional Integration and Development," *German Marshall Fund of the United States* (2015): 2, http://www.jstor.org/stable/resrep18854.
11. Central Intelligence Agency (CIA), *The World Factbook: Ethnic Groups*, 2018, https://www.cia.gov/library/publications/resources/the-world-factbook/fields/400.html#PM
12. Isabeau J. Belisle Dempsey, "Framing the Center: Belize and Panamá within the Central American Imagined Community," *SUURJ: Seattle University Undergraduate Research Journal* 4, no. 13 (2020): 87, https://scholarworks.seattleu.edu/suurj/vol4/iss1/13
13. Pete Wilkinson, "Tourism —The Curse of the Nineties? Belize —An Experiment to Integrate Tourism and the Environment," *Community Development Journal* 27 (1992): 386.
14. Carol Key and Vijayan K. Pillai, "Tourism and Ethnicity in Belize: A Qualitative Study," *International Review of Modern Sociology* 33, no. 1 (2007): 133.
15. Ibid., 139.
16. Ibid.
17. Joseph O. Palacio, *The Garifuna: A Nation Across Borders* (Benque Viejo del Carmen, Belize: Cubola Productions, 2005), 145.
18. Young and Young, "The Impact of the Anglo-Guatemalan Dispute on the Internal Politics of Belize," 9.
19. Young and Young, "The Impact of the Anglo-Guatemalan Dispute on the Internal Politics of Belize," 11; Josef L. Kunz, "Guatemala vs. Great Britain: In Re Belice," *The American Journal of International Law* 40, no. 2 (1946): 385, doi:10.2307/2193198.
20. Young and Young, "The Impact of the Anglo-Guatemalan Dispute on the Internal Politics of Belize," 12.
21. Ibid.
22. Tony Thorndike, "The Conundrum of Belize: An Anatomy of a Dispute," *Social and Economic Studies* 32, no. 2 (1983): 65.
23. Young and Young, "The Impact of the Anglo-Guatemalan Dispute on the Internal Politics of Belize," 21.
24. O. Nigel Bolland, *Colonialism and Resistance in Belize: Essays in Historical Sociology* (Belize City: Cubola, 1988), 214.

25. Anthony J. Payne, "The Belize Triangle: Relations with Britain, Guatemala and the United States," *Journal of Interamerican Studies and World Affairs* 32, no. 1 (199): 124, doi:10.2307/166131

CHAPTER THREE: A BRIEF HISTORY OF GUATEMALA

1. Susanne Jonas and Nestor Rodríguez, *Guatemala-U.S. Migration: Transforming Regions* (Austin: University of Texas Press, 2014), 27.
2. "The Pre-Columbian History of Guatemala," *Science* 6, no. 149 (2001): 514.
3. Hattula Moholy-Nagy, *Historical Archaeology at Tikal, Guatemala*, Tikal Reports, no. 37, Philadelphia: University Museum Publications, 2012.
4. Franco D. Rossi, William A Saturno, and Heather Hurst, "Maya Codex Book Production and the Politics of Expertise: Archaeology of a Classic Period Household at Xultun, Guatemala," *American Anthropologist* 117, no. 1 (2015): 116–32.
5. W. George Lovell and Christopher H. Lutz, "'A Dark Obverse': Maya Survival in Guatemala: 1520–1994," *Geographical Review* 86, no. 3 (1996): 400.
6. Dennis Tedlock, "Reading the Popul Vuh," *Conjunctions* 3 (1982): 176.
7. Aridjis Homero, "Foreword: All was a Feathered Dream." In *Popol Vuh: A Retelling*, by Ian Stavans (Brooklyn, NY: Restless Books, xxxi).
8. Lovell and Lutz, "'A Dark Obverse': Maya Survival in Guatemala: 1520–1994," 400–401.
9. Edward F. Fischer and R. McKenna Brown, *Maya Cultural Activism in Guatemala* (Austin: University of Texas Press, Institute of Latin American Studies, 1996), 8.
10. Catherine Komisaruk, *Labor and Love in Guatemala: The Eve of Independence* (Palo Alto: Stanford University Press, 2013), 4.
11. Ibid., 7.
12. Brianna Leavitt-Alcántara, *Alone at the Altar: Single Women and Devotion in Guatemala, 1670–1870* (Palo Alto: Stanford University Press, 2018), 22.
13. Martha Few, *Women Who Live Evil Lives: Gender, Religion, and the Politics of Power in Colonial Guatemala* (Austin: University of Texas Press, 2002); Leavitt-Alcántara, *Alone at the Altar*, to mention a few.
14. Timothy Hawkins, "A War of Words: Manuel Montúfar, Alejandro Marure, and the Politics of History in Guatemala," *The Historian* 64, no. 3/4 (2002): 514.
15. Severo Martínez Peláez, *La Patria del Criollo: An Interpretation of Colonial Guatemala* (Durham, NC: Duke University Press, 2009).
16. Marta Casaús Arzú, "El Genocidio: La máxima expresión del racismo en Guatemala: Una interpretación histórica y una reflexión." *Nuevo Mundo Mundos Nuevos* [En ligne], Colloques, September 23, 2009: 17, accessed November 27, 2021, https://journals.openedition.org/nuevomundo/57067; "El racismo va a ser un elemento clave en el nuevo Estado liberal oligárquico, en donde el indígena—que durante la Colonia estaba reconocido jurídicamente como un grupo socio-racial y gozaba de cierta autonomía para garantizar la buena marcha del Estado corporativo—pierde todos sus derechos y pasa a ser invisibilizado."
17. W. George Lovell, "The Century After Independence: Land and Life in Guatemala, 1821–1920," *Canadian Journal of Latin American and Caribbean Studies / Revue Canadienne Des études Latino-américaines Et Caraïbes* 19, no. 37/38 (1994): 244.

18. Ralph Lee Woodward, *Rafael Carrera and the Emergence of the Republic of Guatemala, 1821–1871* (Athens: University of Georgia Press, 1993), 106.

19. Julie A. Charlip and E. Bradford Burns, *Latin America: An Interpretive History*, 9ᵗʰ ed. (Upper Saddle River, NJ: Prentice Hall, 2011), 124.

20. Greg Grandin, *The Blood of Guatemala: A History of Race and Nation* (Durham, NC: Duke University Press, 2000), 110.

21. Leavitt-Alcántara, *Alone at the Altar: Single Women and Devotion in Guatemala, 1670–1870*, 202.

22. Lovell, "The Century After Independence: Land and Life in Guatemala, 1821–1920," 246.

23. Grandin, *The Blood of Guatemala: A History of Race and Nation,* 111.

24. Ibid.

25. Charles D. Brockett, "An Illusion of Omnipotence: U.S Policy toward Guatemala, 1954–1960," *Latin American Politics and Society* 44, no.1 (2002): 92.

26. Charlip and Burns, *Latin America: An Interpretive History,* 233.

27. Richard H. Immerman, "Guatemala as Cold War History," *Political Science Quarterly* 95, no. 4 (1981): 630.

28. Ibid., 631.

29. Gustavo Palma, "Un presente al que no se llega y un pasado que no nos abandona. Las falencias sociales que se resisten a desaparecer. Geopolítica, democracia inconclusa y exclusión social. Guatemala, 1944–2019," in *Laberintos y bifurcaciones. Historia inmediata de México y América Central, 1940–2020*, ed. Ronny Viales (San José: Universidad de Costa Rica—Centro de Investigaciones Históricas de América Central, 2021), 76; "Puede afirmarse, sin lugar a dudas, que en las últimas décadas del siglo pasado y en las casi dos del actual siglo XXI, el accionar político y económico de y en Guatemala ha estado determinado por la agenda estratégica y los intereses estadounidenses."

30. Ibid.

31. Charlip and Burns, *Latin America: An Interpretive History,* 235.

32. Greg Grandin, "Everyday Forms of State Decomposition: Quetzaltenango, Guatemala, 1954," *Bulletin of Latin American Research* 19, no. 3 (2000): 303–20.

33. Stephen Kinzer, *Overthrow: America's Century of Regime Change from Hawaii to Iraq* (New York: Times Books/Henry Holt, 2006), 6.

34. Immerman, "Guatemala as Cold War History," 642.

35. Frederick W. Marks, "The CIA and Castillo Armas in Guatemala, 1954: New Clues to an Old Puzzle," *Diplomatic History* 14, no. 1 (1990): 85, http://www.jstor.org.proxy.seattleu.edu/stable/24912032.

36. Aviva Chomsky, *Central America's Forgotten History: Revolution, Violence, and the Roots of Migration* (Boston: Beacon Press, 2021), 82.

37. Charlip and Burns, *Latin America: An Interpretive History,* 238.

38. Brockett, "An Illusion of Omnipotence: U.S Policy toward Guatemala, 1954–1960," 103.

39. Grandin, "Everyday Forms of State Decomposition: Quetzaltenango, Guatemala, 1954," 319.

40. Siobhán Lloyd, "Guatemala," *Socialist Lawyer* 64 (2013): 39.

41. Brockett, "An Illusion of Omnipotence: U.S Policy toward Guatemala, 1954–1960," 107.

42. Lloyd, "Guatemala," 39.

43. Rosemary Thorp, Corinne Caumartin, and George Gray-Molina, "Inequality, Ethnicity, Political Mobilisation and Political Violence in Latin America: The Cases of Bolivia, Guatemala and Peru," *Bulletin of Latin American Research,* 25, no. 4 (2006): 463, http://www.jstor.org.proxy.seattleu.edu/stable/27733878.
44. Douglas Farah, "Papers Show U.S. Role in Guatemalan Abuses," *The Washington Post,* March 11, 1999, https://www.washingtonpost.com/wp-srv/inatl/daily/march99/guatemala11.htm
45. Cheryl Rubenberg, "Israel and Guatemala: Arms, Advice and Counterinsurgency," *MERIP Middle East Report* 140 (1986): 20, doi:10.2307/3012026.
46. Charlip and Burns, *Latin America: An Interpretive History,* 286.
47. Victoria Sanford, "From *I, Rigoberta* to the Commissioning of Truth: Maya Women and the Reshaping of Guatemalan History," *Cultural Critique* 47 (2001): 29.
48. Commission for Historical Clarification (CEH), *Guatemala Memory of Silence: Conclusions and Recommendations,* 1999, https://hrdag.org/wp-content/uploads/2013/01/CEHreport-english.pdf; Victoria Sanford, *Buried Secrets: Truth and Human Rights in Guatemala* (Basingstoke, UK: Palgrave Macmillan, 2003).
49. Randall Janzen, "From Less War to More Peace: Guatemala's Journey since 1996," *Peace Research* 40, no. 1 (2008): 63.
50. Jonas and Rodríguez, *Guatemala-U.S. Migration: Transforming Regions,* 61.
51. See David Carey and M. Gabriela Torres, "Precursors to Femicide: Guatemalan Women in a Vortex of Violence," *Latin American Research Review* 45, no. 3 (2010); Catherine Nolin Hanlon and Finola Shankar, "Gendered Spaces of Terror and Assault: The Testimonio of REMHI and the Commission for Historical Clarification in Guatemala," *Gender, Place & Culture* 7, no. 3 (2000); Beatriz Manz, "The Continuum of Violence in Post-war Guatemala," *Social Analysis,* 52, no. 2 (2008); Victoria Sanford, "From Genocide to Feminicide: Impunity and Human Rights in Twenty-First Century Guatemala," *Journal of Human Rights* 7 (2008). Gender-based violence is defined as "any act that results in, or is likely to result in physical, sexual, or psychological harm or suffering to women [and people with non-dominant gender identities], including threats of such acts, coercion or arbitrary deprivation of liberty, whether occurring in public or private life." Nancy Felipe Russo and Angela Pirlott, "Gender-based Violence: Concepts, Methods, and Findings," *Annals of the New York Academy of Sciences* 1087 (2006): 181.
52. Gender Equality Observatory for Latin America and the Caribbean, "Femicide, the Most Extreme Expression of Violence against Women," oig.cepal website, November 15, 2018, accessed July 20, 2019, https://oig.cepal.org/sites/default/files/nota_27_eng.pdf
53. Karen Musalo and Blaine Bookey, "Crimes without Punishment: An Update on Violence against Women and Impunity in Guatemala," *Social Justice* 40, no. 4 (2014): 107; Serena Cosgrove and Kristi Lee, "Persistence and Resistance: Women's Leadership and Ending Gender-Based Violence in Guatemala," *Seattle Journal for Social Justice* 14, no. 2 (2015): 309.
54. Grupo Guatemalteco de Mujeres (GGM), "Datos estadísticos: Muertes Violentas de Mujeres-MVM y República de Guatemala Actualizado (20/05/19)," *GGM* website, May 20, 2019, accessed July 20, 2019, http://ggm.org.gt/wp-content/uploads/2019/06/Datos-Estad%C3%ADsticos-MVM-ACTUALIZADO-20-DE-MAYO-DE-2019.pdf

55. Ibid.

56. Comisión Internacional contra la Impunidad en Guatemala (CICIG), "Diálogos por el fortalecimiento de la justicia y el combate a la impunidad en Guatemala," CICIG website, accessed August 12, 2019, https://www.cicig.org/comunicados-2019-c/informe-dialogos-por-el-fortalecimiento-de-la-justicia/

57. Shannon Drysdale Walsh and Cecilia Menjívar, "'What Guarantees Do We Have?' Legal Tolls and Persistent Impunity for Femicide in Guatemala," *Latin American Politics and Society* 58, no. 4 (2016): 40, https://doi.org/10.1111/laps.12001.

58. Cosgrove and Lee, "Persistence and Resistance: Women's Leadership and Ending Gender-Based Violence in Guatemala."

59. Fischer and Brown, *Maya Cultural Activism in Guatemala*, 5.

60. Ibid., 15.

61. Walter Flores and Miranda Rivers, "Frenar la corrupción después del conflicto: Movilización anticorrupción en Guatemala," *Special Reports, 482* (Washington: United States Institute of Peace, 2021), 3; "La comisión estaba encargada de ayudar a las instituciones del estado en la investigación y el desmantelamiento de grupos de seguridad ilegales y organizaciones de seguridad clandestinas que desde hacía tiempo amenazaban la democracia y la paz en Guatemala."

62. Santiago Bastos, "¿Exclusiones renovadas? Tierra y migración en el siglo XXI," in *Colección Lectura a Fondo 2* (Guatemala: Agencia Española de Cooperación para el Desarrollo, 2017), 22. "Las remesas contribuyen a los sistemas de sustento de los 773,899 hogares que, en 2004, recibieron cada uno como promedio Q.2,240 mensuales a través de ellas, lo que equivale a haber contado con los ingresos de casi dos salarios mínimos más al mes en cada hogar. De este modo, la propia población rural emigrante de Guatemala acaba subsidiando al Estado en su papel de 'lucha contra la pobreza.'"

CHAPTER FOUR: A BRIEF HISTORY OF EL SALVADOR

1. Susanne Jonas and Nestor Rodríguez, *Guatemala-U.S. Migration: Transforming Regions* (Austin: University of Texas Press, 2014), x.

2. Luis Noe-Bustamente, Antonio Flores, and Sono Shah, "Facts on Hispanics of Salvadoran origin in the United States, 2017," *Pew Research Center Hispanic Trends* (2017): 1, accessed October 19, 2019, https://www.pewresearch.org/hispanic/fact-sheet/u-s-hispanics-facts-on-salvadoran-origin-latinos/

3. Ignacio Ellacuría, SJ; Ignacio Martín-Baró, SJ; Segundo Montes, SJ; Juan Ramón Moreno, SJ; Joaquín López y López, SJ; Amando López, SJ; Elba Ramos (housekeeper); and Celina Ramos (housekeeper's 16-year-old daughter).

4. Kathryn E. Sampeck, "Late Postclassic to Colonial Transformations of the Landscape in the Izalcos Region of Western El Salvador," *Ancient Mesoamerica*, 21, no. 2 (2010): 261, http://www.jstor.org.proxy.seattleu.edu/stable/26309197

5. John Beverly, "El Salvador," *Social Text* 5 (1982): 56.

6. Ibid., 56–57.

7. Mary Wilhelmine Williams, "The Ecclesiastical Policy of Francisco Morazán and the Other Central American Liberals," *The Hispanic American Historical Review* 3, no. 2 (1920): 121; doi:10.2307/2518428.

8. Equipo Maiz, *Historia de El Salvador: De como los guanacos no sucumbieron a los*

infames ultrajes de españoles, criollos, gringos y otras plagas (San Salvador: Algier's Impresores S.A. de C.V, 1989), 58.

9. Paul D. Almeida, *Waves of Protest: Popular Struggle in El Salvador, 1925–2005* (Minneapolis: University of Minnesota Press, 2008), 4.

10. Carlos Velásquez Carrillo, "La reconsolidación del régimen oligárquico en El Salvador: Los ejes de la transformación neoliberal." In *Concentración económica y poder político en América Latina*, ed. Lisa North, Blanca Rubio, Alberto Acosta, and Carlos Pastor (Buenos Aires: Consejo Latinoamericano de Ciencias Sociales, 2020), 182; "tanto la economía nacional como las decisiones del poder político, alternando la presidencia entre miembros de sus propios círculos familiares."

11. James Dunkerley, *The Long War: Dictatorship and Revolution in El Salvador* (London: Junction Books, 1982), 7.

12. Mo Hume, "The Myths of Violence: Gender, Conflict, and Community in El Salvador," *Latin American Perspectives* 35, no. 5 (2008): 69, http://www.jstor.org.proxy.seattleu.edu/stable/27648120.

13. Robert Armstrong and Janet Shenk, *El Salvador: The Face of Revolution* (Boston: South End Press, 1999), 5.

14. Elisabeth J. Wood, "Civil War and the Transformation of Elite Representation in El Salvador," in *Conservative Parties, the Right, and Democracy in Latin America* (Baltimore: Johns Hopkins University Press, 2000), 228.

15. M. Dolores Albiac, "Los Ricos más Ricos de El Salvador," *Estudios Centroamericanos* 54, no. 612 (1999): 841.

16. Beverly, "El Salvador," 58.

17. Ralph Lee Woodward, "The Rise and Decline of Liberalism in Central America: Historical Perspectives on the Contemporary Crisis," *Journal of Interamerican Studies and World Affairs* 26, no. 3 (1984): 296. doi:10.2307/165672.

18. Equipo Maiz, *Historia de El Salvador: De como los guanacos no sucumbieron a los infames ultrajes de españoles, criollos, gringos y otras plagas*, 76.

19. Ibid., 79.

20. Ibid., 80.

21. Jeffrey L. Gould and Aldo Lauria-Santiago, *To Rise in Darkness: Revolution, Repression, and Memory in El Salvador, 1920–1932* (Durham, NC: Duke University Press, 2008), 211.

22. Ibid., xxiii.

23. Serena Cosgrove, *Leadership from the Margins: Women and Civil Society Organizations in Argentina, Chile, and El Salvador* (Piscataway, NJ: Rutgers University Press, 2010), 78–79.

24. Rolando Ruiz, "Los sucesos de 1932: ¿Complot comunista, motín indígena o protesta subalterna? Una revisión historiográfica," *Revista de Humanidades*, 5, no. 3 (2014):136 (San Salvador: Universidad de El Salvador), http://ri.ues.edu.sv/id/eprint/7791/2/7.pdf; "El recuerdo del levantamiento es la causa del temor anticomunista casi paranoico que se ha apoderado de la nación desde entonces. Dicho temor se expresa en la acusación de comunista que se lanza contra cualquier movimiento de reforma, por más modesto que sea."

25. Equipo Maiz, *Historia de El Salvador: De como los guanacos no sucumbieron a los infames ultrajes de españoles, criollos, gringos y otras plagas*, 92.

26. For a copy of Archbishop Romero's letter, see: https://griid.files.wordpress.com/2020/03/4a042-romeroe28099slettertopresidentcarter.pdf

27. Aviva Chomsky, *Central America's Forgotten History: Revolution, Violence, and the Roots of Migration* (Boston: Beacon Press, 2021), 132.

28. Cosgrove, *Leadership from the Margins,* 83.

29. Ibid., 85.

30. Quoted in Cosgrove, *Leadership from the Margins,* 84.

31. Terry Lynn Karl, "El Salvador's Negotiated Revolution," *Foreign Affairs* 71, no. 2 (1992), doi:10.2307/20045130; A. Rabasa et al., "Counterinsurgency Transition Case Study: El Salvador," in *From Insurgency to Stability: Volume II: Insights from Selected Case Studies,* (Santa Monica, CA: RAND Corporation, 2010) 75–116, http://www.jstor.org.proxy.seattleu.edu/stable/10.7249/mg1111-2osd.12

32. Equipo Maiz, *Historia de El Salvador: De como los guanacos no sucumbieron a los infames ultrajes de españoles, criollos, gringos y otras plagas,* 136.

33. Chris Norton, "Salvador's Duarte backs down on peace talks, further weakening his influence," *The Christian Science Monitor,* January 25, 1985, accessed January 12, 2022, https://www.csmonitor.com/1985/0125/osiege.html

34. Equipo Maiz, *Historia de El Salvador: De como los guanacos no sucumbieron a los infames ultrajes de españoles, criollos, gringos y otras plagas,* 143.

35. Ibid., 151.

36. Ralph Sprenkels, *After Insurgency: Revolution and Electoral Politics in El Salvador* (Notre Dame, IN: University of Notre Dame Press, 2018), 2.

37. Ibid., 5.

38. Edelberto Torres-Rivas, *Revoluciones sin cambios revolucionarios: Ensayos sobre la crisis en Centroamérica* (Guatemala: F&G Editores, 2011).

39. Sprenkels, *After Insurgency,* 330.

40. Almeida, *Waves of Protest,* 2.

41. Ibid., 209.

42. María Candelaria Navas, "Los movimientos de mujeres y feministas en la transición de posguerra y su aporte a los cambios culturales en El Salvador," *Revista Realidad,* 151 (2018): 84; ". . . con ello, se fueron construyendo espacios institucionales para solventar problemáticas relacionadas con la subordinación femenina en la Asamblea Legislativa, donde funciona el Grupo Parlamentario de Mujeres, Unidades Municipales de la Mujer creadas en alcaldías y Políticas Municipales de Equidad de Género."

43. Cosgrove, *Leadership from the Margins,* 88–89.

44. Rose J. Spalding, "From the Streets to the Chamber: Social Movements and the Mining Ban in El Salvador," *European Review of Latin American and Caribbean Studies | Revista Europea de Estudios Latinoamericanos y del Caribe,* no. 106 (2018): 47–74, https://doi.org/10.32992/erlacs.10377

45. Gene Palumbo and Elisabeth Malkin, "Mining Ban in El Salvador Prizes Water Over Gold," *The New York Times,* March 29, 2017.

46. Sonja Wolf, "Subverting Democracy: Elite Rule and the Limits to Political Participation in Post-War El Salvador," *Journal of Latin American Studies* 41, no. 3 (2009): 430, doi:10.1017/S0022216X09990149.

47. Mike Anastario, *Parcels: Memories of Salvadoran Migration* (Piscataway, NJ: Rutgers University Press, 2019), 42.

48. Ricardo Roque Baldovinos, "Nayib Bukele: Populismo e implosión democrática en El Salvador," *Andamios* 18, no. 46 (2021): 242–243; "Bukele fue capaz de montar una estrategia que le permitió ganar en primera vuelta una contienda en que enfrentaba a los dos partidos emblemáticos del régimen de la Posguerra, con más experiencia, recursos y, aparentemente, arraigo territorial"

49. Gabriel Labrador and Julia Gararrete, "Bukele Responds to Avalanche of International Criticism: 'The People Voted for This,'" *NACLA,* May 7, 2021, accessed November 29, 2021, https://nacla.org/news/2021/05/07/bukele-international-criticism-technical -coup

CHAPTER FIVE: A BRIEF HISTORY OF HONDURAS

1. Gloria Lara Pinto and George Hasemann, "Honduras antes del año 1500: Una visión regional de su evolución cultural tardía," *Revista de Arqueología Americana* 8 (1993): 21; "Podemos concluir que el Valle de Naco en el periodo entre el 1300 y 1500 de C. se había convertido en un territorio multiétnico, en donde existía un predominio anterior a la conquista de probable origen nahua pipil. Los chontales del documento de 1539 podrían ser hablantes de maya o lenca o ambas cosas, puesto que ya hemos visto que bajo este apelativo eran incluidos ambos grupos por los nahua pipiles y esto estaría también en consonancia con la indicación ya discutida sobre las tres lenguas habladas en el Valle Naco en 1525."

2. Ibid, 30.

3. Ibid., 32, 37.

4. Ibid., 41.

5. Scott Brady, "Honduras' Transisthmian Corridor: A Case of Undeveloped Potential in Colonial Central America," *Revista Geográfica* 133 (2003): 128.

6. Ronald N. Sheptak, "Colonial Masca in Motion: Tactics of Persistence of a Honduran Indigenous Community" (doctoral dissertation, Leiden University, 2013), 70.

7. Brady, "Honduras' Transisthmian Corridor: A Case of Undeveloped Potential in Colonial Central America," 139.

8. Taylor E. Mack, "Contraband Trade Through Trujillo, Honduras, 1720s–1782," *Yearbook (Conference of Latin Americanist Geographers)* 24 (1988): 46.

9. Ibid.

10. Tyler Shipley, "The New Canadian Imperialism and the Military Coup in Honduras," *Latin American Perspectives* 40, no. 5 (2013), 45.

11. Mark B. Rosenberg, "Narcos and Politicos: The Politics of Drug Trafficking in Honduras," *Journal of Interamerican Studies and World Affairs* 30, no. 2/3 (1988): 143.

12. Héctor Pérez-Brignoli, "El Fonógrafo En Los Trópicos: Sobre El Concepto de Banana Republic En La Obra de O. Henry," *Iberoamericana (2001-)* 6, no. 23 (2006): 127, http://www.jstor.org/stable/41676097.

13. Molly Todd, "Race, Nation, and West Indian Immigration to Honduras, 1890–1940 (review)," *Journal of World History* 23, no. 2 (2012): 452.

14. Ibid.

15. Philip L. Shepherd, "The Tragic Course and Consequences of U.S. Policy in Honduras," *World Policy Journal* 2, no. 1 (1984): 135.

16. Suyapa Portillo Villeda, *Roots of Resistance: A Story of Gender, Race, and Labor on the North Coast of Honduras* (Austin: University of Texas Press, 2021), 56.
17. Thomas M. Leonard, *The History of Honduras* (Santa Barbara, CA: ABC-CLIO, 2011), 129.
18. Portillo Villeda, *Roots of Resistance*, 192.
19. Portillo Villeda, *Roots of Resistance*, 201.
20. Ralph Lee Woodward, "The Rise and Decline of Liberalism in Central America: Historical Perspectives on the Contemporary Crisis," *Journal of Interamerican Studies and World Affairs* 26, no. 3 (1984): 306, doi:10.2307/165672.
21. Shepherd, "The Tragic Course and Consequences of U.S. Policy in Honduras," 124.
22. Ibid., 116, 118.
23. Ibid., 127–128.
24. Jordan Swanson, "Unnatural Disasters: Public Health Lessons from Honduras," *Harvard International Review* 22, no. 1 (2000): 32.
25. Ibid., 33.
26. Ibid., 34.
27. Shipley, "The New Canadian Imperialism and the Military Coup in Honduras," 48.
28. Ibid.
29. Ibid., 49.
30. Thomas Legler, "Learning the Hard Way: Defending Democracy in Honduras," *International Journal* 65, no. 3 (2010): 611–612.
31. Ibid., 606.
32. Ibid., 608.
33. Shipley, "The New Canadian Imperialism and the Military Coup in Honduras," 50.
34. Ibid., 51.
35. Organization of American States, "Mission to Support the Fight against Corruption and Impunity in Honduras: About the Mission," 2019, http://www.oas.org/en/spa/dsdsm/maccih/new/mision.asp
36. Amelia Frank-Vitale and Margarita Núñez Chaim, "'Lady Frijoles': Las caravanas centroamericanas y el poder de la hípervisibilidad de la migración indocumentada," *Entre Diversidades* 7, no. 1 (2020): 55.
37. Ibid., 53.
38. Portillo Villeda, *Roots of Resistance*, 246.
39. Ibid., 217.
40. Mario Posas, "Movimientos Sociales en Honduras," in *Antología Del Pensamiento Hondureño Contemporáneo*, ed. Ramón Romero (Buenos Aires, Argentina: CLACSO, 2019), https://doi.org/10.2307/j.ctvnp0kc9.16
41. Cecilia Menjívar and Shannon Drysdale Walsh, "The Architecture of Feminicide: The State, Inequalities, and Everyday Gender Violence in Honduras," *Latin American Research Review* 52 (2017): 223.
42. Posas, "Movimientos Sociales en Honduras," 274.
43. María José Méndez, "'The River Told Me': Rethinking Intersectionality from the World of Berta Cáceres." *Capitalism Nature Socialism* 29, no. 1 (2018): 13.
44. Christopher A. Loperena, "Honduras Is Open for Business: Extractivist Tourism as Sustainable Development in the Wake of Disaster?" *Journal of Sustainable Tourism* 25, no. 5 (2017).

45. Ibid., 625.

46. Posas, "Movimientos Sociales en Honduras," 275.

47. Global Witness, "Honduras: The Deadliest Country in the World for Environmental Activism," *Global Witness,* March 14, 2017, https://www.globalwitness.org/en/campaigns/environmental-activists/honduras-deadliest-country-world-environmental-activism/

48. Tierra de Resistentes, "Los resistentes in datos," 2021, accessed February 3, 2022, https://tierraderesistentes.com/es/datos/

49. Meghan Krausch, "They Are Killing Our Leaders One by One," *The Progressive,* October 2, 2019, https://progressive.org/latest/Honduran-indigenous-protesting-logging-killed-Krausch-191002/

CHAPTER SIX: A BRIEF HISTORY OF NICARAGUA

1. William M. Denevan, "The Pristine Myth: The Landscape of the Americas in 1492," *Annals of the Association of American Geographers*, 82, no. 3 (1992): 370.

2. Linda Newson, "The Depopulation of Nicaragua in the Sixteenth Century," *Journal of Latin American Studies* 14, no. 2 (1982): 253. http://www.jstor.org/stable/156458

3. Ibid., 264.

4. Jaime Biderman, "The Development of Capitalism in Nicaragua: A Political Economic History." *Latin American Perspectives,* 10, no. 1 (1983): 9, https://www.jstor.org/stable/2633361

5. Francis Merriman Stanger, "National Origins in Central America," *The Hispanic American Historical Review* 12, no. 1 (1932): 41, doi:10.2307/2506428.

6. Robert Holden, *Armies without Nations: Public Violence and State Formation in Central America, 1821–1960* (New York: Oxford University Press, 2004), 80.

7. Ibid.

8. Luis Roniger, *Transnational Politics in Central America* (Gainesville: University of Florida Press, 2013), 46.

9. Biderman, "The Development of Capitalism in Nicaragua," 11.

10. Craig S. Revels, "Coffee in Nicaragua: Introduction and Expansion in the Nineteenth Century," *Yearbook (Conference of Latin Americanist Geographers)* 26 (2000): 17–28.

11. Edmund T. Gordon, *Disparate Diasporas: Identity and Politics in an African Nicaraguan Community* (Austin: University of Texas Press, 1998), 63.

12. Deborah Robb Taylor, *The Times and Life of Bluefields: An Intergenerational Dialogue* (Managua, Nicaragua: Academia de Geografia e Historia de Nicaragua, 2005), 32.

13. Gordon, *Disparate Diasporas*, ix.

14. Serena Cosgrove, José Idiáquez, Leonard Joseph Bent, and Andrew Gorvetzian, *Surviving the Americas: Garifuna Persistence from Nicaragua to New York City* (Cincinnati: University of Cincinnati Press, 2021).

15. Ibid., 38.

16. Gordon, *Disparate Diasporas*, 57.

17. Ibid., 61.

18. Ibid.

19. Ibid., 63.

20. George Evans, "The Deaths of Somoza," *World Literature Today* 8, no. 3 (2007): 38.

21. Lawrence A. Clayton, "The Nicaragua Canal in the Nineteenth Century: Prelude to American Empire in the Caribbean," *Journal of Latin American Studies* 19, no. 2 (1987): 326.

22. Jeffrey H. Solomon and ‫ج, ن,ﻧﻮﻣﻮﻟﻮﺳ‬, "Tortured History: Filibustering, Rhetoric, and Walker's 'War in Nicaragua'/ ‫ﺧﻴﺮاﺗﻟا ﺑﺎﻟﻐﻼﺑﻠاو ﺑﺬﻋﻤﻟا: اﻟﻘﺮﺗﻨﺼﺔ وﻛﺎﺗﻜﻮ ﺑﺎﺗﻜﻮ رﻛﻮو ﻧﻊ اﻟﺤﺮﺑ ﻓﻲ‬ ‫اوﺟﺎراﻛﻴﻦ‬," *Alif: Journal of Comparative Poetics* 31 (2011): 105, https://www.jstor.org/stable/23216049.

23. Solomon and ‫ج, ن,ﻧﻮﻣﻮﻟﻮﺳ‬, "Tortured History," 108.

24. Ibid.

25. Michel Gobat, *Confronting the American Dream: Nicaragua under U.S. Imperial Rule* (Durham, NC: Duke University Press, 2007), 40.

26. Joseph O. Baylen, "Sandino: Patriot or Bandit?" *The Hispanic American Historical Review* 31, no. 3 (1951): 407.

27. Gobat, *Confronting the American Dream*; Michael Schroeder and David C. Brooks, "Caudillismo Masked and Modernized: The Remaking of the Nicaraguan State via the Guardia Nacional, 1925–1936," *Middle Atlantic Review of Latin American Studies* 2, no. 2 (2018): 6, https://doi.org/10.23870/marlas.169.

28. Schroeder and Brooks, "Caudillismo Masked and Modernized," 6–7.

29. Evans, "The Deaths of Somoza," 36.

30. Schroeder and Brooks, "Caudillismo Masked and Modernized," 32.

31. Walter LaFeber, *Inevitable Revolutions: The United States in Central America* (New York: W.W. Norton, 1993), 226.

32. LaFeber, *Inevitable Revolutions*, 226.

33. Ibid., 227.

34. Ibid.

35. Ibid., 226.

36. "Thousands dead as quakes strike Nicaraguan city." *New York Times.* December 24, 1972. https://www.nytimes.com/1972/12/24/archives/thousands-dead-as-quakes-strike-nicaraguan-city-capital-battered.html

37. LaFeber, *Inevitable Revolutions,* 227.

38. Ibid.

39. Ibid., 229.

40. Ibid., 229–232.

41. Ibid., 233.

42. Richard L. Harris, "The Revolutionary Transformation of Nicaragua," *Latin American Perspectives* 14, no. 1 (1987): 10.

43. Ibid., 6.

44. Rosario Montoya, *Gendered Scenarios of Revolution: Making New Men and New Women in Nicaragua, 1975–2000* (Tucson: University of Arizona Press, 2012), 10.

45. Verónica Rueda Estrada, "Movilizaciones campesinas en Nicaragua (1990-2018): De los Rearmados a los Autoconvocados," *Cuadernos Intercambio* 16, no. 2 (2019): 4, https://revistas.ucr.ac.cr/index.php/intercambio/article/view/37499/38535; "Las primeras medidas tuvieron el objetivo de erradicar a los grandes terratenientes, principalmente de la zona del Pacífico, estatizar los medios de producción y, con ello, reorganizar las actividades económicas a través de cooperativas de producción."

46. Harris, "The Revolutionary Transformation of Nicaragua," 10.

47. Joseph Betz, "Sandinista Nicaragua as a Deweyan Social Experiment," *Transactions of the Charles S. Peirce Society* 36, no. 1 (2000): 41.

48. William Blum, *Killing Hope: U.S. Military and CIA Interventions since World War II* (London: Zed Books, 2014), 293.

49. Richard Sobel, "Contra Aid Fundamentals: Exploring the Intricacies and the Issues," *Political Science Quarterly (Academy of Political Science)* 110, no. 2 (1995).

50. Roger Peace, "Winning Hearts and Minds: The Debate Over U.S. Intervention in Nicaragua in the 1980s," *Peace & Change* 35, no. 1 (2010): 8, doi:10.111 1/j.1468–0130.2009.00611.

51. María Teresa Blandón, "Los cuerpos del feminismo nicaragüense," in *Antología del pensamiento crítico nicaragüense contemporáneo*, ed. Juan Pablo Gómez and Camilo Antillón (Buenos Aires: Consejo Latinoamericano de Ciencias Sociales, 2017), 357; "Las experiencias vividas por las feministas nicaragüenses durante la década revolucionaria (1979–1989) contribuyeron al reconocimiento—aunque no fuera totalmente consciente en su tiempo—de cómo el género y la clase se intersectan y condicionan la vida de las mujeres, como expresión de la articulación de dos sistemas de dominación —el capitalista y el patriarcal. . . ."

52. Mitchell A. Seligson and John A. Booth, "Political Culture and Regime Type: Evidence from Nicaragua and Costa Rica," *The Journal of Politics* 55, no. 3 (1993): 778, https://doi.org/10.2307/2132001.

53. Mark Everingham, "Neoliberalism in a New Democracy: Elite Politics and State Reform in Nicaragua," *The Journal of Developing Areas* 32, no. 2 (1998): 244–245, https://www.jstor.org/stable/4192756.

54. Karen Kampwirth, "Abortion, Antifeminism, and the Return of Daniel Ortega: In Nicaragua, Leftist Politics?" *Latin American Perspective* 35, no. 6 (2008): 122, https://www.jstor.org/stable/27648142

55. Kai M. Thaler, "Nicaragua: A Return to Caudillismo." *Journal of Democracy* 28, no. 2 (2017): 158, https://doi.org/10.1353/jod.2017.0032.

56. Ibid., 160.

57. As an example of applying institutional pressure and repressive measures against higher education, the Nicaraguan government has targeted the Universidad Centroamericana, the Jesuit university in Managua, for its critical thinking and freedom of thought, and, in retaliation, the half of the university's budget covered by the government has been cut. There's frequently a police cordon around the university, and the new laws that the government has passed to punish organizations seen as traitors means that the UCA is functioning without accreditation or permissions.

58. Amaru Ruiz and Mónica López Baltodano, "Las luchas del movimiento ambientalista de Nicaragua en el siglo XXI," in *Anhelos de un nuevo horizonte: Aportes para una Nicaragua democrática*, ed. Alberto Cortés Ramos, Umanzor López, and Ludwig Moncada (San José: Facultad Latinoamericana de Ciencias Sociales, 2020), 615; "Esta expansión de la agenda ambiental ha sido posible sobre todo en este siglo, gracias al avance de las comunicaciones y al internet."

59. José Luis Rocha, "Tres años de represión y exilio de los nicaragüenses: 2018–2021," CETRI, November 12, 2021, 15, accessed November 23, 2021, https://www.cetri.be/Tres-anos-de-represion-y-exilio-de

60. Joshua Partlow, "They fled violence in Nicaragua by the thousands. What awaits them in Costa Rica?" *The Washington Post*, September 2, 2018, accessed October 19, 2019, https://www.washingtonpost.com/world/the_americas/they-fled-violence-in -nicaragua-by-the-thousands-what-awaits-them-in-costa-rica/2018/09/01/51d3f7ee -a62c-11e8-ad6f-080770dcddc2_story.html?noredirect=on&utm_term= .939c446dfc13

61. Erin S. Finzer, "Modern Women Intellectuals and the Sandino Rebellion: Carmen Sobalvarro and Aura Rostand," *Latin American Research Review* 56, no. 2 (2021): 468, https://doi.org/10.25222/larr.878

62. Lottie Cunningham Wren, "Pueblos indígenas y afrodescendientes. La lucha por sus derechos humanos," in *Anhelos de un nuevo horizonte: Aportes para una Nicaragua democrática*, ed. Alberto Cortés Ramos, Umanzor López, and Ludwig Moncada, 633-646 (San José: Facultad Latinoamericana de Ciencias Sociales, 2020).

63. The Observatory for the Protection of Human Rights Defenders (OPHRD), *Nicaragua: Joint briefing: A Year of Violence against Those Defending the Rights of the Mayangna and Miskitu Indigenous Peoples*, January 29, 2021, accessed November 30, 2021, https://www.omct.org/en/resources/urgent-interventions/nicaragua-briefing -conjunto-un-a%C3%B1o-de-violencia-sistem%C3%A1tica-contra-quienes-defienden -los-derechos-ind%C3%ADgenas

64. The Oakland Institute, "Nicaragua's Failed Revolution: The Indigenous Struggle for Saneamiento," 2020: 6, accessed November 30, 2021, https://www.oaklandinstitute. org/sites/oaklandinstitute.org/files/nicaraguas-failed-revolution.pdf

65. Jennifer Goett, "Beyond Left and Right: Grassroots Social Movements and Nicaragua's Civic Insurrection," *LASA FORUM*, 49, no. 4 (2019): 20.

66. Sam Jones, "Nicaragua, 'A feeling of déjà vu': Author Sergio Ramirez on ex-comrade Ortega and Nicaraguan history repeating." The Guardian, September 18, 2021, accessed December 2, 2021, https://www.theguardian.com/world/2021/sep/18 /sergio-ramirez-interview-nicaragua-ortega-novel

67. Inter-American Commission on Human Rights, "Nicaragua: Concentración del poder y debilitamiento del Estado de Derecho," 2021: 15, accessed January 25, 2022, https:// www.oas.org/es/cidh/informes/pdfs/2021_Nicaragua-ES.pdf. "328 víctimas fatales en el contexto de la crisis y 1,614 personas que fueron privadas de la libertad; además, más de 136 personas permanecen privadas de la libertad; 150 estudiantes expulsados; más de 405 profesionales de la salud despedidos; y más de 103,600 nicaragüenses exiliados."

68. Rocha, "Tres años de represión y exilio de los nicaragüenses," 3; "Acicateados por el hambre y por el miedo se han ido decenas de miles de nicaragüenses. Cambiaron de país porque desesperaron de cambiar el país."

CHAPTER SEVEN: A BRIEF HISTORY OF COSTA RICA

1. Frederick W. Lange and Richard M. Accola, "Metallurgy in Costa Rica," *Archaeology* 32, no. 5 (1979): 33, http://www.jstor.org/stable/41726374.

2. D. K. M. K, "Costa Rica and the Invasion: Difficulties of a Central American Democracy," *The World Today* 11, no. 3 (1955): 130.

3. Edelberto Torres-Rivas, *History and Society in Central America* (Austin: University of Texas Press, 1993), 9.

4. Tord Høvik and Solveig Aas, "Demilitarization in Costa Rica: A Farewell to Arms?" *Journal of Peace Research* 18, no. 4 (1981): 339.
5. Iván Molina and Steven Palmer, "Popular Literacy in a Tropical Democracy: Costa Rica 1850–1950," *Past & Present* 184 (2004): 173.
6. Steven Palmer, "Getting to Know the Unknown Soldier: Official Nationalism in Liberal Costa Rica, 1880–1900," *Journal of Latin American Studies* 25, no. 1 (1993): 48.
7. Torres-Rivas, *History and Society in Central America,* 17.
8. Ibid.
9. Ibid.
10. Palmer, "Getting to Know the Unknown Soldier," 45.
11. Ibid.
12. Ibid., 51.
13. Ronald N. Harpelle, "Racism and Nationalism in the Creation of Costa Rica's Pacific Coast Banana Enclave," *The Americas* 56, no. 3 (2000): 32.
14. Høvik and Aas, "Demilitarization in Costa Rica," 335.
15. James L. Huesmann, "The Chinese in Costa Rica, 1855–1897," *The Historian* 53, no. 4 (1991): 711.
16. Huesmann, "The Chinese in Costa Rica, 1855–1897," 714.
17. Benjamín N. Narváez, "Re-envisioning Caribbean Costa Rica: Chinese-West Indian Interaction in Limón during the Late Nineteenth and Early Twentieth Centuries," *New West Indian Guide* 95 (2021): 2.
18. David Díaz Arias and Ronald Soto Quirós, "*Mestizaje*, indígenas e identidad nacional en Centroamérica: De la Colonia a las Repúblicas Liberales," *Cuaderno de Ciencias Sociales* 143 (2007): 57.
19. Harpelle, "Racism and Nationalism in the Creation of Costa Rica's Pacific Coast Banana Enclave," 30.
20. Ibid., 40.
21. Huesmann, "The Chinese in Costa Rica, 1855–1897," 715.
22. Ibid., 718.
23. Narváez, "Re-envisioning Caribbean Costa Rica," 8.
24. Samuel M. Otterstrom, "Nicaraguan Migrants in Costa Rica during the 1990s: Gender Differences and Geographic Expansion," *Journal of Latin American Geography* 7, no. 2 (2008): 8.
25. Høvik and Aas, "Demilitarization in Costa Rica," 340.
26. Ibid.
27. Harpelle, "Racism and Nationalism in the Creation of Costa Rica's Pacific Coast Banana Enclave," 41.
28. Høvik and Aas, "Demilitarization in Costa Rica," 336.
29. Ibid.
30. D. K. M. K, "Costa Rica and the Invasion," 134.
31. D. K. M. K, "Costa Rica and the Invasion," 130.
32. Russell Leigh Sharman, "Re/Making La Negrita: Culture as an Aesthetic System in Costa Rica," *American Anthropologist* 108, no. 4 (2006): 849.
33. Kyle Longley, "Peaceful Costa Rica, the First Battleground: The United States and the Costa Rican Revolution of 1948," *The Americas* 50, no. 2 (1993): 170.
34. Ibid., 175.

35. Ibid., 70–71.
36. Ibid., 67.
37. Ibid., 69.
38. Michelle Christian, "'. . . Latin America without the Downside': Racial Exceptionalism and Global Tourism in Costa Rica," *Ethnic and Racial Studies* 36, no. 10 (2013): 1600.
39. Víctor Hugo Acuña Ortega, "La invención de la diferencia costarricense, 1810–1870," *Antología del Pensamiento Crítico Costarricense Contemporáneo* (Buenos Aires, Argentina: Consejo Latinoamericano de Ciencias Sociales, 2019), 55.
40. Narváez, "Re-envisioning Caribbean Costa Rica," 213.
41. Lisa Campo-Engelstein and Karen Meagher, "Costa Rica's 'White Legend': How Racial Narratives Undermine its Health Care System," *Developing World Bioethics* 11, no. 2 (2011): 100.
42. Christian, "'. . . Latin America without the downside,'" 1603.
43. Campo-Engelstein and Meagher, "Costa Rica's 'White Legend,'" 100.
44. Campo-Engelstein and Meagher, "Costa Rica's 'White Legend,'" 104.
45. Aránzazu Robles Santana, "¿Ciudadanas? Mujeres indígenas en Costa Rica: Problemática historia e historiográfica sobre su acceso a la ciudadanía," *Diálogos, Revista Electrónica de Historia* 13, no. 2 (2012): 58.
46. Ibid., 52–53.
47. Otterstrom, "Nicaraguan Migrants in Costa Rica during the 1990s: Gender Differences and Geographic Expansion," 7.
48. Natalia Zamora and Vilma Obando, "Biodiversity and Tourism in Costa Rica," March 2001, accessed February 3, 2022, https://www.cbd.int/doc/nbsap/tourism/CostaRica (Tourism).pdf
49. Zamora and Obando, "Biodiversity and Tourism in Costa Rica"; Crist Inman, "Tourism in Costa Rica: The Challenge of Competitiveness," March 2002, accessed February 3, 2022, https://www.incae.edu/sites/default/files/cen653.pdf; Lynn R. Horton, "Buying Up Nature: Economic and Social Impacts of Costa Rica's Ecotourism Boom," *Latin American Perspectives* 36, no. 3 (2009): 93.
50. Lara Moragrega Martín, "Tourist Expansion and Development of Rural Communities: The Cast of Monteverde, Costa Rica," *Mountain Research and Development* 24, no. 3 (2004): 202.
51. Carol Key and Vijayan K. Pillai, "Tourism and Ethnicity in Belize: A Qualitative Study," *International Review of Modern Sociology* 33, no. 1 (2007): 133.
52. Michael J. Miller, "Biodiversity Policy Making in Costa Rica: Pursing Indigenous and Peasant Rights," *The Journal of Environment & Development* 15, no. 4 (2006).
53. Donald Rojas, "Indígenas Ticos Pierden Tierras," *Ambien-Tico*, October 10, 2001, accessed 27, 2021, https://www.ambientico.una.ac.cr/revista-ambientico/indigenas-ticos-pierden-tierras/
54. Miller, "Biodiversity Policy Making in Costa Rica," 359.
55. Robles Santana, "¿Ciudadanas? Mujeres indígenas en Costa Rica," 55.
56. Ibid., 54.
57. Ibid., 56.
58. Open Government Partnership, "Results of Early Open Government Partnership Initiatives," 2016: 1, http://www.opengovpartnership.org/sites/default/files/case-study_Results-OGP-Early-Initiatives_20161201_2.pdf

59. Joshua Partlow, "They fled violence in Nicaragua by the thousands. What awaits them in Costa Rica?" *The Washington Post*, September 2, 2018, accessed October 19, 2019, https://www.washingtonpost.com/world/the_americas/they-fled-violence-in-nicaragua-by-the-thousands-what-awaits-them-in-cota-rica/2018/09/01/51d3f7ee-a62c-11e8-ad6f-080770dcddc2_story.html?noredirect=on&utm_term=.939c446dfc13

CHAPTER EIGHT: A BRIEF HISTORY OF PANAMA

1. The World Bank, "The World Bank in Panama," 2016, accessed February 2, 2018, http://www.worldbank.org/en/country/Panama/overview
2. International Monetary Fund, "Report for Selected Countries and Subjects," 2018, accessed February 2018.
3. Adam C. J. Menzies and Mikael J. Haller, "Embedded Craft Production at the Late Pre-Columbian (A.D. 900—1522) Community of He4 (El Hatillo), Central Region of Panama," *Canadian Journal of Archaeology* 36, no. 1 (2012): 111.
4. Samir S. Patel, "Pirates of the Original Panama Canal," *Archaeology* 66, no. 2 (2013): 35.
5. Menzies and Haller, "Embedded Craft Production at the Late Pre-Columbian," 110.
6. Patel, "Pirates of the Original Panama Canal," 32.
7. Ibid.
8. Richard G. Cooke and Beatriz Elena Rovira, "Historical Archaeology in Panama City," *Archaeology* 36, no. 2 (1983): 51.
9. Peter M. Sanchez, "The End of Hegemony? Panama and the United States," *International Journal on World Peace* 19, no. 3 (2002): 63.
10. Augustus Campbell and Colin D. Campbell, "Crossing the Isthmus of Panama, 1849: The Letters of Dr. Augustus Campbell," *California History* 78, no. 4 (1999): 227.
11. Cooke and Rovira, "Historical Archaeology in Panama City," 51.
12. James Brown Scott, "The Treaty Between Colombia and the United States," *The American Journal of International Law* 15, no. 3 (1921): 435.
13. Noel Maurer and Carlos Yu, "What T. R. Took: The Economic Impact of the Panama Canal, 1903–1937," *The Journal of Economic History* 68, no. 3 (2008): 710.
14. Dimitrios Theodossopoulos, "With or Without Gringos: When Panamanians Talk about the United States and Its Citizens," *The International Journal of Social and Cultural Practice* 54, no. 1 (2010): 54.
15. Maurer and Yu, "What T. R. Took," 689.
16. Rodolfo Sabonge and Ricardo J. Sánchez, "El Canal de Panamá en la economía de América Latina y el Caribe," *CEPAL – Colección Documentos de proyectos* (2009): 22.
17. Brown Scott, "The Treaty Between Colombia and the United States," 430.
18. Ibid., 431.
19. I. Roberto Eisenmann, "The Struggle against Noriega," *Journal of Democracy* 1, no. 1 (1990): 42.
20. Lester D. Langley, "Negotiating New Treaties with Panama: 1936," *The Hispanic American Historical Review* 48, no. 2 (1968): 222.
21. Langley, "Negotiating New Treaties with Panama: 1936," 229.
22. Peter M. Sanchez, "The End of Hegemony? Panama and the United States," *International Journal on World Peace* 19, no. 3 (2002): 67.

23. Ibid.

24. Julie Velásquez Runk, "Indigenous Land and Environmental Conflicts in Panama: Neoliberal Multiculturalism, Changing Legislation, and Human Rights," *Journal of Latin American Geography* 11, no. 2 (2012): 24.

25. Sanchez, "The End of Hegemony? Panama and the United States," 68.

26. Theodossopoulos, "With or Without Gringos," 54.

27. Guillermo Castro Herrera, "On Cattle and Ships: Culture, History and Sustainable Development in Panama," *Environment and History* 7, no. 2 (2001): 211.

28. Sanchez, "The End of Hegemony? Panama and the United States," 73.

29. Richard L. Millett, "The Aftermath of Intervention: Panama 1990," *Journal of Interamerican Studies* 32, no. 1 (1990): 2.

30. Sanchez, "The End of Hegemony? Panama and the United States," 76.

31. Eisenmann, "The Struggle Against Noriega"; Millett, "The Aftermath of Intervention: Panama 1990."

32. Eisenmann, "The Struggle Against Noriega," 44.

33. Sanchez, "The End of Hegemony? Panama and the United States," 80–81.

34. Sanchez, "The End of Hegemony? Panama and the United States," 81.

35. Ibid.

36. Millett, "The Aftermath of Intervention: Panama 1990," 7.

37. Ibid., 8.

38. Ibid.

39. Velásquez Runk, "Indigenous Land and Environmental Conflicts in Panama," 25.

40. Georges Priestley and Alberto Barrow, "El movimiento negro en Panamá: Una interpretación histórica y política, 1994–2004," *Política e identidad: Afrodescendientes en México y América Central* (2010): 5.

41. Ibid., 10.

42. Ibid., 20.

43. Ibid., 31.

44. Lok Siu, "Cultural Citizenship of Diasporic Chinese in Panama," *Amerasia Journal* 28, no. 2 (2002): 189–190, doi:10.17953/amer.28.2.117j7810478075h2.

45. Velásquez Runk, "Indigenous Land and Environmental Conflicts in Panama."

46. Anthony J., Bebbington, Laura Aileen Sauls, Herman Rosa, Benjamin Fash, and Denise Humphreys Bebbington, "Conflicts over Extractivist Policy and the Forest Frontier in Central America," *European Review of Latin American and Caribbean Studies/Revista Europea de Estudios Latinoamericanos y Del Caribe*, no. 106 (2018): 121, https://www.jstor.org/stable/26608622.

47. Joan Martínez-Alier, "Conflictos ambientales en Centroamérica y las Antillas: Un rápido toxic tour," *Ecología Política* 60 (2020): 48; Marco A. Gandaseguí, "Una historia política de Panamá: Movimientos populares y militarismo en Panamá," *Revista Conjeturas Sociológica* 2, no. 4 (2014): 15.

48. Velásquez Runk, "Indigenous Land and Environmental Conflicts in Panama," 25.

49. Barney Warf, "Tailored for Panama: Offshore Banking at the Crossroads of the Americas," *Geografiska Annaler. Series B, Human Geography* 84, no. 1 (2002): 37.

50. Ibid., 41.

NOTES

CHAPTER NINE: THINKING IN HISTORICAL PERSPECTIVE
ABOUT CENTRAL AMERICA TODAY

1. Edelberto Torres-Rivas, *History and Society in Central America* (Austin: University of Texas Press, 1993), 28.

2. Ralph Lee Woodward, *Rafael Carrera and the Emergence of the Republic of Guatemala, 1821–1871* (Athens: University of Georgia Press, 1993), xiii.

3. James Quesada, "A Brief History of Nicaragua," in *Higher Education at the Crossroads of State Repression and Neoliberal Reform in Nicaragua: Reflections from a University under Fire in Nicaragua*, ed. Wendi Bellanger, Serena Cosgrove, and Irina Carlota Silber (New York: Routledge, 2022).

4. "Troops Occupy El Salvador's Legislature to Back President's Crime Package," *NPR*, February 10, 2020, accessed January 12, 2022, https://www.npr.org/2020/02/10/804407503/troops-occupy-el-salvadors-legislature-to-back-president-s-crime-package

5. "Joe Biden's other headache: Democracy is quickly eroding in Central America," *The Economist*, August 28, 2021, 26.

6. Omar Herrera Rodríguez, "La geopolítica contemporánea de Estados Unidos y el fin de Centroamérica," *Temas de Nuestra América* 33, no. 62 (2017): 82–83; "Bajo estas nuevas coordenadas geopolíticas, cualquier proyecto social alternativo, debe considerar el ensanchamiento de los límites espaciales. Si bien, Centroamérica es una promesa y un horizonte para muchos, esta no puede dares sin considerar que está circunscrita a un espacio mayor de control, vigilancia y represión."

7. Aviva Chomsky, *Central America's Forgotten History: Revolution, Violence, and the Roots of Migration* (Boston: Beacon Press, 2021), 38.

8. Rodríguez, "La geopolítica contemporánea de Estados Unidos y el fin de Centroamérica," 71.

9. Marisa León-Gómez Sonet, "Immigration Policy Must Look Beyond the Border," *NACLA*, June 8, 2021, accessed November 23, 2021, https://nacla.org/news/2021/06/08/immigration-policy-must-look-beyond-border

10. Martínez-Alier, "Conflictos ambientales en Centroamérica y las Antillas: un rápido toxic tour," *Ecología Política*, 60 (2020): 44; "La presencia de empresas extractivistas de Canadá o Estados Unidos es una constante en la región, pero también aparecen empresas europeas y, cada vez más, chinas."

11. Monserrat Sagot, "(Re) Definiendo las identidades y la acción política: Multitudes diversas, sujetos colectivos y movimientos sociales en la Centroamérica del nuevo milenio," (Conferencia Inaugural del Ciclo Lectivo del 2007 Escuela de Antropología y Sociología Universidad de Costa Rica, San José, Costa Rica, 2007), 13; "Esto otorgaría a los nuevos movimientos una radicalidad de una naturaleza diferente, ya que sus luchas tienen como objetivo transformar lo cotidiano de los actores en el aquí y en el ahora y no necesariamente en un futuro lejano. De tal forma, la emancipación comienza ahora o no comienza nunca... la emancipación por la que luchan estos nuevos actores es ante todo personal, social y cultural."

12. Ibid., 3.

13. Rosario Montoya, *Gendered Scenarios of Revolution: Making New Men and New Women in Nicaragua, 1975–2000*, 1st ed. (Tucson: University of Arizona Press, 2012), 7.

14. Alberto Martín Álvarez, "Desafiando la hegemonía neoliberal: ideologías de cambio radical en la Centroamérica de posguerra," *Historia Actual Online* 25 (2011): 116; "Cuál es la finalidad de un partido revolucionario si la revolución ya no es un proyecto posible."

15. Martín Álvarez, "Desafiando la hegemonía neoliberal," 117.

16. Martín Álvarez, "Desafiando la hegemonía neoliberal," 120.

17. Sagot, "(Re) Definiendo las identidades y la acción política," 6; "Estos nuevos movimientos se han convertido en lugares de producción de identidades que se resisten a la normalización, es decir, a ser parte de la norma unitaria, que desconfían del poder totalitario, sea de quien sea, y de los discursos 'universalizantes.' Se ha producido así una politización de otras áreas de la vida, que antes no eran consideradas como terreno para la acción política."

18. Charles R. Hale, "Does Multiculturalism Menace? Governance, Cultural Rights and the Politics of Identity in Guatemala," *Journal of Latin American Studies* 34 (2002): 499.

19. José Luis Rocha, "Tres años de represión y exilio de los nicaragüenses: 2018–2021," 5, *CETRI,* November 12, 2021, accessed November 23, 2021, https://www.cetri.be /Tres-anos-de-represion-y-exilio-de; "los centroamericanos que son castigados por querer trabajar donde no nacieron."

20. Ibid., 2. "A mayor violencia, mayor migración."; "La migración de las dos décadas que hacen de bisagra en el cambio de siglo fue acicateada por motivos económicos, por la inestabilidad política que en Honduras se profundizó tras el golpe de Estado de 2009 y por las múltiples violencias que se desplegaron en las tres naciones del norte de Centroamérica: entre otras, las protagonizadas por las poderosas pandillas trasnacionales llamadas 'maras,' la persecución de activistas indígenas y ambientalistas, y el sicariato al servicio de los narcos y de los acaparadores de tierras para proyectos turísticos, mineros, hidroeléctricos, inmobiliarios y especulativos."

21. Ibid.

22. Carlos Sandoval-García, "Nicaraguan Immigration to Costa Rica: Tendencies, Policies, and Politics," *LASAForum* Vol. xlvi, no. 4 (Fall 2015): 7.

23. María Jesús Mora, "Costa Rica Has Welcoming Policies for Migrants, but Nicaraguans Face Subtle Barriers," *Migration Policy Institute*, November 5, 2021, https://www. migrationpolicy.org/article/costa-rica-nicaragua-migrants-subtle-barriers

24. Sonet, "Immigration Policy Must Look Beyond the Border."

25. Giovanni Batz, "U.S. Policy Toward Central America Continues Legacy of Displacement," *NACLA*, April 29, 2021, accessed November 23, 2021, https://nacla.org /news/2021/04/28/us-policy-central-america-migration-displacement

BIBLIOGRAPHY

Acuña Ortega, Víctor Hugo. "La invención de la diferencia costarricense, 1810–1870." In *Antología del Pensamiento Crítico Costarricense Contemporáneo*, edited by Montserrat Sagot and David Díaz Arias, 45–73. Buenos Aires, Argentina: Consejo Latinoamericano de Ciencias Sociales, 2019.

Acuña Ortega, Víctor. "Centroamérica: Raíces autoritarias y brotes democráticos." *Envío* 170 (1996): 1–16.

Aguilar-Støen, Mariel. "Beyond Transnational Corporations, Food and Biofuels: The Role of Extractivism and Agribusiness in Land Grabbing in Central America." *Forum for Development Studies* 43, no. 1 (2016): 155–75.

Albiac, M. Dolores. "Los ricos más ricos de El Salvador." *ECA: Estudios Centroamericanos* 54, no. 612 (1999): 841–864.

Almeida, Paul D. *Waves of Protest: Popular Struggle in El Salvador, 1925–2005*. Minneapolis: University of Minnesota Press, 2008.

Anastario, Mike. *Parcels: Memories of Salvadoran Migration*. Piscataway, NJ: Rutgers University Press, 2019.

Archbishop Oscar A. Romero to President Jimmy Carter (February 17, 1980). Accessed December 5, 2021. https://griid.files.wordpress.com/2020/03/4a042-romeroe28099 slettertopresidentcarter.pdf

Armbruster-Sandoval, Ralph. "Globalization and Transnational Labor Organizing: The Honduran Maquiladora Industry and the Kimi Campaign." *Journal of Latin American Studies* 35 no. 2 (2003): 279–310.

Armstrong, Robert, and Janet Shenk. *El Salvador: The Face of Revolution*. Boston: South End Press, 1999.

Arriola, Elvia R. "Gender, Globalization and Women's Issues in Panama City: A Comparative Inquiry." *The University of Miami Inter-American Law Review* 41, no. 1 (2009): 19–41.

Babcock, Elizabeth C., and Dennis Conway. "Why International Migration Has Important Consequences for the Development of Belize." *Yearbook (Conference of Latin Americanist Geographers)* 26 (2000): 71–86.

Barry, Tom. *El Salvador: A Country Guide*. Albuquerque, NM: The Inter-Hemispheric Education Resource Center, 1990.

Bastos, Santiago. "¿Exclusiones renovadas? Tierra y migración en el siglo XXI." In *Colección Lectura a Fondo 2*, 5–33. Guatemala: Agencia Española de Cooperación para el Desarrollo, 2017.

Batz, Giovanni. "U.S. Policy Toward Central America Continues Legacy of Displacement." *NACLA*, April 29, 2021. Accessed November 23, 2021, https://nacla.org/news /2021/04/28/us-policy-central-america-migration-displacement

Baylen, Joseph O. "Sandino: Patriot or Bandit?" *The Hispanic American Historical Review* 31, no. 3 (1951): 394–419.

BBC News. "Nicaragua Timeline." 2012. http://news.bbc.co.uk/2/hi/americas/1225283.stm

Bebbington, Anthony J., Laura Aileen Sauls, Herman Rosa, Benjamin Fash, and Denise Humphreys Bebbington. "Conflicts over Extractivist Policy and the Forest Frontier in Central America." *European Review of Latin American and Caribbean Studies/Revista Europea de Esudios Latinoamreicanos y Del Caribe*, no. 106 (2018): 103–32. https://www.jstor.org/stable/26608622.

Belisle Dempsey, Isabeau J. "Framing the Center: Belize and Panamá within the Central American Imagined Community." *SUURJ: Seattle University Undergraduate Research Journal* 4, no. 13 (2020). https://scholarworks.seattleu.edu/suurj/vol4/iss1/13

Betz, Joseph. "Sandinista Nicaragua as a Deweyan Social Experiment." *Transactions of the Charles S. Peirce Society* 36, no. 1 (2000): 25–47.

Beverly, John. "El Salvador." *Social Text* 5 (1982): 55–72.

Biderman, Jaime. "The Development of Capitalism in Nicaragua: A Political Economic History." *Latin American Perspectives* 10, no. 1 (1983): 7–32. http://www.jstor.org.proxy.seattleu.edu/stable/2633361

Blandón, María Teresa. "Los cuerpos del feminismo nicaragüense." In *Antología del pensamiento crítico nicaragüense contemporáneo*, edited by Juan Pablo Gómez and Camilo Antillón, 353–370. Buenos Aires: Consejo Latinoamericano de Ciencias Sociales, 2017.

Blum, William. "Killing Hope: U.S. Military and CIA Interventions since World War II." London: Zed Books, 2014.

Bolland, O. Nigel. *Colonialism and Resistance in Belize: Essays in Historical Sociology*. Belize City: Cubola, 1988.

Bonner, Donna M. "Garifuna Children's Language Shame: Ethnic Stereotypes, National Affiliation, and Transnational Immigration as Factors in Language Choice in Southern Belize." *Language in Society* 30, no. 1 (2001): 81–96.

Booth, John A., Christine J. Wade, and Thomas W. Walker. *Understanding Central America: Global Forces, Rebellion, and Change*. Boulder, CO: Westview Press, 2015.

Bourgois, Philippe. "The Black Diaspora in Costa Rica: Upward Mobility and Ethnic Discrimination." *Nieuwe West-Indische Gids / New West Indian Guide* 60, no. 3/4 (1986): 149–165.

Brady, Scott. "Honduras' Transisthmian Corridor: A Case of Undeveloped Potential in Colonial Central America." *Revista Geográfica* 133 (2003): 127–151.

Brockett, Charles D. "An Illusion of Omnipotence: U.S Policy toward Guatemala, 1954–1960." *Latin American Politics and Society* 44, no. 1 (2002): 91–126.

Brown Scott, James. "The Treaty Between Colombia and the United States." *The American Journal of International Law* 15, no. 3 (1921): 430–439.

Brysk, Alison. "Global Good Samaritans? Human Rights Policy in Costa Rica." *Global Governance* 11, no. 4 (2005): 445–466.

Camarota, Steven A., and Karen Zeigler. *Central American Immigrant Population Increased Nearly 28-Fold since 1970*. November 1, 2018. https://cis.org/Report/Central-American-Immigrant-Population-Increased-Nearly-28Fold-1970

Campbell, Augustus, and Colin D. Campbell. "Crossing the Isthmus of Panama, 1849: The Letters of Dr. Augustus Campbell." *California History* 78, no. 4 (1999): 226–237.

Campo-Engelstein, Lisa, and Karen Meagher. "Costa Rica's 'White Legend': How Racial Narratives Undermine its Health Care System." *Developing World Bioethics* 11, no. 2 (2011): 99–107.

Carey, David, and M. Gabriela Torres. "Precursors to Femicide: Guatemalan Women in a Vortex of Violence." *Latin American Research Review* 45, no. 3 (2010): 142–164.

Casas-Zamora, Kevin. "The Travails of Development and Democratic Governance in Central America." policy paper. *Foreign Policy at Brookings*, Number 28 (June 2011).

Casaús Arzú, Marta. "El Genocidio: La máxima expresión del racismo en Guatemala: Una interpretación histórica y una reflexión." *Nuevo Mundo Mundos Nuevos* [En ligne]. Colloques, September 23, 2009. Accessed November 27, 2021. https://journals.openedition.org/nuevomundo/57067

Castro Herrera, Guillermo. "On Cattle and Ships: Culture, History and Sustainable Development in Panama." *Environment and History* 7, no. 2 (2001): 201–217.

Castro, Juan, and Manuela Lavinas Picq. "Stateness as Landgrab: A Political History of Maya Dispossession in Guatemala." *American Quarterly* 69, no. 4 (2017): 791–799.

Central Intelligence Agency (CIA). The World Factbook: Ethnic Groups. 2018. https://www.cia.gov/the-world-factbook/field/ethnic-groups/

Chanda, Areendam, C. Justin Cook, and Louis Putterman. "Persistence of Fortune: Accounting for Population Movements, There Was No Post-Columbian Reversal." *American Economic Journal: Macroeconomics* 6, no. 3 (2014): 1–28.

Charlip, Julie A., and E. Bradford Burns. *Latin America: An Interpretive History.* 9th Ed. Upper Saddle River, NJ: Prentice Hall, 2011.

Chomsky, Aviva. *Central America's Forgotten History: Revolution, Violence, and the Roots of Migration.* Boston: Beacon Press, 2021.

Christian, Michelle. "'. . . Latin America without the downside': Racial Exceptionalism and Global Tourism in Costa Rica." *Ethnic and Racial Studies* 36, no. 10 (2013): 1599–1619.

Clayton, Lawrence A. "The Nicaragua Canal in the Nineteenth Century: Prelude to American Empire in the Caribbean." *Journal of Latin American Studies* 19, no. 2 (1987): 323–352.

Comisión Interamericana de Derechos Humanos. *Nicaragua: Concentración del poder y debilitamiento del Estado de Derecho.* Organización de Estados Americanos, OEA/Ser.L/V/II (2021). Accessed November 23, 2021. http://www.oas.org/es/cidh/informes/pdfs/2021_Nicaragua-ES.pdf

Comisión Internacional contra la Impunidad en Guatemala (CICIG). "Diálogos por el fortalecimiento de la justicia y el combate a la impunidad en Guatemala." 2019. Accessed August 12, 2019. https://www.cicig.org/comunicados-2019-c/informe-dialogos-por-el-fortalecimiento-de-la-justicia/

Commission for Historical Clarification (CEH). *Guatemala Memory of Silence: Conclusions and Recommendations.* 1999. https://hrdag.org/wp-content/uploads/2013/01/CEHreport-english.pdf

Cooke, Richard G., and Beatriz Elena Rovira. "Historical Archaeology in Panama City." *Archaeology* 36, no. 2 (1983): 51–57.

Cosgrove, Serena. *Leadership from the Margins: Women and Civil Society Organizations in Argentina, Chile, and El Salvador.* Piscataway, NJ: Rutgers University Press, 2010.

Cosgrove, Serena, and Benjamin W. Curtis. *Understanding Global Poverty: Causes, Solutions, and Capabilities.* 2nd ed. New York: Routledge, 2022.

Cosgrove, Serena, José Idiáquez, Leonard Joseph Bent, and Andrew Gorvetzian. *Surviving the Americas: Garifuna Persistence from Nicaragua to New York City.* Cincinnati: University of Cincinnati Press, 2021.

Cosgrove, Serena, and Kristi Lee. "Persistence and Resistance: Women's Leadership and Ending Gender-Based Violence in Guatemala." *Seattle Journal for Social Justice* 14, no. 2 (2015): 309–332.

Cunin, Elisabeth, and Odile Hoffmann. "From Colonial Domination to the Making of the Nation: Ethno-Racial Categories in Censuses and Reports and their Political Uses in Belize, 19th-20th Centuries." *Caribbean Studies* 41, no. 2 (2013): 31–60.

Cunningham Wren, Lottie. "Pueblos indígenas y afrodescendientes. La lucha por sus derechos humanos". In *Anhelos de un nuevo horizonte: aportes para una Nicaragua democrática*, edited by Alberto Cortés Ramos, Umanzor López and Ludwig Moncada, 633-646. San José: Facultad Latinoamericana de Ciencias Sociales, 2020.

D. K. M. K. "Costa Rica and the Invasion: Difficulties of a Central American Democracy." *The World Today* 11, no. 3 (1955): 129–138.

Denevan, William M. "The Pristine myth: The Landscape of the Americas in 1492." *Annals of the Association of American Geographers* 82, no. 3 (1992): 369–385.

Denevan, William M., ed. *The Native Population of the Americas in 1492*. Madison: University of Wisconsin Press, 1992.

Díaz Arias, David, and Ronald Soto Quirós. "*Mestizaje*, indígenas e identidad nacional en Centroamérica: De la Colonia a las Repúblicas Liberales." *Cuaderno de Ciencias Sociales* 143 (2007). San José, Costa Rica: Sede Académica Costa Rica.

Díaz Arias, David, and Viales, Ronny J. "Sociedad imaginada: el ideario político de la integración excluyente en Centroamérica: 1821–1870." In *Historia de las desigualdades sociales en América Central. Una visión interdisciplinaria siglos XVIII- XXI*, edited by Ronny J. Viales and David Díaz Arias, 197- 218. San José, Costa Rica: Universidad de Costa Rica Centro de Investigaciones Históricas de América Central, 2016.

Donato, Katherine M. "U.S. Migration from Latin America: Gendered Patterns and Shifts." *Annals of the American Academy of Political and Social Science* 630 (2010): 78–92.

Dunkerley, James. *The Long War: Dictatorship and Revolution in El Salvador*. London: Junction Books, 1982.

Dym, Jordana. *From Sovereign Villages to National States: City, State, and Federation in Central America, 1759–1839*. Albuquerque: University of New Mexico Press, 2006.

Dym, Jordana, and Christophe Belaubre. *Politics, Economy, and Society in Bourbon Central America, 1759–1821*. Boulder: University Press of Colorado, 2007.

Easterly, William, and Ross Levine. "The European Origins of Economic Development." *Journal of Economic Growth* 21 (2016): 225–257.

Education Policy and Data Center. *Violence Threatens Educational Gains in Central America*. Accessed October 19, 2019. https://www.epdc.org/epdc-data-points/violence-threatens-educational-gains-central-america

Eisenmann, I. Roberto. "The Struggle Against Noriega." *Journal of Democracy* 1, no. 1 (1990): 41–46.

Elvir, Lety. *Women's Poems of Protest and Resistance: Honduras, 2009–2014*. Washington, DC: Casasola LLC, 2015.

England, Sarah. *Afro Central Americans in New York City: Garifuna Tales of Transnational Movements in Racialized Space*. Gainesville: University Press of Florida, 2006.

Equipo Maiz. *Historia de El Salvador: De como los guanacos no sucumbieron a los infames ultrajes de españoles, criollos, gringos y otras plagas*. San Salvador: Algier's Impresores S.A. de C.V, 1989.

Equipo Maiz. *Los acuerdos de paz*. San Salvador, 1992.

Erquicia, José Heriberto, and Rina Cáceres. *Relaciones interétnicas: Afrodescendientes en Centroamérica*. San Salvador: Universidad Tecnológica de El Salvador, 2017.

Euraque, Darío A. "Apuntes para una historiografía del *mestizaje* en Honduras." *Iberoamericana (2001-)* 5, no. 19 (2005): 105–117.

Evans, George. "The Deaths of Somoza." *World Literature Today* 81, no. 3 (2007): 36–43.

Everingham, Mark. "Neoliberalism in a New Democracy: Elite Politics and State Reform in Nicaragua." *The Journal of Developing Areas* 32, no. 2 (1998): 237–264. http://www.jstor.org.proxy.seattleu.edu/stable/4192756

Everitt, J. C. "The Torch is Passed: Neocolonialism in Belize." *Caribbean Quarterly* 33, no. 3/4 (1987): 42–59.

Farah, Douglas. "Papers Show U.S. Role in Guatemalan Abuses." *The Washington Post*. March 11, 1999. https://www.washingtonpost.com/wp-srv/inatl/daily/march99/guatemala11.htm

Few, Martha. *Women Who Live Evil Lives: Gender, Religion, and the Politics of Power in Colonial Guatemala*. Austin: University of Texas Press, 2002.

Finzer, Erin S. "Modern Women Intellectuals and the Sandino Rebellion: Carmen Sobalvarro and Aura Rostand." *Latin American Research Review* 56, no. 2 (2021): 457–71. https://doi.org/10.25222/larr.878.

Fischer, Edward F., and R. McKenna Brown. *Maya Cultural Activism in Guatemala*. Austin: University of Texas Press, Institute of Latin American Studies, 1996.

Flores, Walter, and Miranda Rivers. "Frenar la corrupción después del conflicto: Movilización anticorrupción en Guatemala." *Special Reports* 482. Washington: United States Institute of Peace, 2021.

Foster, Lynn V. *A Brief History of Central America*. 2nd ed. New York: Checkmark Books, 2007.

Frank-Vitale, Amelia, and Margarita Núñez Chaim. 2020. "'Lady Frijoles': Las caravanas centroamericanas y el poder de la hípervisibilidad de la migración indocumentada." *Entre Diversidades* 7, no. 1 (14) (2020): 37- 61.

Gabriel, S., and V. M. Satish. "U.S. Intervention in Nicaragua: A Success or Failure?" *The Indian Journal of Political Science* 51, no. 4 (1990): 565–579. http://www.jstor.org.proxy.seattleu.edu/stable/41855523

Gandaseguí, Marco A. "Una historia política de Panamá: Movimientos populares y militarismo en Panamá." In *Revista Conjeturas Sociológicas*. San Salvador: Universidad de El Salvador, 2014.

Gender Equality Observatory for Latin America and the Caribbean. "Femicide, the Most Extreme Expression of Violence against Women." oig.cepal website, November 15, 2018. Accessed July 20, 2019. https://oig.cepal.org/sites/default/files/nota_27_eng.pdf

Global Impunity Dimensions. *GII-2017 Global Impunity Index*. August 2017. https://www.udlap.mx/cesij/files/IGI-2017_eng.pdf

Global Witness. "Honduras: The Deadliest Country in the World for Environmental Activism." Global Witness. March 14, 2017. https://www.globalwitness.org/en/campaigns/environmental-activists/honduras-deadliest-country-world-environmental-activism/

Gobat, Michel. *Confronting the American Dream: Nicaragua under U.S. Imperial Rule*. Durham, NC: Duke University Press, 2007.

Goett, Jennifer. "Beyond Left and Right: Grassroots Social Movements and Nicaragua's Civic Insurrection." *LASA FORUM* 49, no. 4 (2019): 25–31.

Gómez Menjívar, Jennifer Carolina. "Precious Water, Priceless Words, Fluidity and Mayan Experience on the Guatemalan-Belizean Border." *Diálogo* 19, no. 1 (2016): 23–32.

Gordillo, Enrique, and Tania Sagastume. "Historia económica de Guatemala, 1944-2000." In *Historia de Guatemala, 1944- 2000,* edited by Gustavo Berganza, 186–247. Guatemala: Asociación de Investigación y Estudios Sociales–, 2004.

Gordon, Edmund T. *Disparate Diasporas: Identity and Politics in an African Nicaraguan Community.* Austin: University of Texas Press, Institute of Latin American Studies, 1998.

Gould, Jeffrey L., and Aldo Lauria-Santiago. *To Rise in Darkness: Revolution, Repression, and Memory in El Salvador, 1920–1932.* Durham, NC: Duke University Press, 2008.

Gould, Jeffrey. "Gender, Politics, and the Triumph of *Mestizaje* in Early 20th Century Nicaragua." *Journal of Latin American Anthropology* 2, no. 1 (1996): 4–33.

Grandin, Greg. "Everyday Forms of State Decomposition: Quetzaltenango, Guatemala, 1954." *Bulletin of Latin American Research* 19, no. 3 (2000): 303–20.

Grandin, Greg. *The Blood of Guatemala: A History of Race and Nation.* Latin America Otherwise. Durham, NC: Duke University Press, 2000.

Grupo Guatemalteco de Mujeres (GGM). "Datos estadísticos: Muertes Violentas de Mujeres-MVM y República de Guatemala Actualizado (20/05/19)." *GGM* website, May 20, 2019. Accessed July 20, 2019. http://ggm.org.gt/wp-content/uploads/2019/06/Datos-Estad%C3%ADsticos-MVM-ACTUALIZADO-20-DE-MAYO-DE-2019.pdf

Gudmundson, Lowell, and Héctor Lindo-Fuentes. *Central America, 1821–1871: Liberalism before Liberal Reform.* Tuscaloosa: University of Alabama Press, 1995.

Gudmundson, Lowell, and Justin Wolfe. *Blacks and Blackness in Central America: Between Race and Place.* Durham, NC: Duke University Press, 2010.

Guerrón-Montero, Carla. "Racial Democracy and Nationalism in Panama." *Ethnology* 45, no. 3 (2006): 209–228.

Hale, Charles R. "Does Multiculturalism Menace? Governance, Cultural Rights and the Politics of Identity in Guatemala." *Journal of Latin American Studies* 34 (2002): 485–524.

Hamilton, Nora and Norma Stoltz Chinchilla. "Central American Migration: A Framework for Analysis." *Latin American Research Review* 26, no. 1 (1991): 75–110.

Hammond, Norman. "The Prehistory of Belize." *Journal of Field Archaeology* 9, no. 3 (1982): 349–362.

Harpelle, Ronald N. "Racism and Nationalism in the Creation of Costa Rica's Pacific Coast Banana Enclave." *The Americas* 56, no. 3 (2000): 29–51.

Harris, Richard L. "The Revolutionary Transformation of Nicaragua." *Latin American Perspectives* 14, no. 1 (1987): 3–18.

Hawkins, Timothy. "A War of Words: Manuel Montúfar, Alejandro Marure, and the Politics of History in Guatemala." *The Historian* 64, no. 3/4 (2002): 513–533.

Herrera Rodríguez, Omar. "La geopolítica contemporánea de Estados Unidos y el fin de Centroamérica." *Temas de Nuestra América* 33, no. 62 (2017): 65- 84.

Herrera, Robinson A. "'Por Que No Sabemos Firmar': Black Slaves in Early Guatemala." *The Americas* 57, no. 2 (2000): 247–267.

Holden, Robert. *Armies without Nations: Public Violence and State Formation in Central America, 1821–1960*. New York: Oxford University Press, 2004.

Homero, Aridjis. "Foreword: All was a Feathered Dream." In *Popol Vuh: A Retelling*, by Ian Stavans. Brooklyn, NY: Restless Books, xiii-xxxii.

Hornbeck, J. F. "The Dominican Republic-Central America- United States Free Trade Agreement (CAFTA- DR): Developments in Trade and Investment." *Congressional Research Service*, April 9, 2012. doi:https://fas.org/sgp/crs/row/R42468.pdf.

Horton, Lynn R. "Buying Up Nature: Economic and Social Impacts of Costa Rica's Ecotourism Boom." *Latin American Perspectives* 36, no. 3 (2009): 93–107.

Høvik, Tord, and Solveig Aas. "Demilitarization in Costa Rica: A Farewell to Arms?" *Journal of Peace Research* 18, no. 4 (1981): 333–351.

Huesmann, James L. "The Chinese in Costa Rica, 1855–1897." *The Historian* 53, no. 4 (1991): 711–720.

Hume, Mo. "The Myths of Violence: Gender, Conflict, and Community in El Salvador." *Latin American Perspectives* 35, no. 5 (2008): 59–76. http://www.jstor.org.proxy .seattleu.edu/stable/27648120.

Immerman, Richard H. "Guatemala as Cold War History." *Political Science Quarterly* 95, no. 4 (1981): 629–653.

Inman, Crist. "Tourism in Costa Rica: The Challenge of Competitiveness." March 2002. Accessed February 3, 2022. https://www.incae.edu/sites/default/files/cen653.pdf

Inter-American Commission on Human Rights. "Nicaragua: Concentración del poder y debilitamiento del Estado de Derecho." 2021. Accessed January 25, 2022. https:// www.oas.org/es/cidh/informes/pdfs/2021_Nicaragua-ES.pdf

International Monetary Fund. "Report for Selected Countries and Subjects." 2018. Accessed February 2018.

Janzen, Randall. "From Less War to More Peace: Guatemala's Journey since 1996." *Peace Research* 40 no. 1 (2008): 55–75.

"Joe Biden's Other Headache; Central America." *The Economist*, August 28, 2021, 26.

Johnson, Melissa A. "The Making of Race and Place in Nineteenth-Century British Honduras." *Environmental History* 8 no. 4 (2003): 598–617.

Jonas, Susanne, and Nestor Rodríguez. *Guatemala-U.S. Migration: Transforming Regions*, Austin: University of Texas Press, 2014.

Kampwirth, Karen. "Abortion, Antifeminism, and the Return of Daniel Ortega: In Nicaragua, Leftist Politics?" *Latin American Perspectives* 35 no. 6 (2008): 122–136. http:// www.jstor.org.proxy.seattleu.edu/stable/27648142

Karl, Terry Lynn. "El Salvador's Negotiated Revolution." *Foreign Affairs* 71, no. 2 (1992): 147–164. doi:10.2307/20045130.

Karlsson, Marianna, Bob van Oort, and Bård Romstad. "What We Have Lost and Cannot Become: Societal Outcomes of Coastal Erosion in Southern Belize." *Ecology and Society* 20, no. 1 (2015): 1–14.

Key, Carol, and Vijayan K. Pillai. "Tourism and Ethnicity in Belize: A Qualitative Study." *International Review of Modern Sociology* 33, no. 1 (2007): 129–150.

Kinzer, Stephen. *Overthrow: America's Century of Regime Change from Hawaii to Iraq*. New York: Times Books/Henry Holt, 2006.

Komisaruk, Catherine. *Labor and Love in Guatemala: The Eve of Independence*. Palo Alto: Stanford University Press, 2013.

Kramer, Wendy, W. George Lovell, and Christopher H. Lutz. "Encomienda and Settlement: Towards a Historical Geography of Early Colonial Guatemala." *Yearbook (Conference of Latin Americanist Geographers)* 16 (1990): 67–72.

Kunz, Josef L. "Guatemala vs. Great Britain: In Re Belice." *The American Journal of International Law* 40, no. 2 (1946): 383–90. doi:10.2307/2193198.

Labrador, Gabriel, and Julia Gararrete. "Bukele Responds to Avalanche of International Criticism: 'The People Voted for This.'" *NACLA*, May 7, 2021. Accessed November 29, 2021. https://nacla.org/news/2021/05/07/bukele-international-criticism-technical -coup

LaFeber, Walter. *Inevitable Revolutions: The United States in Central America*. New York: W.W. Norton, 1993.

Lange, Frederick W., and Richard M. Accola. "Metallurgy in Costa Rica." *Archaeology* 32, no. 5 (1979): 26–33. http://www.jstor.org.proxy.seattleu.edu/stable/41726374

Lange, Matthew, James Mahoney, and Matthias Vom Hau. "Colonialism and Development: A Comparative Analysis of Spanish and British Colonies." *American Journal of Sociology* 111, no. 5 (2006): 1412–1462. https://doi.org/10.1086/499510

Langley, Lester D. *The Banana Wars: United States Intervention in the Caribbean, 1898–1934*. Wilmington, DE: Scholarly Resources, 2002.

Langley, Lester D. "Negotiating New Treaties with Panama: 1936." *The Hispanic American Historical Review* 48, no. 2 (1968): 220–233.

Lara Pinto, Gloria, and George Hasemann. "Honduras antes del año 1500: Una visión regional de su evolución cultural tardía." *Revista de Arqueología Americana* 8 (1993): 9–49.

Larson, Elizabeth M. "Nicaraguan Refugees in Costa Rica from 1980–1993." *Yearbook (Conference of Latin Americanist Geographers)* 19 (1993): 67–79.

Leavitt-Alcántara, Brianna. *Alone at the Altar: Single Women and Devotion in Guatemala, 1670–1870*. Palo Alto, CA: Stanford University Press, 2018.

Legler, Thomas. "Learning the Hard Way: Defending Democracy in Honduras." *International Journal* 65, no. 3 (2010): 601–618.

Lentz, Mark W. "Black Belizeans and Fugitive Mayas: Interracial Encounters on the Edge of Empire, 1750–1803." *The Americas* 70, no. 4 (2014): 645–675.

Leogrande, William M. "Making the Economy Scream: U.S. Economic Sanctions against Sandinista Nicaragua." *Third World Quarterly* 17, no. 2 (1996): 329–348.

Leonard, Thomas M. *The History of Honduras*. Santa Barbara, CA: ABC-CLIO, 2011.

León-Gómez Sonet, Marisa. "Immigration Policy Must Look Beyond the Border." *NACLA*, June 8, 2021. Accessed November 23, 2021. https://nacla.org/news /2021/06/08/immigration-policy-must-look-beyond-border

Lloyd, Siobhán. "Guatemala." *Socialist Lawyer* 64 (2013): 38–40.

Longley, Kyle. "Peaceful Costa Rica, the First Battleground: The United States and the Costa Rican Revolution of 1948." *The Americas* 50, no. 2 (1993): 149–175.

Looper, Matthew G. "New Perspectives on the Late Classic Political History of Quirigua, Guatemala." *Ancient Mesoamerica* 10, no. 2 (1999): 263–280.

Loperena, Christopher A. "Honduras Is Open for Business: Extractivist Tourism as Sustainable Development in the Wake of Disaster?" *Journal of Sustainable Tourism* 25, no. 5 (2017): 618–633.

Lovell, W. George, and Christopher H. Lutz. "'A Dark Obverse': Maya Survival in Guatemala: 1520–1994." *Geographical Review* 86, no. 3 (1996): 398–407.

Lovell, W. George, and Christopher H. Lutz. "The Historical Demography of Colonial Central America." *Yearbook (Conference of Latin Americanist Geographers)* 17/18 (1990): 127–138.

Lovell, W. George. "The Century After Independence: Land and Life in Guatemala, 1821, 1920." *Canadian Journal of Latin American and Caribbean Studies / Revue Canadienne Des études Latino-américaines Et Caraïbes* 19, no. 37/38 (1994): 243–260.

Lundgren, Nancy. "Children, Race, and Inequality: The Colonial Legacy in Belize." *Journal of Black Studies* 23, no. 1 (1992): 86–106.

Lutz, Christopher H. *Santiago de Guatemala, 1541–1773: City, Caste, and the Colonial Experience*. Norman: University of Oklahoma Press, 1994.

Mack, Taylor E. "Contraband Trade Through Trujillo, Honduras, 1720s–1782." *Yearbook (Conference of Latin Americanist Geographers)* 24 (1988): 45–56.

Macpherson, Anne S. "Citizens v. Clients: Working Women and Colonial Reform in Puerto Rico and Belize, 1932–45." *Journal of Latin American Studies* 35, no. 2 (2003): 279–310.

Manz, Beatriz. "The Continuum of Violence in Post-war Guatemala." *Social Analysis* 52, no. 2 (2008): 151–164.

Marks, Frederick W. "The CIA and Castillo Armas in Guatemala, 1954: New Clues to an Old Puzzle." *Diplomatic History* 14, no. 1 (1990): 67–86. http://www.jstor.org.proxy.seattleu.edu/stable/24912032

Martín Álvarez, Alberto. "Desafiando la hegemonía neoliberal: Ideologías de cambio radical en la Centroamérica de posguerra." *Historia Actual Online* 25 (2011): 111- 123.

Martín, Lara Moragrega. "Tourist Expansion and Development of Rural Communities: The Cast of Monteverde, Costa Rica." *Mountain Research and Development* 24, no. 3 (2004): 202–205.

Martínez Peláez, Severo. *La Patria del Criollo: An Interpretation of Colonial Guatemala*. Durham, NC: Duke University Press, 2009.

Martínez Peñate, Oscar. *El Salvador: Historia General*. San Salvador: Editorial Nuevo Enfoque Impreso, 2002.

Martínez-Alier, Joan. "Conflictos ambientales en Centroamérica y las Antillas: Un rápido toxic tour." *Ecología Política* 60 (2020): 43- 54.

Maurer, Noel, and Carlos Yu. "What T. R. Took: The Economic Impact of the Panama Canal, 1903–1937." *The Journal of Economic History* 68, no. 3 (2008): 686–721.

McSweeney, Kendra. "A Demographic Profile of the Tawahka Amerindians of Honduras." *Geographical Review* 92, no. 3 (2002): 398–414.

Meding, Holger M. "Historical Archives of the Republic of Panama." *Latin American Research Review* 34 (1999): 129–142.

Méndez, María José. "'The River Told Me': Rethinking Intersectionality from the World of Berta Cáceres." *Capitalism Nature Socialism* 29, no. 1 (2018): 7–24.

Menjívar, Cecilia, and Shannon Drysdale Walsh. "The Architecture of Feminicide: The State, Inequalities, and Everyday Gender Violence in Honduras." *Latin American Research Review* 52 (2017): 221–240.

Menzies, Adam C. J., and Mikael J. Haller. "Embedded Craft Production at the Late Pre-Columbian (A.D. 900—1522) Community of He4 (El Hatillo), Central Region of Panama." *Canadian Journal of Archaeology* 36, no. 1 (2012): 198–140.

Miller, Michael J. "Biodiversity Policy Making in Costa Rica: Pursing Indigenous and Peasant Rights." *The Journal of Environment & Development* 15, no. 4 (2006): 359–381.

Millett, Richard L. "The Aftermath of Intervention: Panama 1990." *Journal of Interamerican Studies* 32, no. 1 (1990): 1–15.

Moberg, Mark. "Structural Adjustment and Rural Development: Inferences from a Belizean Village." *The Journal of Developing Areas* 27, no. 1 (1992): 1–20.

Moholy-Nagy, Hattula. *Historical Archaeology at Tikal, Guatemala.* Tikal Reports, no. 37. Philadelphia: University Museum Publications, 2012.

Molina, Iván, and Steven Palmer. "Popular Literacy in a Tropical Democracy: Costa Riva 1850–1950." *Past & Present* 184 (2004): 169–207.

Montgomery, Tommie Sue. *Revolution in El Salvador: From Civil Strife to Civil Peace.* San Francisco: Westview Press, 1995.

Montoute, Annita. "CARICOM's External Engagements: Prospects and Challenges for Caribbean Regional Integration and Development." German Marshall Fund of the United States, 2015. http://www.jstor.org/stable/resrep18854

Montoya, Rosario. *Gendered Scenarios of Revolution: Making New Men and New Women in Nicaragua, 1975–2000.* 1st ed. Tucson: University of Arizona Press, 2012.

Mora, María Jesús. "Costa Rica Has Welcoming Policies for Migrants, but Nicaraguans Face Subtle Barriers," Migration Policy Institute. November 5, 2021. https://www.migrationpolicy.org/article/costa-rica-nicaragua-migrants-subtle-barriers

Murray, Kevin. "El Salvador: Peace on Trial." Oxford: Oxfam Publications, 1997.

Musalo, Karen, and Blaine Bookey. "Crimes without Punishment: An Update on Violence against Women and Impunity in Guatemala." *Social Justice* 40, no. 4 (2014): 106–17.

Narváez, Benjamín N. "Re-envisioning Caribbean Costa Rica: Chinese-West Indian Interaction in Limón during the Late Nineteenth and Early Twentieth Centuries." *New West Indian Guide* 95 (2021): 1–32.

Narváez, Benjamín N. "The Power and Pitfalls of Patronage: Chinese Immigrants in Costa Rica during the Era of Exclusion, 1897–1943." *Journal of Migration History* 6 (2020): 209–235.

Navas, María Candelaria. "Los movimientos de mujeres y feministas en la transición de posguerra y su aporte a los cambios culturales en El Salvador." *Revista Realidad* 151 (2018): 63–88.

Nelson, Diane M. "Perpetual Creation and Decomposition: Bodies, Gender, and Desire in the Assumptions of a Guatemalan Discourse of *Mestizaje*." *Journal of Latin American Anthropology* 4, no. 1 (1998): 74–111.

Newson, Linda A. "The Demographic Impact of Colonization." In *The Cambridge Economic History of Latin America*, edited by Victor Bulmer-Thomas, John Coatsworth, and Roberto Cortes-Conde, 143–184. Cambridge, UK: Cambridge University Press, 2005.

Newson, Linda. "The Depopulation of Nicaragua in the Sixteenth Century," *Journal of Latin American Studies* 14, no. 2 (1982): 53–286. http://www.jstor.org/stable/156458

Noe-Bustamente, Luis, Antonio Flores, and Sono Shah. "Facts on Hispanics of Salvadoran Origin in the United States, 2017." *Pew Research Center.* Hispanic Trends, 2017. Accessed October 19, 2019. https://www.pewresearch.org/hispanic/fact-sheet/u-s-hispanics-facts-on-salvadoran-origin-latinos/

Nolin Hanlon, Catherine, and Finola Shankar. "Gendered Spaces of Terror and Assault: The Testimonio of REMHI and the Commission for Historical Clarification in Guatemala." *Gender, Place & Culture* 7, no. 3 (2000): 265–286.

Norton, Chris. "Salvador's Duarte backs down on peace talks, further weakening his influence." *The Christian Science Monitor.* January 25, 1985. Accessed January 13, 2022. https://www.csmonitor.com/1985/0125/osiege.html

Oakland Institute. "Nicaragua's Failed Revolution: The Indigenous Struggle for Saneamiento." 2020. Accessed November 30, 2021. https://www.oaklandinstitute.org/sites /oaklandinstitute.org/files/nicaraguas-failed-revolution.pdf

Observatory for the Protection of Human Rights Defenders (OPHRD). *Nicaragua: Joint Briefing: A Year of Violence against Those Defending the Rights of the Mayangna and Miskitu Indigenous Peoples.* January 29, 2021. Accessed November 30, 2021. https:// www.omct.org/en/resources/urgent-interventions/nicaragua-briefing-conjunto -un-a%C3%B1o-de-violencia-sistem%C3%A1tica-contra-quienes-defienden-los -derechos-ind%C3%ADgenas

O'Connor, Allison, Jeanne Batalova, and Jessica Bolter. "Central American Immigrants in the United States." *Migration Policy Institute,* August 15, 2019. Accessed January 31, 2022. https://www.migrationpolicy.org/article/central-american -immigrants-united-states-2017

Open Government Partnership. "Results of Early Open Government Partnership Initiatives." 2016. http://www.opengovpartnership.org/sites/default/files/case-study _Results-OGP-Early-Initiatives_20161201_2.pdf

Organization of American States. "Mission to Support the Fight against Corruption and Impunity in Honduras: About the Mission." 2019. http://www.oas.org/en/spa /dsdsm/maccih/new/mision.asp

Orozco, Manuel. *Recent Trends in Central American Migration.* 2018. https://www .thedialogue.org/wp-content/uploads/2018/05/Recent-Trends-in-Central-American -Migration-1.pdf

Otterstrom, Samuel M. "Nicaraguan Migrants in Costa Rica during the 1990s: Gender Differences and Geographic Expansion." *Journal of Latin American Geography* 7, no. 2 (2008): 7–33.

Palacio, Joseph O. *The Garifuna: A Nation Across Borders.* Benque Viejo del Carmen, Belize: Cubola Productions, 2005.

Palma, Gustavo. "Un presente al que no se llega y un pasado que no nos abandona. Las falencias sociales que se resisten a desaparecer. Geopolítica, democracia inconclusa y exclusión social. Guatemala, 1944–2019." In *Laberintos y bifurcaciones. Historia inmediata de México y América Central, 1940–2020,* edited by Ronny Viales, 69–141. San José: Universidad de Costa Rica—Centro de Investigaciones Históricas de América Central, 2021.

Palmer, Steven. "Getting to Know the Unknown Soldier: Official Nationalism in Liberal Costa Rica, 1880–1900." *Journal of Latin American Studies* 25, no. 1 (1993): 45–72.

Palumbo, Gene, and Elisabeth Malkin. "Mining Ban in El Salvador Prizes Water Over Gold." *The New York Times.* March 29, 2017.

Partlow, Joshua. "They fled violence in Nicaragua by the thousands. What awaits them in Costa Rica?" *The Washington Post,* September 2, 2018. Accessed October 19,

2019. https://www.washingtonpost.com/world/the_americas/they-fled-violence-in
-nicaragua-by-the-thousands-what-awaits-them-in-costa-rica/2018/09/01/51d3f7ee
-a62c-11e8-ad6f-080770dcddc2_story.html?noredirect=on&utm_term
=.939c446dfc13

Patch, Robert. *Indians and the Political Economy of Colonial Central America, 1670–1810*.
Norman: University of Oklahoma Press, 2013.

Patel, Samir S. "Pirates of the Original Panama Canal." *Archaeology* 66, no. 2 (2013): 30–37.

Pattridge, Blake D. "The Catholic Church in Revolutionary Guatemala, 1944–54: A
House Divided." *Journal of Church and State* 36, no. 3 (1994): 527–540.

Payne, Anthony J. "The Belize Triangle: Relations with Britain, Guatemala and the
United States." *Journal of Interamerican Studies and World Affairs* 32, no. 1 (1990):
119–35. doi:10.2307/166131.

Peace, Roger. "Winning Hearts and Minds: The Debate Over U.S. Intervention
in Nicaragua in the 1980s." *Peace & Change* 35, no. 1 (2010): 1–38. doi:10.111
1/j.1468-0130.2009.00611

Penny, H. Glenn. "Latin American Connections: Recent Work on German Interactions
with Latin America." *Central European History* 46 (2013): 362–394.

Penny, H. Glenn. "Migrant Knowledge to Fugitive Knowledge? German Migrants and
Knowledge Production in Guatemala, 1880s - 1945." *Geschichte und Gesellschaft* 43
(2017): 381–412.

Pérez-Brignoli, Héctor. "El Fonógrafo En Los Trópicos: Sobre El Concepto de Banana
Republic En La Obra de O. Henry." *Iberoamericana (2001-)* 6, no. 23 (2006): 127–41.
http://www.jstor.org/stable/41676097

Pérez-Brignoli, Héctor. *El laberinto centroamericano. Los hilos de la historia*. San José,
Costa Rica: Centro de Investigaciones Históricas de América Central, 2017.

Pew Research Center. "Religion in Latin America: Widespread Change in a Historically
Catholic Region." November 13, 2014. https://www.pewforum.org/2014/11/13
/religion-in-latin-america/

Portillo Villeda, Suyapa. *Roots of Resistance: A Story of Gender, Race, and Labor on the
North Coast of Honduras*. Austin: University of Texas Press, 2021.

Posas, Mario. "Movimientos Sociales en Honduras." In *Antología Del Pensamiento Hondureño Contemporáneo*, edited by Ramón Romero, 259–92. Buenos Aires: CLACSO,
2019. https://doi.org/10.2307/j.ctvnp0kc9.16

Preston-Werner, Theresa. "'Gallo Pinto': Tradition, Memory, and Identity in Costa Rican
Foodways." *Journal of American Folklore* 122, no. 483 (2009): 11–27.

Priestley, Georges, and Alberto Barrow. "El movimiento negro en Panamá: Una interpretación histórica y política, 1994–2004." In *Política e identidad: Afrodescendientes
en México y América Central*, edited by Odile Hoffman, 129–155. México: Centro de
Estudios y Centroamericanos, 2010.

Prunier, Delphine Marie, and Sergio Salazar. "Fronteras Centroamericanas Y Movilidad
En 2020. Una Región De Fracturas Y Desigualdades Impactada Por El COVID-19."
Estudios Fronterizos (2021): np.

Quesada, James. "A Brief History of Nicaragua." In *Higher Education at the Crossroads
of State Repression and Neoliberal Reform in Nicaragua: Reflections from a University
under Fire in Nicaragua,* edited by Wendi Bellanger, Serena Cosgrove, and Irina
Carlota Silber. New York: Routledge, 2022.

Rabasa, Angel, John Gordon, Peter Chalk, Audra K. Grant, K. Scott McMahon, Stephanie Pezard, Caroline Reilly, David Ucko, and S. Rebecca Zimmerman. "Counterinsurgency Transition Case Study: El Salvador." In *From Insurgency to Stability: Volume II: Insights from Selected Case Studies,* 75–116. Santa Monica, CA: RAND Corporation, 2010. http://www.jstor.org.proxy.seattleu.edu/stable/10.7249/mg1111-2osd.12

Revels, Craig S. "Coffee in Nicaragua: Introduction and Expansion in the Nineteenth Century." *Yearbook (Conference of Latin Americanist Geographers)* 26 (2000): 17–28.

Robb Taylor, Deborah. *The Times and Life of Bluefields: An Intergenerational Dialogue.* Managua: Academia de Geografia e Historia de Nicaragua, 2005.

Robles Santana, Aránzazu. "¿Ciudadanas? Mujeres indígenas en Costa Rica: Problemática historia e historiográfica sobre su acceso a la ciudadanía." *Diálogos, Revista Electrónica de Historia* 13, no. 2 (2012): 48–67.

Rocha, José Luis. "Evolución de la ilegalidad migratoria de los Centroamericanos vista desde un censo, la geopolítica y los modelos migratorios." In *Migraciones en América Central: políticas, territorios y actores,* edited by Carlos Sandoval, 119–139. San José: Universidad de Costa Rica, 2016.

Rocha, José Luis. "Tres años de represión y exilio de los nicaragüenses: 2018–2021," CETRI, November 12, 2021. Accessed November 23, 2021. https://www.cetri.be/Tres -anos-de-represion-y-exilio-de

Rocha, José Luis. *Expulsados de la globalización: Políticas migratorias y deportados centroamericanos.* Managua: IHNCA-UCA, 2010.

Rojas, Donald. "Indígenas Ticos Pierden Tierras." *Ambien-Tico,* October 10, 2001. Accessed January 13, 2022. https://www.ambientico.una.ac.cr/revista-ambientico /indigenas-ticos-pierden-tierras/

Romero Vargas, Germán. *Las estructuras sociales de Nicaragua en el siglo XVIII.* Managua: Vanguardia, 1988.

Romero Vargas, Germán. *Las sociedades del Atlántico en Nicaragua en los siglos XVII y XVIII.* Managua: Fondo de Promoción Cultural-BANIC, 1995.

Roniger, Luis. *Transnational Politics in Central America.* Gainesville: University of Florida Press, 2013.

Roque Baldovinos, Ricardo. "Nayib Bukele: Populismo e implosión democrática en El Salvador." *Andamios* 18, no. 46 (2021): 231- 253.

Rosenberg, Mark B. "Narcos and Politicos: The Politics of Drug Trafficking in Honduras." *Journal of Interamerican Studies and World Affairs* 30, no. 2/3 (1988): 143–165.

Rossi, Franco D., William A Saturno, and Heather Hurst. "Maya Codex Book Production and the Politics of Expertise: Archaeology of a Classic Period Household at Xultun, Guatemala." American Anthropologist 117, no. 1 (2015): 116–32.

Rubenberg, Cheryl. "Israel and Guatemala: Arms, Advice and Counterinsurgency." *MERIP Middle East Report* 140 (1986): 16–44. doi:10.2307/3012026

Rueda Estrada, Verónica. "Movilizaciones campesinas en Nicaragua (1990- 2018): De los Rearmados a los Autoconvocados." *Cuadernos Intercambio* 16, no. 2 (2019):1–33. https://revistas.ucr.ac.cr/index.php/intercambio/article/view/37499/38535

Ruhl, Mark J. "Agrarian Structure and Political Stability in Honduras." *Journal of Interamerican Studies* 26, no. 1 (1984): 33–68.

Ruiz, Amaru, and Mónica López Baltodano. "Las luchas del movimiento ambientalista de Nicaragua en el siglo XXI." In *Anhelos de un nuevo horizonte: aportes para una*

Nicaragua democrática, edited by Alberto Cortés Ramos, Umanzor López, and Ludwig Moncada, 609- 632. San José: Facultad Latinoamericana de Ciencias Sociales, 2020.

Russo, Nancy Felipe, and Angela Pirlott. "Gender-based Violence: Concepts, Methods, and Findings." *Annals of the New York Academy of Sciences* 1087 (2006): 178–205.

Sabonge, Rodolfo, and Ricardo J. Sánchez. "El Canal de Panamá en la economía de América Latina y el Caribe." In *CEPAL – Colección Documentos de proyectos*. Santiago de Chile: United Nations, 2009.

Sagot, Monserrat. "(Re) Definiendo las identidades y la acción política: multitudes diversas, sujetos colectivos y movimientos sociales en la Centroamérica del nuevo milenio." Conferencia Inaugural del Ciclo Lectivo del 2007 Escuela de Antropología y Sociología Universidad de Costa Rica, San José, Costa Rica, 2007.

Sampeck, Kathryn E. "Late Postclassic to Colonial Transformations of the Landscape in the Izalcos Region of Western El Salvador." *Ancient Mesoamerica* 21, no. 2 (2010): 261–282. http://www.jstor.org.proxy.seattleu.edu/stable/26309197

Sanchez, Peter M. "The End of Hegemony? Panama and the United States." *International Journal on World Peace* 19, no. 3 (2002): 57–89.

Sandoval-García, Carlos. "Nicaraguan Immigration to Costa Rica: Tendencies, Policies, and Politics," LASA Forum, Vol. xlvi, no. 4 (Fall 2015): 7–10.

Sanford, Victoria. "From Genocide to Feminicide: Impunity and Human Rights in Twenty-First Century Guatemala." *Journal of Human Rights* 7 (2008): 104–122.

Sanford, Victoria. *Buried Secrets: Truth and Human Rights in Guatemala*. Basingstoke, UK: Palgrave Macmillan, 2003.

Sanford, Victoria. "From *I, Rigoberta* to the Commissioning of Truth: Maya Women and the Reshaping of Guatemalan History." *Cultural Critique* 47 (2001): 16–53.

Schroeder, Michael, and David C. Brooks. "Caudillismo Masked and Modernized: The Remaking of the Nicaraguan State via the Guardia Nacional, 1925–1936." *Middle Atlantic Review of Latin American Studies* 2, no. 2 (2018): 1–32. https://doi.org/10.23870/marlas.169

Seligson, Mitchell A., and John A. Booth. "Political Culture and Regime Type: Evidence from Nicaragua and Costa Rica." *The Journal of Politics* 55 no. 3 (1993): 777–792. http://www.jstor.org.proxy.seattleu.edu/stable/2132001

Sellers-García, Sylvia. *Distance and Documents at the Spanish Empire's Periphery*. Redwood City: Stanford University Press, 2013.

Sharman, Russell Leigh. "Re/Making La Negrita: Culture as an Aesthetic System in Costa Rica." *American Anthropologist* 108, no. 4 (2006): 842–853.

Shepherd, Philip L. "The Tragic Course and Consequences of U.S. Policy in Honduras." *World Policy Journal* 2, no. 1 (1984): 109–154.

Sheptak, Russell N. "Colonial Masca in Motion: Tactics of Persistence of a Honduran Indigenous Community." Doctoral dissertation, Leiden University. 2013.

Shipley, Tyler. "The New Canadian Imperialism and the Military Coup in Honduras." *Latin American Perspectives* 40, no. 5 (2013): 44–61.

Sieder, Rachel. "The Politics of Exception and Military Reformism (1972–1978)." *Journal of Latin American Studies* 27, no. 1 (1995): 99–127.

Siu, Lok. "Cultural Citizenship of Diasporic Chinese in Panama." *Amerasia Journal* 28, no. 2 (2002): 181–202. doi: 10.17953/amer.28.2.117j7810478075h2.

Sobel, Richard. "Contra Aid Fundamentals: Exploring the Intricacies and the Issues." *Political Science Quarterly (Academy of Political Science)* 110, no. 2 (1995): 287.

Solomon, Jeffery H., and سولومون, ج. "Tortured History: Filibustering, Rhetoric, and Walker's 'War in Nicaragua' / التاريخ المعذب: القرصنة والبلاغة وكوتكاو ركوو نع الرحلا في اوجاراكيذ. *Alif: Journal of Comparative Poetics* 31 (2011): 105–132. http://www.jstor.org.proxy.seattleu.edu/stable/23216049

Soto Quirós, Ronaldo. "Discursos y políticas de inmigración en Costa Rica: 1862–1943." *Iberoamericana (2001-)* 19 (2005): 119–133.

Spalding, Rose J. "From the Streets to the Chamber: Social Movements and the Mining Ban in El Salvador." *European Review of Latin American and Caribbean Studies | Revista Europea de Estudios Latinoamericanos y del Caribe*, no. 106 (2018): 47–74. https://doi.org/10.32992/erlacs.10377

Sprenkels, Ralph. *After Insurgency: Revolution and Electoral Politics in El Salvador.* Notre Dame, IN: University of Notre Dame Press, 2018.

Stanger, Francis Merriman. "National Origins in Central America." *The Hispanic American Historical Review* 12 no. 1 (1932): 18–45. doi:10.2307/2506428

Sullivan-González, Douglass. "'A Chosen People': Religious Discourse and the Making of the Republic of Guatemala, 1821–1871." *The Americas* 54, no. 1 (1997): 17–38.

Sutter, Paul S. "Triumphalism and Unruliness during the Construction of the Panama Canal." *RCC Perspectives* 3 (2015): 19–24.

Swanson, Jordan. "Unnatural Disasters: Public Health Lessons from Honduras." *Harvard International Review* 22, no. 1 (2000): 32–35.

Tedlock, Dennis. "Reading the Popul Vuh." *Conjunctions* 3 (1982): 176–185.

Thaler, Kai M. "Nicaragua: A Return to Caudillismo." *Journal of Democracy* 28, no. 2 (2017): 157–69. https://doi.org/10.1353/jod.2017.0032

"The Pre-Columbian History of Guatemala." *Science* 6, no. 149 (2001): 514–515.

Theodossopoulos, Dimitrios. "With or Without Gringos: When Panamanians Talk about the United States and Its Citizens." *The International Journal of Social and Cultural Practice* 54, no. 1 (2010): 52–70.

Thorndike, Tony. "The Conundrum of Belize: An Anatomy of a Dispute." *Social and Economic Studies* 32, no. 2 (1983): 65–102.

Thorp, Rosemary, Corinne Caumartin, and George Gray-Molina. "Inequality, Ethnicity, Political Mobilisation and Political Violence in Latin America: The Cases of Bolivia, Guatemala and Peru." *Bulletin of Latin American Research* 25, no. 4 (2006), 453–480. http://www.jstor.org.proxy.seattleu.edu/stable/27733878

"Thousands dead as quakes strike Nicaraguan city." December 24, 1972. *New York Times.* Accessed January 25, 2022. https://www.nytimes.com/1972/12/24/archives /thousands-dead-as-quakes-strike-nicaraguan-city-capital-battered.html

Tienda, Marta, and Susana M. Sánchez. "Latin American Immigration to the United States." *Daedalus* 142, no. 3 (2013): 48–64.

Todd, Molly. "Race, Nation, and West Indian Immigration to Honduras, 1890–1940 (review)." *Journal of World History* 23, no. 2 (2012): 451–454.

Torres-Rivas, Edelberto. *Revoluciones sin cambios revolucionarios: Ensayos sobre la crisis en Centroamérica.* Guatemala: F&G Editores, 2011.

Torres-Rivas, Edelberto. *History and Society in Central America.* Austin: University of Texas Press, 1993.

Transparency International. *Corruption Perceptions Index 2018*. 2018. https://www
.transparency.org/cpi2018

United States Agency for International Development (USAID). "U.S. Foreign Aid
by Country: Nicaragua." 2017. Explorer.usaid.gov/cd/NIC?fiscal_year=2017
&measure=Disbursements.

U.S. Embassy in Nicaragua. "History of Diplomatic Relations (1911-Present)." Accessed
October 19, 2019. ni.usembassy.gov/our-relationship/policy-history/current-issues/

Vásquez Ruiz, Rolando. "Los sucesos de 1932: ¿Complot comunista, motín indígena o
protesta subalterna? Una revisión historiográfica." *Revista de Humanidades* 5, no. 3
(2014): 133–196. http://ri.ues.edu.sv/id/eprint/7791/2/7.pdf

Velásquez Carrillo, Carlos. "La reconsolidación del régimen oligárquico en El Salvador:
Los ejes de la transformación neoliberal." In *Concentración económica y poder político
en América Latina*, edited by Lisa North, Blanca Rubio, Alberto Acosta, and Carlos
Pastor, 180- 215. Buenos Aires: Consejo Latinoamericano de Ciencias Sociales, 2020.

Velásquez Runk, Julie. "Indigenous Land and Environmental Conflicts in Panama: Neoliberal Multiculturalism, Changing Legislation, and Human Rights." *Journal of Latin
American Geography* 11, no. 2 (2012): 21–47.

Walsh, Shannon Drysdale, and Cecilia Menjívar. "'What Guarantees Do We Have?' Legal
Tolls and Persistent Impunity for Femicide in Guatemala." *Latin American Politics
and Society* 58, no. 4 (2016): 31–55. https://doi.org/10.1111/laps.12001

Warf, Barney. "Tailored for Panama: Offshore Banking at the Crossroads of the Americas." *Geografiska Annaler. Series B, Human Geography* 84, no. 1 (2002): 33–47.

Wilkinson, Pete. "Tourism—The Curse of the Nineties? Belize—An Experiment to Integrate
Tourism and the Environment." *Community Development Journal* 27 (1992): 386–395.

Williams, Mary Wilhelmine. "The Ecclesiastical Policy of Francisco Morazán and the
Other Central American Liberals." *The Hispanic American Historical Review* 3, no. 2
(1920): 119–43. doi:10.2307/2518428

Wingartz Plata, Oscar. "Nicaragua: Una Historia de Avances y Retrocesos." *Revista de
Historia de América* 142 (2010): 25–35.

Wolf, Sonja. "Subverting Democracy: Elite Rule and the Limits to Political Participation
in Post-War El Salvador." *Journal of Latin American Studies* 41, no. 3 (2009): 429–465.
http://www.jstor.org.proxy.seattleu.edu/stable/27744162

Wood, Elisabeth J. "Civil War and the Transformation of Elite Representation in El Salvador." In *Conservative Parties, the Right, and Democracy in Latin America*, 223–254.
Baltimore: Johns Hopkins University Press–, 2000.

Woodward, Ralph Lee. *Central America, A Nation Divided*. 3rd ed. New York: Oxford
University Press, 1999.

Woodward, Ralph Lee. *Rafael Carrera and the Emergence of the Republic of Guatemala,
1821–1871*. Athens: University of Georgia Press, 1993.

Woodward, Ralph Lee. "The Rise and Decline of Liberalism in Central America: Historical Perspectives on the Contemporary Crisis." *Journal of Interamerican Studies and
World Affairs* 26, no. 3: 291–312, 1984. doi:10.2307/165672.

World Bank. "The World Bank in Panama." 2016. Accessed February 2, 2018. http://
www.worldbank.org/en/country/Panama/overview

World Justice Project. *Rule of Law Index 2014 Report*. https://worldjusticeproject.org
/sites/default/files/documents/RuleofLawIndex2014.pdf

World Justice Project. *Rule of Law Index 2015 Report.* https://worldjusticeproject.org/sites/default/files/documents/roli_2015_0.pdf

World Justice Project. *Rule of Law Index 2016 Report.* https://worldjusticeproject.org/sites/default/files/documents/RoLI_Final-Digital_0.pdf

World Justice Project. *Rule of Law Index 2017–2018 Report.* https://worldjusticeproject.org/sites/default/files/documents/WJP-ROLI-2018-June-Online-Edition_0.pdf

World Justice Project. *Rule of Law Index 2019 Report.* https://worldjusticeproject.org/sites/default/files/documents/WJP_RuleofLawIndex_2019_Website_reduced.pdf

Young, Alma H., and Dennis H. Young. "The Impact of the Anglo-Guatemalan Dispute on the Internal Politics of Belize." *Latin American Perspectives* 15, no. 2 (1988): 6–30.

Zamora, Natalia, and Vilma Obando. "Biodiversity and Tourism in Costa Rica." March 2001. Accessed February 3, 2022. https://www.cbd.int/doc/nbsap/tourism/CostaRica (Tourism).pdf

Zong, Jie, and Jeanne Batalova. "Central American Immigrants in the United States." *Migration Policy Institute,* September 2, 2015. Accessed January 24, 2022. https://www.migrationpolicy.org/article/central-american-immigrants-united-states-2013

ACKNOWLEDGMENTS

The acknowledgments section is often the last part of a manuscript that authors turn in, due to the mad rush involved in finishing up a manuscript, and yet, it's the part that requires tracking the contributions of many people over time, especially in our case. We've been working on this project for more than four years, and the list of people in Central America and beyond who provided reading suggestions or gave us feedback on different chapters is long. Please know that in between these lines there is so much gratitude on our part for all the assistance we've received along the way; a book project like this one is never a solitary project, but one born of community. Also, we know that our work rests on the shoulders of scholars across the Americas and beyond whose research, analysis, and scholarship allowed us to write this book. To all, our most sincere thanks! Ultimately, though, we are responsible for the content of this book and any errors that it may contain.

We'd like to begin by thanking the Central American scholars who read early drafts or made suggestions about material we should consult. We are particularly grateful to José Alberto Idiáquez, SJ, president of the Universidad Centroamericana in Managua, Nicaragua, for being the first person to read a draft of the manuscript. His close reading of this set of short histories and his valuable edits and suggestions were an important catalyst for continuing. The authors also thank Dr. Ana Marina Tzul Tzul and Laura Orozco from the Universidad Rafael Landívar (Quetzaltenango Campus) as well as Marielos Torres and historian Julián Gonzalez at the Universidad Centroamericana "José Simeón Cañas" in San Salvador, El Salvador. A special shout-out to Irina Carlota Silber at the City College of New York for research about El Salvador, Victoria Sanford at Lehman College for research about Guatemala, and Lori Maddox at ELAW for her close read of the Belize chapter. We are very grateful to the expert research support of Fiore Bran Aragón who gathered research from over twenty Central American scholars for inclusion in the book. We thank the scholars who contributed resources from across Central America: Víctor Hugo Acuña (Universidad de Costa Rica), Ronny Viales Hurtado (Universidad de Costa Rica), Alberto Cortés Ramos (Universidad de Costa Rica), Cristofer Rodríguez (Asistente de Investigación del Dr. Víctor Hugo Acuña), Allan Martell (Louisiana State University), Roberto Deras (Universidad Centroamericana "José Simeón Cañas"), Amparo

Marroquín Parducci (Universidad Centroamericana "José Simeón Cañas"), Xiomara Avendaño Rojas (Universidad de El Salvador), Sergio Palencia Frener (City University of New York), José Cal Montoya (Universidad San Carlos de Guatemala), Jorge Amaya (Universidad Nacional de Honduras), José Cardona Amaya (Universidad Nacional de Honduras), Edwin Matamoros (Instituto de Historia de Nicaragua y Centroamérica from the Universidad Centroamericana in Managua), Eimeel Castillo (University of Michigan), María Fernanda Zeledón (Universidad Autónoma Metropolitana México), Ruth Matamoros (University of Texas-Austin), Larry Montenegro Baena (Movimiento por la Descolonización de la Mosquitia), Carlos Guevara-Mann (Florida State University, Panama Campus), and Victor Ortíz Salazar (Universidad de Panamá). Fiore also identified important online resources and databases that are listed in the open access version of the book. *¡¡Gracias mil a todes por sus aportes!!*

This book would never have come to fruition if not for the financial support and subject-matter expertise of the Seattle International Foundation. From co-founder Bill Clapp's insistence that policy makers and educators across the United States need a book like this, to important feedback from former executive director Arturo Aguilar and current executive director Adriana Beltrán, we thank you. We are also grateful to SIF staff who contributed insights and suggestions along the way: Natalia Lozano, Diana Campos, Eric Olson, Julie Sponsler, Olga Vnodchenko, and John Wachter. A special shout-out to Peter Bloch García for being a good shepherd in a key moment.

Both authors thank Seattle University and Seattle University's Central America Initiative for their commitment to the project. Our thanks to Joseph Orlando and the Provost's Office at Seattle University for their support of this project. At Seattle University, we also extend our deepest gratitude to the librarians at the Lemieux Library, especially Rick Block, for superhero powers to track down English- and Spanish-language resources about the history of Central America.

For a manuscript to become a book, it needs champions in the publishing world. We would like to express our sincere thanks to the team at University of Cincinnati Press (UCP), including its fearless leader Elizabeth (Liz) Scarpelli, amazing assistant managing editor Sarah Muncy, persistent editorial assistant Alex Nash, and tech savvy Luke Beckwith. When UCP sent this manuscript out for external review, the feedback was simultaneously positive and constructive. We are grateful to the anonymous external readers for their recognition of the potential contributions of a book like this as well as for new readings and suggestions we've included, particularly encouragement to expand the introduction and include Central American trends and the concepts historians and other scholars use to interpret past and current events in the region. We would also like to thank Meg Krausch for their excellent copyediting and close read of the manuscript.

On a personal note: Serena thanks Marty for being a critical interlocutor and steadfast companion, unstintingly generous with support. I hope that the next generation starting with Meme, Alex, Raquel, Erik, and young people in Central America and beyond, who care about the region, find this book a useful and accessible resource. Serena also thanks David Leyse and Layna McAllister for providing a beautiful and hospitable writing retreat. Isabeau thanks Mom and Dad for their encouragement and commiseration, doled out plentifully as needed during this writing journey. Isabeau also thanks co-author, Serena, for her years of mentorship and friendship; and offers thanks in advance for all the years to come. And, most importantly, we both want to express our deepest and most heartfelt gratitude to all of our readers. Whether you are reading these chapters for a class or the book just happened to catch your eye, you are an equal partner in our endeavor to share Central America's stories, and it means so much to have you walk with us. Thank you. *Gracias mil.*

In solidarity,
Serena and Isabeau

INDEX

ABOUT THE AUTHORS

SERENA COSGROVE, PhD, (she/her) is an Associate Professor in International Studies and director of the Latin American & Latinx Studies program at Seattle University. She also serves as the faculty coordinator of Seattle University's Central America Initiative.

ISABEAU J. BELISLE DEMPSEY (they/them) is half-Belizean and graduated from Seattle University in 2019 with a double major in International Studies and Spanish.